PASSCHENDAELE
1917

PASSCHENDAELE
1917

THE TOMMIES' EXPERIENCE OF
THE THIRD BATTLE OF YPRES

ROBERT J. PARKER

AMBERLEY

First published 2017

Amberley Publishing
The Hill, Stroud
Gloucestershire, GL5 4EP

www.amberley-books.com

Copyright © Robert J. Parker, 2017

The right of Robert J. Parker to be identified
as the Author of this work has been asserted in
accordance with the Copyrights, Designs and
Patents Act 1988.

ISBN 978 1 4456 5571 0 (hardback)
ISBN 978 1 4456 5572 7 (ebook)

British Library Cataloguing in Publication Data.
A catalogue record for this book is available
from the British Library.

Map illustration by Thomas Bohm, User Design,
Illustration and Typesetting.
Typesetting and Origination by Amberley
Publishing.
Printed in the UK.

CONTENTS

PROLOGUE: THE HORROR
THAT WAS PASSCHENDAELE

On 31 July 1917, the Battle of Passchendaele, officially the Third Battle of Ypres, began. Twelve divisions of the British Second and Fifth Armies under General Sir Douglas Haig, plus allied French soldiers, stormed 'over the top' at 03:50. Preceded by an unprecedented artillery barrage of over 3,000 guns, over half of which were listed as heavy guns, and firing over four-and-a-half-*million* shells, the British attack swiftly overran many of the Day One objectives until met by vigorous German counter-attacks. Even more significantly, they faced a steady rainfall that was to intensify throughout the day and virtually halt any possibility of further advance.

This sequence of events would continue for nearly the next four months: thunderous artillery barrages, advancing British infantry, German counter attacks, slight territorial gains, and torrential rain. The combination would lead to the infamous hell of Passchendaele – a battle within a battle, as human beings sought to wage war while fending off the elements of rain and cold over a mud-soaked stretch of Flanders in south-western Belgium. It would go down in history as one of the costliest, bitterest, and perhaps most futile engagements in a war that has come to personify futility.

It was an absolute nightmare. Often we would have to stop and wait for up to half-an-hour, because all the time the duckboards were being blown up and men being blown off the track or simply slipping off – because we were all in full marching order with gas-masks and rifles, and some were carrying machine guns and extra ammunition ... an explosion nearby or just the slightest thing would knock a man off balance and he would go off the track and right down into the muck ... It had taken us more than twelve hours to get there ... We went over onto this morass, straight into a curtain of rain and mist and shells, for we were caught between two barrages ... Well of course, we lost direction right away ... the machine gun fire from the German positions was frightful. They were simply spraying bullets all over the place. We could hardly move because the mud was so heavy ... with people being hit and falling and splashing down all around you ... casualties were heavy ... We were there for more than twenty-four hours and the rain and the shelling never stopped the whole time.

This is East Lancashire Regiment Lieutenant P. King's description of an attack across the mud- and rain-soaked swamp of water-filled shell holes that was typical of the nearly four-month horror endured by both British and German soldiers during the Battle of Passchendaele.[1]

The noted and honoured 20th-century archaeologist Sir Mortimer Wheeler was an officer in the Royal Artillery during the Great War and saw considerable action at the battle of Passchendaele. In a letter to his wife written home on 29 October 1917, Mortimer vividly wrote of what hundreds of thousands of British and German soldiers were enduring on a daily basis:

I cannot attempt to describe the conditions under which we are fighting. Anything I could write about them would seem an exaggeration but would, in reality, be miles below the truth. The whole battlefield for miles is a congested mess of sodden, rain-filled shell holes which are being added to every moment. The mud is not so much mud as a fathomless, sticky morass. The shell holes, where they do not actually merge into one another, are divided only by a few inches of this glutinous mud. There is no cover and it is of course impossible to dig. If it were not for the cement pillboxes left by the Boche, not a thing could live for many hours. The guns are in the open and – most phantastic of all – many of them are in full view of the Boche. I must not say much about my own battery's position but to give you some idea of it, our gun was in water up to its breech and when it recoiled, the breech splashed under water. The gunners work thigh-deep in water.[2]

Mortimer omits the brutality of the wounds and death, but his description certainly sets the scene for the conditions that the Battle of Passchendaele was being fought under; literally day and night, and week after blood- and rain-soaked week. What was neglected (and probably destined for censure had it been included) was this later report from another British artillery battery report, as their crew contended with the miserable conditions of the interminably pitiless Flanders rain and mud:

The (gun crew) batteries had no daily life, but rather a daily death, while their experiences – day in, and day out – were invariably the same. Morning, noon, and night, the men were splashing about in mud, trying to keep their ammunition clean and their guns serviceable; daily they were shelled, sometimes with long deliberate bombardments, sometimes in hurricane shell-storms which descended on them for forty minutes or so, two or three times a day. They were always wet, always cold; they continually saw the guns and ammunition, which they had spent hours in cleaning and preparing, blown to bits in the passing of a second; they helped to bring up more guns, more ammunition, and saw, in the serving of these new guns, their mates blown to pieces, shattered, torn. They grew to believe that relief would never come.[3]

The mud and the blood of Flanders have soaked the history of Passchendaele with a legacy of death and despair. Why was the Battle for Passchendaele, the Third Battle of Ypres, ever fought? Lacking any defined objective of tactical value, why was it allowed to continue for such an inexplicably unconscionable amount of time?

Noted poet Siegfried Sassoon, who experienced the thick of the Flanders fighting conditions, summed up the feeling of many who fought and suffered there: 'I died in hell – (They called it Passchendaele).' For it was more than just another questionable engagement conducted during a savagely vicious and circumstantial war, but a confrontation that forced soldiers on both sides to continually endure the indescribably foul and tortuous conditions of a life-and-death struggle while labouring against the unremitting elements of torrential rain, amid oceans of mud.

C. A. Bill of the 15th Battalion, Royal Warwickshire Regiment related how:

For the first few miles we moved along a single duckboard track laid down on a vast sea of mud. Movement was difficult and slow, although separate up and down tracks were in use. By the time we had reached the end of the duckboards night had fallen and guides from the front line met us to lead us as best as they could on solid ground between the maze of water-filled shell-holes. Into these many men fell and got soaked in the foul water, and were fortunate indeed if they were seen and hauled out and saved from almost certain drowning, weighed down as they were by their heavy equipment. Picture the puny efforts of a small fly to cross the pudding basin full of batter and you have some idea of the hopelessness of the man who has missed the track and become bogged in the appalling mud which appeared to have no solid bottom. A party of 'A' company men passing up to the front line found such a man bogged (down) to above the knees. The united efforts of four of them with rifles beneath his armpits, made not the slightest impression, and to dig, even if shovels had been available, would be impossible, for there was no foothold. Duty compelled them to move on up to the line, and when two days later they passed down that way the wretched fellow was still there; but only his head was now visible and he was raving mad.[4]

Such was an ordinary soldier's witness to the literal edge of life and death during the four-month battle that raged through the waterlogged fields of south western Belgium.

Fought in the summer and autumn of 1917 the Battle of Passchendaele has become, along with the horrors of the Verdun and the Somme campaigns, the epitome of the Great War's ruthless slaughter of thousands of hapless young men for no discernible goal or gain. Fought under the most abominable conditions, and consuming approximately a quarter million British and Commonwealth soldiers, the Battle of Passchendaele has been debated and vilified ever since for its seemingly maniacal wastage of men, machines, and morale – and for the purpose of, at best, the most dubious justifications of necessity. The amount of sacrifice and effort required for the endurance of nearly four months of an unimaginable nightmare of mud, blood, and death can barely be described in words and pictures. Such was the excruciatingly hideous ordeal experienced by those who fought and died there, that today the word 'Passchendaele' alone evokes vivid images of a mud-choked, rain-soaked moonscape of lifeless craters and desolate landscape. It is, indeed, no exaggeration or myth.

German soldiers on the other side of 'no man's land' suffered equally and responded with nearly identical comments, as German officer Ernst Junger said:

The heavy rains of the past few days had turned the crater field into a morass, deep enough, especially around the Paddlebach, to endanger life. On my wanderings, I would regularly pass solitary and abandoned corpses; often it was just a head or a hand that was left protruding from the dirty level of the crater. Thousands have come to rest in such a way.[5]

And a German Musketeer of the 231st Bavarian Infantry Regiment put it most succinctly when he commented:

> The whole earth is ploughed by the exploding shells and the holes are filled with water, and if you do not get killed by shells you may drown in the craters. Everybody is rushing, running, trying to escape almost certain death.[6]

As at Verdun and the Somme, the question is forever posed: why and how did this single location take on such an importance that the British high command was willing to expend nearly a quarter million casualties to conquer a low ridge containing a tiny, obscure, and completely destroyed Belgian village named Passchendaele? What was the military significance or geographic importance of this position that such a massive and horrific sacrifice designated it vitally essential for capture? Was this a tactical or strategic prize worth the extravagant investment of men, material, frustration, and grief?

British General and Commander-in-Chief Sir Douglas Haig was again looking for a breakthrough on the Western Front, just as he had envisioned a similar achievement the year before at the Battle of the Somme. This time the piercing of the German lines was imagined for an area of Belgium that would lead to the North Sea coast and the linkage with amphibious British forces to drive the German submarine fleet off of the ports near the entrance to the nearby English Channel. Envisioning that successful manoeuvre, Haig would follow through with a sweeping wheel around the northern German flank that would roll up the German army and provide the Allies with victory. It was a grand scheme.

On 20 June, a little more than a week before the campaign was scheduled to commence, Haig addressed British Prime Minister David Lloyd George and his war cabinet in London. Haig predicted that a victory in Flanders might possibly lead to a German collapse and as good as promised the Prime Minister that there would be no intention of entering into another tremendous offensive involving heavy losses.[7] This was of course in reference to the previous year's debacle at the Battle of the Somme, where almost an entire army of freshly recruited volunteers for 'King and Country' had been sacrificed in an ineffectual six-month slug-fest to break through the German lines in north western France. Lloyd George, and presumably also Haig, did not desire a repeat of this disaster that had accomplished nothing other than the gradual attrition of the combating armies through enormous and continuous casualties. But to Haig, the war of attrition was a legitimate strategic device for success and was currently being won by the Allies; he was convinced that Germany's collapse was imminent, and victory was in sight.

Unfortunately, the Third Battle of Ypres (Passchendaele), as had happened at the First (1914) and Second (1915) Battles of Ypres, became hopelessly bogged down by the tenacity of the German army's defence and the relentless deluge of rain that turned the flat, featureless, Flanders battlefield into a quagmire of mud, slimy water, and endless swamp that flooded every nook and cranny of the former farm fields. It was not what Haig had imagined or had planned, but this battle, as the others before it, soon took on a dynamic all of its own. The pursuit of the conquest of Passchendaele village and its adjoining ridge (all 60 metres/200 feet in height of it) became an obsession for Haig, who would not quit the battle until the village and ridge were taken.

The supposition and the subsequent decision to pursue this objective to such extreme lengths were widely broached and discussed at the time, and have been hotly debated ever since. What cannot be questioned by anyone, however, were the appalling conditions from July to November of the Flanders front, and the enormous casualties that were incurred to complete this bitterly contested conquest. In fact, Haig's judgment became singularly clouded by the fervour of his cherished belief that the Germans were on the brink of collapse and defeat. At a meeting of war correspondents on 9 October, Haig assured one and all that the offensive was practically through the enemy's defences and the enemy has only 'flesh and blood against us'.

That German 'flesh and blood' was definitely infused with an ironclad quality since it required another month of repeated attacks and corresponding casualties to gain the last several hundred yards and seize the village and ridge of Passchendaele. For whatever ambiguous gain and purpose this final achievement can be presented, it was responsible for another substantial payment of over 60,000 killed and wounded – the type of tactical slaughter that Haig had promised not to embark upon. To this bill can be added the frightful conditions and the environmental horror in which the concluding assault alone produced 16,000 casualties. But for Haig, the securing of the now unidentifiable remains of the ruin and rubble of Passchendaele village had been accomplished.

A Flanders offensive had been on Haig's agenda since he had assumed command of the British Army in December of 1915. Haig had pressed for Flanders over the Somme in 1916, but reluctantly gave in to the persistent desires of the French high command to launch an attack in France. Politically, the 1917 Flanders decision had been challenged from the start by Prime Minister David Lloyd George, already no friend of Haig's due to the catastrophe of the Somme battle the previous year. Lloyd George was fearful – and rightfully so – that Haig would embark upon another dreadful squandering of men and material in a reckless waste of resources. This is exactly what the Flanders offensive would evolve into and although with less human loss than at the Somme, still at a tragically considerable cost in life.

Although no shrinking violet in his aggressive desire to defeat Germany, the Prime Minister was on record as being opposed to Haig's seemingly wanton waste of manpower. However, Lloyd George was at a loss for either a replacement for Haig, whom he would have enjoyed sacking, or a viable alternative strategy with which to pursue the war against Germany in a vigorous fashion. In fact, even the British Chief of the Imperial General Staff (CIGS) General Sir William Robertson, and as such Haig's immediate supervisor in London, had commented upon the Flanders offensive, 'I confess I stick to it more because I see nothing better, and because my instinct prompts me to stick to it, than because of any good argument by which I can support it.'[8]

From this difficult logic came forth the reluctant approval and initiation of Haig's Passchendaele Campaign. He believed in fighting the Germans and wearing them down, even at the mutual cost and attrition of his own army. Haig's faith in the Flanders 1917 offensive then persisted through the agony of confronting the combined adversaries of the determined German army and the appallingly atrocious weather. Haig's staunch expectation of success never flagged, and for him always, a victory could be won and the war ended.

Although probably apocryphal and without documented foundation, the oft-quoted comment by Haig's Chief of Staff, General Sir Launcelot Kiggell, emphasises the madness that Passchendaele descended into. When confronted with his first sight of the waterlogged moonscape of swampy, muddy shell-holes that was the battlefield, Kiggell was reported to have burst into tears and said: 'Good God, did we really send our men out to fight in this?' And the response from his escorting guide was: 'It gets worse further on.'[9]

Even if not spoken by Kiggell, as some attribute it to General Sir John Davidson, another member of Haig's staff at Passchendaele, it reflects a deeper truth and speaks volumes as to the misery, death, and futility that became Passchendaele.

I

WHY PASSCHENDAELE?

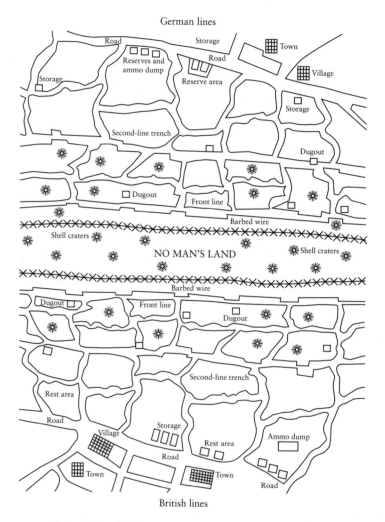

Typical Trench alignment.

To fully comprehend why the Battle of Passchendaele was fought requires tracing the background of the Great War itself. Understanding how and why the Great War was able to engage and seduce the world's major nations into a brutal and devastating blood-letting helps to explain the horror that Passchendaele would become and the enduring infamy it still retains. Attempting to discover any discernible meaning for either the Great War, or the Battle of Passchendaele, requires probing for underlying explanations in order to somehow make sense of what was taking place during 1914–1918. Passchendaele was not fought in a vacuum; it was an extension of the madness that was the Great War – what we now call the First World War. Passchendaele, therefore, must be framed within the episodes that led up to the Great War and the stalemate conditions that existed along the Western Front after three years of ferocious fighting.

These were events conducted on a colossal scale of endeavour. Much of today's political, social and technological world was largely spawned by the Great War. From mechanical technology to social disruption, from re-drawn boundaries to global politics, the Great War generated and established the world that we now inhabit. Among the greatest and most profound results was the Great War's disturbing lack of a definitive conclusion, in and of itself, a disaster for the next generation. It was to virtually ensure the inevitability of the Second World War and the convulsive world events, results, and implications that were fostered by that drama. Militarily, the Great War dramatically altered the method of waging war – introducing a shocking capacity for mortal violence and a seismic upheaval in mankind's behaviour, ingenuity, and potential for self-destruction. The Great War extended and amplified the evolution of waging war on a national basis. It increased the totality of a society's engagement of war by utilising every aspect of military and civilian resource. Every individual, soldier or civilian, and every branch of social function within a nation, would be required to participate and sacrifice in order to outlast equally likeminded opponents demonstrating similar resolve. The Great War, and the great battles that came to define the war, would be fought until there was neither blood nor treasure left for a nation to invest in the struggle. Every man, commodity and piece of equipment would serve merely as a cog in this industrialised war of attrition. The victor would suffer as much as the defeated, but in the process of mutual devastation, one side would eventually claim to be the last man standing and declare victory. Once engaged in this apocalyptic catastrophe, there could be no turning back – a war would be fought until an enemy capitulated, a victory was proclaimed, and a triumph could be declared. Today's observers who recognise this obsessive commitment by the combatants, coupled with the belligerent's equally stubborn determination, will begin to comprehend the motivation, even if not accepting the justification, for the Great War's pattern of seemingly suicidal behaviour and the increasingly deadly path that was followed.

The Great War evolved out of several diverse situations that *should not* have generated a continental war – and certainly not led to the global disaster that it became. Historians have written countless books as to why the First World War should never have taken place. But due to a lack of effective statesmanship, coupled with defiant and foolish brinkmanship, the European continent allowed itself to be plunged into a war that would disrupt and then devastate its culture, society, wealth, and stability. Merely stating the obvious, that the Great War was a mistake, does not alter the fact that it did take place, thereby leading Europe down the inexorable path to all of the Great War's manifold consequences. The calamity of the Great War is not lessened by the reckless and foolish nature of its conception; quite the contrary, its bastardised birth only underscores the tragedy of its horrific consequences. Scholars have endlessly argued whether the issues in 1914 were critical enough to justify the war that would be fought. This becomes a two-part question and argument: were the issues that led to the war significant enough for Europe to go to war; and once at war, did those same issues have sufficient importance then to justify the war that came to be fought? This book can only mention these bolder questions in passing, but they do precede the nature and duration of the great battles that would become the signature of the Great War's next four years. The more ghastly of these battles: Verdun, Somme, and Passchendaele, were savagely waged within the context of these nebulous issues. This background begins to explain, while not necessarily excusing, the reckless conduct and impact of these titanic clashes. When armies of over one million men embroil themselves in life-and-death battles, often lasting months and resulting in the death and maiming of hundreds of thousands, then some explanation must be introduced as to why such sacrifice was deemed necessary by both the leadership and the members of these organisations.

Following the defeat of Napoleon Bonaparte in 1815 at the Battle of Waterloo, Europe had benefited from a century without a major war being fought. In that time, Europe had prospered and developed as no society ever had before. The advancements in health, science, technology, human rights, cultural achievement and overall societal improvements were dramatic and pervasive. Europe had become the focus for art, invention and prosperity. Its wealth and confidence, reinforced by political and social stability, seemed to be on a permanent track of improvement and growth. There were events that fractured this otherwise upward trend of growth and progress – political revolution, small wars, and the ever-evolving rearrangement of social, political, and economic divisions; however, the reigning attitude was decidedly one of optimism concerning progress, wealth and stability. And peace.

No one envisioned the outbreak of a convulsive war on the scale that would erupt during the summer of 1914. And no one could foresee the depth of devastation, destruction and damage that such a conflict would degenerate into. It was, tquite simply – unimaginable. Both the lack of a definable purpose, and the resultant intensity and duration, were beyond any prediction. But the Great War did erupt, brought on by the culmination of many overheated factors that had been simmering for decades. Several of these factors, in retrospect, would seem to be manageable, or at least not worth the oncoming sacrifice. But the momentum for war became uncontrollable, and once begun, the war took on its own life, to consume and devour any worthy goals – real or imagined.

First was the ideal of nationalism, in which a particular group of people fiercely defend their own borders and guard their own governing agency. Based on such cultural divisions as religion, ethnicity, and politics, nationalism created revolutionary movements throughout Europe. To the nationalist, allegiance to your nation state is the highest of ideals, even to the extent that there is no higher form of devotion than to be willing gloriously to die for it.

The desire to create new nation states for distinctive groups of people was most fervently being felt in the Balkan areas of southern Europe, largely dominated by the Austro-Hungarian Empire. Minority groups craved statehood and were violently pursuing this goal. Several minor Balkan wars had taken place in the early part of the 20th century, although none had grown into a larger war. It was an Austrian dilemma that was considered by the rest of Europe to be prickly, but strictly regional. Austria was reluctant to concede to these groups, and was willing to go to war to prevent a further rise in the formation of independent states carved out of her territory. One such provocateur in this dispute was Serbia, who frequently encouraged, or at least tolerated, some of her more radically minded sympathisers and their corresponding ambitions. Being Slavic and Orthodox Christian, the Serbs were supported and sometimes encouraged by fellow Slavic Orthodox Christians of the more powerful Russian Empire. This, in turn, introduces the second major factor – the formation of entangling alliances.

Europe had crisscrossed herself with a series of alliances that, on paper at least, promised to aid fellow allied nations if attacked by opposing nations that were, in all probability, members of competing alliances. Austria-Hungary had associated herself with the newly formed German Empire under Kaiser Wilhelm II. The state of Germany was a relatively new entity, being formed after Prussia's victory over France in the Franco-Prussian War of 1870–71. Germany's creation had been orchestrated under the diplomatic and military brilliance of Otto von Bismarck, and the new German state had rapidly risen in military, industrial and economic power. Befitting her Prussian core, Germany had trained and equipped one of the world's largest and most modern military organisations, while also becoming a leading producer of industrial goods. Her burgeoning growth in wealth, trade, influence and military power had all of Europe on alert as to her intentions. It was to Germany that Austria, and another recently created nation, Italy, now allied themselves in the formation of the 'Triple Alliance'.

In the creation of modern Germany, France had been defeated and humiliated during the Franco-Prussian War. In the process, France had lost two regional border areas to the new Germany, the districts of Alsace and Lorraine. Known as the 'Grande Revenge', many in France desperately desired to avenge the embarrassing defeat to the Germans and regain their lost possessions. France, therefore, allied herself with the sleeping giant, Russia, a vast nation of unlimited potential but beset by poverty, backwardness and her own political turmoil. Russia's empire, led by the ineffectual Czar Nicholas II, longed to modernise and advance into the industrialised world of the 20th century. Russia's support of Serbia against the Austrian Empire placed her in direct conflict with the Triple Alliance. Further entangling these major powers, Russia's ally, the French, continued to harbour the desire to regain her lost provinces and avenge her earlier defeat to Germany.

Russia and France, and later joined by Great Britain, created the 'Triple Entente', which was formed in order to challenge and offset the power of the German-Austrian alliance. Great Britain was also feeling the growing threat of the new German Empire, as Germany was aggressively contending on the world stage for colonies and global trade. Additionally, Germany was building a notably modern and powerful naval fleet to compete with the British and thereby presenting a challenge to the Royal

Navy's traditional dominance of the oceans. Great Britain also felt responsible for protecting and defending certain smaller and weaker European states. One of these was the small cross-channel nation of Belgium, to whom she was partially obligated by treaty. Such was the complicated pattern of commitments that formed a web of interlocking treaties and alliances.

These alliances would threaten grave consequences when a nation felt challenged or endangered by another nation. The potential to be dragged into an undesired war should have been obvious. Such a dangerous risk materialised in the summer of 1914 when the heir to the Austro-Hungarian throne, Franz Ferdinand, was assassinated while on a tour of the Austrian province of Bosnia and Herzegovina. While riding in an automobile, Ferdinand and his wife were shot dead by a Serbian extremist in the streets of Sarajevo, the capital. The assassin, Gavrilo Princip, was a member of a violent Slavic-Serbian nationalist movement, the Black Hand. This group sought a united nation for all Slavic Serbs of southern Europe. Assassination and terrorist tactics were their principal weapons.

In response, Austria issued Serbia an ultimatum concerning the assassination, blaming Serbia for the murder and the revolutionary climate that initiated the situation. Austria was convinced that Serbia would reject the ultimatum, and supported by her powerful German ally, she prepared to go to war against Serbia. Under the threat of Austria's impending war with Serbia, Russia was induced to defend its smaller ally against the larger Austrian Empire, even though that action could conceivably ignite a chain reaction of responses from other mutual allies. In fact, that is exactly what transpired. Germany supported her ally Austria against Russia and, upon learning of Russia's mobilisation (considered at that time to be an act of war), proceeded to declare war on Russia.

Further complicating the situation was the enormous build-up of military equipment, arms, and trained soldiers, a process that had been going on for decades. Germany's massive military machine relied on the rapid and detailed mobilisation of its army in order to quickly defeat the two major Triple Entente powers: Russia and

France. German's clockwork military requirements demanded a precise and ingenious timetable of railway-based manoeuvres that would provide a holding action against her eastern enemy, Russia, while inaugurating a huge swinging door invasion to sweep into France. This wide flanking tactic would rapidly encircle Paris and quickly defeat France. Accomplishing the defeat of France, the German army would then be poised to return full strength to the east to defeat the huge, but less than nimble, Russian army. Known as the Schlieffen Plan, it had one other dangerous feature: in order to accommodate the movement of the German army into north-western France to encircle Paris, the attacking Germans would need to invade and defeat Belgium. This is exactly what the Germans proceeded to do but by violating Belgian territory, Belgium's ally Great Britain was motivated to enter the war. Great Britain had already felt an obligation to honour her Entente alliance with France and Russia, but was now even more compelled to enter the war in defence of Belgium.

In less than a month following the assassination of Franz-Ferdinand, Europe was at war with itself. Whether the issues or provocations were great enough for such a situation was soon overlooked in the effort to secure a quick victory. This quick victory soon eluded all the engaged participants and set the stage for a prolonged war of attrition. Each team of allied nations arrived heavily armed and mightily prepared, with large populations and stockpiles of weaponry to back them up. These nations were now confronted with the dilemma of how to wage and win a war that featured weapons of unprecedented killing capacity. Europe had placed itself in a diplomatic trap that precluded acceptable or viable alternatives. These combatants would now literally fight their way out of it.

What were these European titans fighting over? That question hangs in the air to this day. Ten million battlefield deaths did not answer the question; instead, that sacrifice only makes the question more urgent and more baffling. More than four years of fighting failed to provide a conclusive outcome and after a twenty-year respite, a rearmed Europe engulfed itself in a Second World War that dwarfed the First.

Going into the Great War, all the combatants envisioned a rapid war that would be over within six months. What would this war resemble? Generals typically refight previous wars before discovering, exploring, and refining the next era of tactics. Before the Great War, the consensus among most political and military leaders was that the war would be violent and brief. They got it half right. Once into the war, the goal was to rapidly win it and extricate themselves from the conflict as soon as possible. But if denied this, what were the strategic and tactical options available to them? The Great War and its ensuing stalemate was the result, and battles such as Verdun, The Somme and Passchendaele became the price of the learning curve as commanders struggled under the burden of new technologies that more efficiently accelerated killing. These questions would haunt all of Europe for those four years, and the world for the next century.

At the outset, the war was fluid and dynamic in the movement of soldiers and equipment. But six months into the war, the situation had deteriorated into a stalemated trench war along the Western Front that stretched 400 miles from the English Channel to the Swiss Alps. The power of the weapons and the size of the armies, continually reinforced by the industrial capacity of 20th-century Europe, would now dictate the strategy and tactics of the battlefield. The Eastern Front, due to its sheer size, allowed for greater mobility of forces, as the huge Russian bear sought to overrun the more efficient German army. Fighting on two fronts was of course an issue in itself for the German army. Even after winning major battles over the Russians in late 1914, the Germans were required to maintain an enormous presence in the east in order to hold back the numerically superior Russian Army.

In the west, after narrowly missing the opportunity to win the war during its opening stages, the Germans dug in to hold onto their captured French and Belgian territory with great tenacity. The French had made initial attacks along the Franco-German border in an attempt to regain their provinces of Alsace and Lorraine, but had been thoroughly repulsed during the early stages of 1914. Along the English Channel and North Sea coasts, the Germans and British had raced to the sea in an all-out effort to out-flank one another. By the end of 1914, the Germans held the North Sea coast as far south as Nieuport, Belgium, using the coast for their submarine bases and the harassment of the vital British shipping lanes. These submarine bases became of paramount importance to both the British and German high command: the Germans as a base for submarine activity, and the British in the attempt to deny the Germans access to the oceans and as a potential hinge to pivot around the German northern flank and sweep across the entire German front. Therefore, the Belgian section of the Western Front extending to the North Sea was of the highest priority owing to its strategic position.

South western Belgium witnessed nearly continuous fighting from the beginning to the end of the war – rarely was it ever quiet. Annually, the area would erupt into a major battle of immense size: the First, Second and Third Battles of Ypres, the latter being referred to as Passchendaele, and the 1918 German and British offensives that finally concluded the war. In particular, the area around the town of Ypres became the focus of this fierce fighting, featuring the infamous 'Salient' that angled deep into the German lines. Thus, the Ypres sector repeatedly became an area of some the most bitter and intense fighting of the war. Extending slightly beyond the tip of the salient lay the village of Passchendaele, and its adjacent towns and ridges, all of which became prizes of the highest value.

In 1914, the Flanders area of Belgium had witnessed the race to the sea and the First Battle of Ypres, as both Germans and British sought to control the Channel ports. The Germans also sought to split the allied Franco-British armies and possibly push on to Paris and win the war, but stiff Allied resistance prevented this and the Germans had to be content with sitting tight and holding onto most of the Belgian coast.

The Second Battle of Ypres, in the spring of 1915, saw a renewed effort by the Germans to pierce the Flanders battlefield with the first use of poisonous gas. Again the Germans sought to break through the British lines and drive a wedge between the allied Franco-Anglo forces, but after some modest gains, they failed.

The Flanders/Ypres area that frequently and heavily contested sector, became the scene and inspiration for a memorable and much quoted poem. During the Second Battle of Ypres, Canadian Medical Officer Colonel John McCrae wrote what was to become one of the most famous poems from the Great War, 'In Flanders Fields'. The poem inspired the image that has become the enduring symbol of the Great War, the poppy.

Trained and enlisted as an artillery soldier early in the war, the forty-two year old McCrae was later, and reluctantly, shifted to his occupational calling as a physician to treat wounded soldiers at the front. It was in this capacity in a medical bunker within the 'Salient', near the Yser Canal, that McCrae learned of the death of his friend Lt Alexis Helmer, killed by a shell that shattered his body to bits. Grief stricken by Helmer's death, McCrae read the service at Helmer's burial and wrote a brief but inspired poem to honour Helmer and the cause for which these soldiers were fighting and dying.

Back in Britain the poem was later published in *Punch* magazine and became enormously popular. The image of the poppy, a flower that blooms abundantly throughout Flanders, emerged as the representation of the war – the deaths, the sacrifice, and the memories of those who had given their lives.

Later in the war, McCrae died of pneumonia while serving as the commanding officer of the Canadian hospital in Boulogne, France. He was buried in the nearby military cemetery in France, but a memorial to him and his famous poem can be found today at the Essex Farm medical bunker station only a few yards from the former front along the Yser Canal in Belgium.

In truth, the short poem is actually a strident call to arms, and a reminder that the Allied cause is worthy of the sacrifice and must be fulfilled. Later, the poppy was chosen by General Douglas Haig as the symbol of the British Legion, as it still is. To this day, the poppy remains the emblem of everything concerning the Great War and its heritage.

So the Flanders/Ypres sector, from the beginning of the war, was an area of major and violent struggle. It was particularly prominent in British General Douglas Haig's focus until usurped by the interruption stemming from the Verdun crisis.

In 1916 the British were called upon to relieve the pressure on French forces defending the fortress area of Verdun in north eastern France. Coaxed by French General Joseph Joffre, British General Haig attacked at the Somme River sector in the north-west central region of France. Haig would have preferred opening an offensive in Belgium but, for the sake of the alliance, went along with the suggestion for the Somme offensive. After a four-month effort to break through the German lines at the Somme, and with only minimal gains to show for the extraordinary loss of life, Haig conceded the lack of progress. He then adjusted his reasoning for waging the Somme battle and declared a victory in the form of attrition – the Germans being unable to match and replace their losses as readily as the Allies. In 1917, Haig dusted off his coveted design for an operation in Flanders, launching three months of attacks that became the Third Battle of Ypres, also known as Passchendaele.

By the summer of 1917, the Allies had failed to win major victories on either the Eastern Front by the Russians, or the Italian front by the Italians (the Italians having changed sides in 1915 to join the Entente Powers/Allies). In 1915 the Allies had tried a different approach by attempting, and failing, to carve an incision through Turkey along the Dardanelles and into the Black Sea. This alternative attempt to open up the war in 1915 had ended in disaster and retreat. With this situation in mind, the Allies returned their attention to the Western Front in Europe. Since bypassing the Western Front in peripheral strategic enterprises had proven fruitless, the Anglo-Franco allies again sought to smash head on directly through the Germans. General Haig and the British high command decided to renew the effort to clear the German submarine threat from the English Channel and North Sea ports, while simultaneously threatening to encircle the northern flank of the German front. Perhaps, with some good fortune, the British could completely outflank the Germans and drive the war into Germany and achieve victory. Such were the grandiose plans of the British in early 1917.

As plans were being drawn up for the Flanders offensive, the circumstances for the campaign became dramatically altered by two significant events: the collapse of the Russian Czarist government and the mutiny of the French army following the aborted and disastrous Neville offensive at the Chemin des Dames in north central France. Both these events would have huge implications for the proposed British offensive in Flanders.

Czar Nicholas II of Russia had abdicated in March of 1917, giving way to a provisional government led by Alexander Kerensky, who promised to continue the war effort against the Germans in support of the Anglo-Franco alliance. This situation remained weakly tenable at best, and the effort would only last for another six months before the collapse of the Kerensky regime during the Bolshevik Revolution. In the autumn of 1917, Vladimir Lenin and the Bolsheviks seized control of Russia with the avowed promise of withdrawing Russia from the war and ending their alliance with France and England. The repercussions of this event would be immediate with regards to the war effort and far-reaching for the future of world history.

Russia's participation in the Great War had wavered as the war progressed but, nonetheless, her presence and influence in the pinning down of a million German soldiers on the Eastern Front remained vital to the Allied cause. Defeats, mutinies, and the Czar's abdication had gradually placed Russia on the brink of defeat; however, under Kerensky, and with support from the Allies, Russia had hung on and remained in the war. Unfortunately for the Allies, during the Passchendaele campaign

Russian assistance would finally come to an end. Upon seizing power, Lenin and his Bolshevik regime would fulfil their promise by negotiating the Treaty of Brest-Litovsk and formally withdrawing Russia from the war.

The Allies were now faced with the upcoming transfer of roughly one million German soldiers and their accompanying equipment from the Eastern to the Western Front. This influx of manpower would help the Central Powers offset the arrival of the newly forming American army to the Western Front. The US had declared war on Germany in April 1917, but would need at least a year to enlist and train an army that by 1918 began arriving in France at the rate of 250,000 soldiers a month. The entry of the US, with its robust industrial capacity and untapped manpower potential, would eventually tilt the war in the Allies' favour, but in the winter of 1916–1917, the feared withdrawal of Russia was of paramount concern to the Allies.

The other desperate factor confronting the Allies in 1917 was the mutiny of the French army following Nivelle's spring offensive. French General Robert Nivelle had confidently promised a war-winning offensive that commenced in April. After limited gains and enormous casualties, the attack disintegrated into disaster. Worse than the battlefield defeat, the French infantry had refused orders to continue to attack. They would defend, but division after division, perhaps over half of all front line divisions, were insisting on a cessation of the fruitless and suicidal attacks against overwhelming machine gun and artillery defences. Many units refused to return to the front lines to relieve other units and many directly disobeyed orders to the point of discarding their rifles. It was a critical situation. The British government and high command were informed, but the news was not generally publicised and never did reach the Germans. In fact, it was not until forty years later, in 1967, that a complete story of the mutiny was finally authorised and released to the public.

As in 1916 at the Somme, the British Army would again be required to conduct a massive offensive to apply steady pressure against the German defences – this time, to shield the French army's dilemma posed by the mutiny. This, however, conveniently fitted in with Haig's desire for a Flanders offensive so he would be more than anxious to conduct it.

For the French, there was considerable work to do if control and stability of their army were to be regained. General Nivelle was removed and relocated to North Africa; General Philippe Petain, the hero of Verdun, was brought in to replace Nivelle as Commander in Chief, with General Ferdinand Foch assuming the position of chief of the general staff. Petain and Foch were both in agreement that for the time being, only limited French attacks would be exercised. The French would concentrate on defending their positions and restoring their shattered morale while waiting for the American army to begin arriving in significant numbers. Initially, Petain brought stability to the situation through a policy of quiet accommodation to the protest. Specific changes included longer and more frequent leaves, a generally lenient response to the men who had mutinied and, most important of all, a cessation of the suicidal offensives that had caused such huge casualties for so little gain. Gradually, over the course of 1917, the French Army regained its discipline and its composure in response to Petain's reforms. Petain did invoke massive arrests, as 3,500 were court-martialled. Of these, 500 were convicted, but most were reprieved, while between 42 and 60 were executed. Petain then instituted a campaign of boosting morale that included reduction of pointless attacks, promises of an army featuring increased use of tanks, and emphasising the arrival of the oncoming American army – the latter two both emerging in large numbers by 1918.[1]

In the meantime, it would be left to the British Army and their summer offensive to apply sustained attacking pressure upon the Germans. This absolute necessity to support the regrouping French during their dire need neatly complemented General Douglas Haig's long-held ambition to initiate a war-winning strategy in Flanders. As in 1916 at the Somme, the British Army was going to be responsible for conducting a significantly larger portion of the ground war than they had ever envisioned. In 1914, the British Expeditionary Force had originally consisted of only six professional infantry divisions and two cavalry divisions to provide support for the Allied left flank. Britain's wartime responsibility had always assumed its major Royal Navy commitment but the growth of its ground force into a million-man army had been unanticipated. It was a huge endeavour to take on the heart of the German army again until the French could recover and the Americans arrived; but for Haig, it was the opportunity he had dreamed of – a sweeping drive to the coast to clear the Germans from the Channel ports in conjunction with the Royal Navy, and then a swing around the northern flank of the German line to at least threaten, if not overwhelm, the entire German position.

Haig's Flanders offensive of 1917 would return the Ypres area to the centre of the fighting that had already seen virtually continuous combat since the outset of the war. Flanders was the site of the two major battles of First and Second Ypres, fought in 1914 and 1915 respectively, which had basically retained the status quo. Now it would once again witness a large-scale battle. The British held the forbidding salient that jutted into the German lines east of Ypres, and this would be used by Haig as a jumping-off point to initiate his offensive. Both strategic need and personal desire allowed Haig the political and military room to plan and conduct this operation. The decision, made in the spring of 1917, began in June with the successful offensive victories at Vimy Ridge in north western France, and Messines in southern Belgium. Both victories had convinced Haig that with proper planning and the massive amount of concentrated artillery that the British now possessed, a breakthrough could be achieved. The size, experience, and power of the current British Army, combined with Haig's firm belief in the imminent breakdown of German morale, suggested that a victory would be his and the war could be won. And so was born the Third Ypres campaign, the Battle of Passchendaele.

2

THE PLAN AND THE TERRAIN

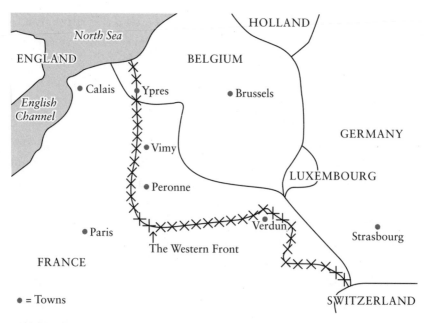

The Western Front.

As described in Chapter One, Flanders had been the scene of constant fighting since the autumn of 1914 and would continue to witness ongoing dramatic activity right through to 1918 and the end of the war. It was the most continuously contested area of the Western Front. Other areas saw peaks of activity: the

Marne battles of 1914 and again in 1918, the Somme in 1916, and Verdun in 1916, but Flanders in western Belgium endured a violent focus of fighting that was relentless in its chronology and devastation.

Strategically the Flanders area was the gateway to the coast where the English Channel meets the North Sea. It was the northerly section of the 400-mile line of trenches that stretched from the North Sea, through Belgium and France, and south to the junction with the Swiss Alps. Despite considerable debate by both politicians and commanders, and occasional forays elsewhere, it was acknowledged by most that the Western Front was where the war would be won or lost. Recognising the importance of the Western Front explained why the positions were so desperately contested during the four-year struggle. Russia and the vast Eastern Front saw mammoth battles and sweeping confrontations for over three years; eventually this front resulted in victory for the Central Powers, but it *did not* determine the outcome of the war. The gains conceded by Russia to the Germans were later handed back in the Treaty of Versailles, nullifying any German conquests and victory on the Eastern Front. Since the Flanders region contained multiple prizes of value, its strategic importance was elevated and the investment to retain or acquire it became greater. The Western Front would determine the outcome of the war.

What were these prizes that would be the cause of such sacrifice? The Channel ports of Ostende and Zeebrugge were of vital importance to the Germans as submarine bases to attack British and Allied shipping. This issue, submarine warfare, would eventually be the downfall of the Germans, since their renewal of unrestricted submarine warfare in the spring of 1917 would bring the United States into the war. The US possessed immense industrial capacity and a potential for raising a fresh and energetic million-man army against the Germans. Likewise, the British sought to regain these Channel ports to prevent the Germans from further access to the sea with their fleet of submarines. Great Britain, as the world's greatest naval power for several centuries, was concerned with anything having to do with the movement of ships and shipping, and it was of the utmost importance for the British to maintain that oceanic superiority.

Besides the Channel ports, Flanders was at the northernmost flank of the 400-mile line of trenches. If *either* opponent could turn or pierce that flank, it would place enormous pressure on the entire Western Front to the south. Both sides understood this significance and both combatants launched offensives seeking to envelop this position and roll up the opposing side. The Germans came very close to executing this plan in their spring offensive of 1918, only to be halted at the Second Battle of the Marne outside of Paris. The Allies then succeeded in their own war-winning counter-offensive of summer and autumn 1918.

The Points of View

The town of Ypres occupied the centre of the Flanders sector, and Ypres became the focal point for much of the war's fighting in Flanders. Jutting due east of Ypres was the infamous salient, an Allied bulge in the German line that, while harassing the Germans, also encouraged the British to widen and expand the position as a jumping off point for any attempt to conduct an offensive. 'The Salient' became synonymous with the horrors of the Western Front and its frighteningly relentless fighting. It had rightfully earned a reputation as one of the most dangerous, difficult, and violent of assignments. Dreaded as a destination by both sides, it was constantly and heatedly contested.

Haig was convinced that the Germans were near collapse and that one more 'big push' would defeat them. In considering another massive offensive, Haig never lost his lust for the Flanders approach on the Western Front. It seemed to offer manifold benefits and opportunities: the eradication of the Germans along the Channel coast ports; the strategically appetising position atop the northern wing of the German line and the threat to roll up the entire German line from north to south; the possibility of breaking through on the northern edge, confronting the Germans with the unenviable decision of either withdrawing their entire line back to Germany or risk being completely enfiladed from the north. Any of these advantages would undoubtedly force the Germans either to seek an armistice or surrender on Allied terms.

Haig was also supremely confident in his army's equipment, preparation, and numerical strength. He again possessed several hundred thousand troops, most of which were well-trained and experienced. His artillery capacity had never been larger or more robust. The Allies were controlling the air with a burgeoning air force and Haig could call upon a stable of the new and improved Mark IV tanks in numbers sufficient that they could adequately support a large offensive. He and his generals were comfortable in the Belgium/Flanders area, having fought much of the war there, and his intelligence reports all indicated that the German army was on the verge of collapse. Factoring in the need to assist the French in providing pressure until they reorganised their mutinous army, along with the urgency to defeat Germany before what could (and did) become the imminent withdrawal of Russia from the war, there appeared no more propitious moment for an all-out offensive in Belgium.

There were, however, some serious doubts on the part of British politicians. Not everyone was convinced of a German collapse. The Germans had put up a stubborn resistance during the spring 1917 Neville offensive in central France, and against the British diversionary segment of that offensive at Arras. The Arras campaign had again witnessed British attacks that were blunted at a cost of heavy casualties. Even with the successful capture of Vimy Ridge by the Canadian Corps, very little meaningful progress had been made and the sacrifice in men and equipment had again been staggering. Another 160,000 British casualties were 'invested' only to learn that, in spite of stronger artillery, better-disciplined creeping barrages, and growing air superiority, a breakthrough on the Western Front would remain elusive. The Germans, contrary to Haig's reports and hopes, were anything but on the brink of collapse. The French Nivelle offensive disaster, and subsequent mutiny, again reflected the stout German fighting capacity. It should also have signalled to Haig that his dream of a breakthrough in Flanders would not be a foregone conclusion and that every indication on the battlefield clearly demonstrated that the Germans remained a most formidable foe.

In England, the Lloyd George government was extremely pessimistic concerning Haig's offensives that squandered thousands of soldiers for little or no visible gains. The threat of Italy or Russia being knocked out of the war led to numerous suggestions for the transfer of soldiers to different fronts. In fact, in November of 1917 at the end of the Passchendaele campaign, General Herbert Plumer and five veteran British divisions of the Passchendaele offensive were indeed sent to Italy (British Expeditionary Force-Italy) to bolster the sagging Italian Front after the Italian defeat at Caporetto. But even though Lloyd George and his War Cabinet gave general approval to Haig in mid-May of 1917 for a summer offensive in Flanders, it was with great reluctance and with the understanding that it would have full support and cooperation from the French.[1] Haig had asked for another 500,000 soldiers that were being held back in England, but the War Cabinet would not give in to Haig's request. Lloyd George was fed up with Haig's strategy of attrition and the depressingly endless casualty lists. Nor were Lloyd George and the War Cabinet enthralled by Haig's belief that a Flanders offensive could be a British 'stand alone' commitment, which the War Cabinet believed would only lead to further massive British casualties for no noticeable gains.[2] Other proposals for renewing former fronts, such as against Turkey, were also rejected, so the Flanders option was acceded to.

Politics

At the start of 1917 it was clear that both British and French leaders were unanimous in their determination to continue the war and achieve victory. Neither government was willing to concede, both believed Germany could and should be defeated, and there was mutual agreement that *attacking* the Germans was the method to gain this victory. In fact, at Verdun, after fending off defeat, the implacable French had counter-attacked to regain the territory lost in the initial months of that year-long struggle. Both Generals Petain and Nivelle had taken the battle to the Germans, using overwhelming artillery support to regain this otherwise inconsequential position.

French General Joseph Joffre had been 'promoted' laterally to an upstairs administrative post because he could not break the stalemate on the Western Front. To begin dislodging the Germans from their hold on French territory, General Robert Nivelle was allowed to pursue his strategy of unfettered attack. This resulted in the disastrous Nivelle/Aisne offensive and the subsequent mutiny of the French soldiers over being ordered to conduct continued suicidal attacks. As at Verdun, Petain was brought in to bring order to the situation and Nivelle was then sacked. In conjunction with Nivelle's offensive, the British had cooperated with their own offensive at Arras. After some initial success, the British again suffered substantial casualties, in fact, the greatest daily average of the war and for no appreciable gain. Labelled as a diversionary attack in support of the Nivelle offensive, it became another five-week-long grind involving the British First, Third, and Fifth Armies. Comprising twenty-five divisions, its cost and commitment appeared as anything but 'diversionary'.

Such was the dilemma for British Prime Minister David Lloyd George, who had become Prime Minister on the strength of his success as minister of munitions – restoring sufficient numbers of dependably performing weapons and ammunition to the British Army in France – and his willingness to fight the war on a more aggressive basis. Lloyd George had assumed office in December of 1916, replacing previous PM Herbert Asquith, who seemed reluctant to wage a total war and demonstrated a growing inability to cope with and administer a mammoth global conflict. That effort demanded a more committed helmsman in charge of the government and Lloyd George offered that willingness to fight. But where was he going to send his armies, and who was to lead them? His faith in Haig was decidedly limited: yes, we need to pound the Germans and attack, but no, we cannot have endless casualties for no gain.

Lloyd George was dubious about any of Haig's plans and sought alternatives. France was suffering a mutiny, Russia was on the verge of cracking, and therefore Britain was indeed responsible for holding up its end, but where and how? Several alternatives were proposed. Both the Balkans and Italy were put forward, and both would be out of Haig's control. Haig would not be removed but he also would not be free to squander thousands more British troops in a wasteful venture. The French government was against these peripheral options and so too were both the French and British military advisors. In the end it was acknowledged by both government and military administrations that engaging the German army on the Western Front would be the most advantageous course to help both Russia and France and would better serve the overall goal of defeating Germany.

General Herbert Plumer had been laying out plans for a Belgian offensive since early in 1916, and Belgium had always been Haig's first choice for offensive operation. If the British were to go onto the offensive in 1917, for all of the above reasons, then Lloyd George and the War Cabinet were going to have to accept both Haig and Belgium for the operation. But Lloyd George, aggressive and determined about the war as he was, remained wary of Haig and his methods. In other words, Lloyd George was in a 'one foot in and one foot out' state of mind. Hence, when the Nivelle offensive began, it was primarily a French operation and a secondary British venture. The initial success with the Canadian capture of Vimy Ridge was most welcome. It was a tactically important piece of high ground that the Germans had commanded since early in the war. Improved tactics and the extraordinary determination of the Canadians had brought a victory. This was how Lloyd George envisioned the war and the defeat of Germany. But the Nivelle offensive, which had optimistically predicted a war-winning breakthrough within forty-eight hours, turned into a disaster and the Battle of Arras in April–May 1917 saw another British expenditure of blood for little gain.

Therefore Plumer's approach to Belgium was examined and considered. It was a methodical approach of step-by-step advancement. It called for the taking of Messines Ridge at the southern edge of the Franco-Belgian boundary, and then a plateau by plateau movement northward until the Belgian coast was reached, whereby British naval and army forces would merge and then push up the coast, clearing the Channel ports of the Germans.

For over a year, Plumer's Second Army had prepared for the taking of the Messines Ridge by secretly mining 20 tunnels deep under the German position and laying powerful quantities of high explosives. The resulting battle was a huge success and Messines Ridge was taken. This achievement increased confidence that the Gheluvelt plateau would be next, followed by the Pilckem Ridge, and finally the Passchendaele Ridge, before moving on to the railhead town of Roulers and then continuing to the coast. It was a conservative approach, with each individual step followed by a week's preparation to reorganise and bring up the guns and supplies for the next step. It would not attempt to be a major breakthrough, but would inflict a costly step-by-step defeat upon the Germans in both casualties and the clearing of the Channel coast.

This plan was rejected by Haig as too conservative and he proposed a new plan. This was to be a grander scheme involving amphibious attacks by the Navy, a powerful sweep up the coast by General Henry Rawlinson's Fourth Army, and a matching sweep out of the Ypres Salient by the Fifth Army, which would join with the Fourth to not only sweep the coast but to turn the entire northern flank of the German Western Front. It required an incredible amount of cooperative effort from multiple military branches that must all successfully dovetail together – also, massive amounts of preparation and equal amounts of good fortune. All of this detailed execution would need to be forthcoming in a synchronised manner. A further consideration was the threat of the weather, which was ultimately to be the unforeseen and unpredicted trump card in the entire operation.

By the time all these proposals had been debated between the Lloyd George government and Haig, the Nivelle offensive had collapsed, the French army had mutinied, and the Czarist Russian government had abdicated. The Russian provisional government offered a hollow promise to continue the war and the Messines Ridge had been taken by Plumer's meticulous planning and execution. Had a Belgian offensive of a more modest kind, as originally proposed by Plumer, been accepted, designed, and enacted, it might have succeeded in freeing the Channel ports. Perhaps, even more optimistically, an opportunity might have presented itself to swing north and east to apply even greater pressure on the German position. But instead, it was well into June of 1917 before Haig was authorised to 'continue his preparations' for a final Flanders offensive and select his general to lead it. Haig's choice was not the more conservative Plumer, but the more sabre flashing style cavalry officer, Hubert Gough, who would be recommended to Lloyd George for final acceptance.[3] Haig did not receive the formal authorisation to attack the Ypres Salient until 25 July, only six days before the actual offensive began.[4] Even then, Lloyd George's greatest fear was that Haig would conduct another version of the previous year's Battle of the Somme and its accompanying horrific toll of casualties for no gain. His fears were well founded.

Flanders

There were serious problems in mounting a large and extravagant offensive in Flanders. The terrain was low, barely above sea level, and carefully maintained for farming and pasture by the centuries-old system of drainage canals, dikes, and ditches. The entire region could easily be inundated by water if there was destruction to the drainage system. This condition could be further exacerbated by heavy rains, which, coupled with the removal of the canal and drainage system through combat, would make the battlefield nearly impossible to negotiate. Haig should have been aware of the fragility of the Flanders landscape, and the vulnerability of the land to damage from a collapse of the drainage system. The ground over which Haig chose to attack could easily be wrecked beyond repair by the destruction of the canal system, or heavy rainfall, or both – which is of course exactly what happened. The pounding inflicted by the mountain of merciless artillery shelling before the major attack even started left the battlefield a hopeless morass of flooded moonscape. This swampy ocean of mud made movement by man, beast, or machine exceedingly difficult, and rendered virtually impossible the forward movement of supplies and weapons that had to attend any advancement of the front. Rain, which began falling on day one of the offensive and continued in record amounts over the next three months, compounded the problems of the already devastated and wrecked landscape.

Realising the terrain's high water table would make entrenchment almost impossible, the Germans chose instead to build countless concrete bunkers and pillboxes to house machine gun nests and inter-linked supporting positions to the rear of their forward lines. Attackers would overrun forward positions only to be pinned down and annihilated by the heavily defended and reinforced second lines. German counter-attacks would then drive the attackers off their initial gains while supported by pre-registered artillery fire. This was the flexible defence plan as conceived by General Eric Ludendorff and his fellow German commanders. It forced attackers to enter a forward killing zone with limited artillery protection, as newly won positions soon extended beyond the range of observable supporting artillery fire. It was an extremely effective tactic at holding ground, forcing attackers to pay a huge price in casualties, and offering only limited opportunity for gain. It was also costly in casualties to the defenders – which the Germans were willing to suffer in order to maintain their positions. It also required well-prepared and trained defending units – which the Germans possessed.

Knowledge of the delicate condition of the Flanders terrain was not new; it was well known for its marginal capacity to divert water. Only slightly above sea level, offering little if any high ground, and protected by its system of dikes, dams, and canals, the fields and farms were prone to flooding due to the clay subsoil that refused to allow water to permeate. Rainwater either sits and puddles on this clay subsoil, or must be diverted into canals and channelled off. When not controlled and redirected off the carefully tended agricultural fields, it turns the otherwise rich farm soil into a quagmire, forming lakes of swampy glutinous mud. If the water is properly run off, the land provides for abundant farms and pastures, but its viability relies upon its water control system. When the massive opening artillery barrage was unleashed in mid-July, four-and-a-half-million shells would be expended to prepare for the opening of the Ypres campaign. This spelled doom not just for the German defenders, but the very landscape that the British attackers would have to cross. After three years of intense fighting in Flanders, and in particular the Salient, the condition of the ground had already been severely disrupted. If and when severe rains arrived, the condition of the pulverised muddy morass would only suffer further deterioration. And come they did – in almost continuous record amounts for the next four months. The results should have been predictable for the British high command; nothing could move or function across the sea of water-laden shell holes. This was to be the Passchendaele battlefield for the next three-and-a-half months.

Belgium

The entire area of Flanders was therefore entirely unsuitable for the waging of a massive Great War-style artillery-dominated trench war. But two factors made it seem to be worth the effort by the British and suggested it as a springboard for offensive action. First, south western Belgium was one of the few remaining areas of Belgium that was not occupied by the Germans, and the British felt compelled to defend this tiny area of their cross-channel ally, an ally they had felt obliged to defend in 1914 at the cost of going to war. To concede Flanders to the Germans was to give up that over which Britain had gone to war. Second, the British were keen to regain control of the Channel ports along the North Sea coast leading out of the English Channel and into the North Sea. These ports had been used by the Germans as submarine bases and their recovery by the Royal Navy was high on the agenda. Therefore, for these reasons, Britain felt obligated to defend Flanders and, if possible, to expand out of it.

The distances for this mission seem incredibly short, and they are. From the Menin Gate in Ypres to the centre of the town of Passchendaele is only six-and-a-half miles, yet it ended up taking three-and-a-half months and nearly 300,000 British casualties to secure that distance. Haig's plan to seize the important railhead of Roulers, behind the German lines, was only a scant 10 miles from the original British front lines. The drive west and north, from Roulers to the coast, was less than 20 miles. Surely a determined offensive, even if not achieving a breakthrough, could at a minimum seize this much territory. Such was the belief and confidence in the spring of 1917 when Haig proposed his plan to the war cabinet. The potential strategic benefits were an added incentive. What Haig again promised not to do, however, was suffer another massive loss of life as had occurred at the Somme in 1916 for no quantifiable gain.

The Plan

Haig chose to develop a complex plan of several strategic goals. This would offer a greater reason for the War Cabinet and Prime Minister Lloyd George to look more favourably at the proposal. The plan would feature the Royal Navy making an amphibious landing on the Channel ports to coincide with an attack by General Henry Rawlinson's Fourth army moving across the Yser canal at the port of Nieuport. The combined coastal operation would then proceed up the coast, merging with Haig's intended breakthrough at Ypres. This powerfully combined force would wipe the coast clear of the Germans, free the ports of Zeebrugge and Ostende, and then begin a sweeping flank attack around the entire German northern flank. Free of the German defences and trench system, Haig's army would then burst into the open and envelop the

German line. Being able to collapse the German positions from the rear would ensure an Allied victory. It was a grand scheme, but undoubtedly much too ambitious considering the previous difficulty in attaining any substantial gains by attacking on the Western Front.

There were several major impediments to this otherwise grand and imaginative strategy. In the light of the conditions of the Ypres Salient, and the history of previous grand offensives by the Allies in 1916 and 1917 under Haig and Nivelle, the chances for success did not look good – the German defences were just too strong, and the British belief in a budding German collapse was wishful thinking. The Germans had already stymied the Nieuport amphibious landings by launching a surprise attack across the Yser River/canal and reducing Rawlinson's Fourth Army from attackers to defenders. The planned amphibious invasion had been set back by the German attack, a lack of available material equipment, and the narrowness of their attack dates due to the dictates of the calendar and corresponding tides. Although looking good on paper, the entire scheme involved too many chances for postponement or failure – and such proved to be the case. This then reduced Haig's offensive to a brute force approach across the mud-soaked fields of Flanders.

In this too, Haig struggled. Originally as previously mentioned he had rejected General Herbert Plumer's plans as too conservative and so decided on a breakthrough. Haig then chose General Hubert Gough, a fellow cavalryman, and more of a tactical 'slasher' in his philosophy of engagement. Gough honestly believed, and spent the rest of his lifetime trying to prove, that Haig wanted him to take a broad front at the Salient and prepare for a breakthrough penetration. Haig denied this and later insisted that Gough was instructed to limit his attack to a narrow focus and shallow depth of conquest. Both men have ample backing to defend their positions. Either way, the initial attacks by Gough proceeded on the idea that the 'Big Push' was to break through the German lines, and as such, that is the way Gough planned and directed the first month of the campaign. When that proved futile, and at high cost in casualties with not enough gain to compensate for the losses, Gough was shunted aside and Herbert Plumer was brought back with the Second Army to lead the advance. Plumer was to change the pace, direction, and ambition of the offensive. Any thought of the 'grand' scheme was dropped and Plumer's original recommendation of 'bite and hold' limited advances was installed.

Such was the confusion as to the fundamental design of the offensive in the summer of 1917, before the Third Battle of Ypres even got under way.

3

THE ARMIES: THE 'TOMMY' AND THE GERMAN SOLDIER

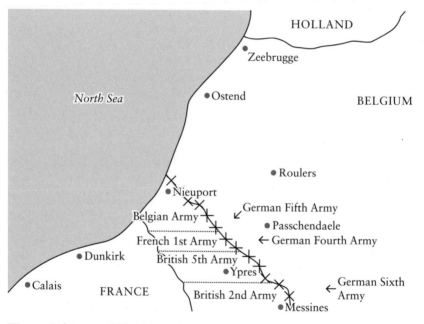

Western Belgium and Flanders spring-summer 1917.

When Great Britain went to war in the summer of 1914, it had a small professional army scattered around the world that numbered roughly a quarter of a million men. About one-third were stationed in India. Britain also had reservists, Territorials, and colonial troops.

When the British Expeditionary Force (BEF) arrived in France to help stem the tide of the German invasion, it consisted of only five infantry divisions and one cavalry division amounting to roughly 100,000 combatants. It was basically wiped out in the first six months of the war. As the war gained momentum, it was clear that a powerful new army would have to be raised and the first call to arms brought in roughly one million volunteers. The United Kingdom had always traditionally relied upon the spirit of volunteerism to fill the ranks of the military. Conscription, the method used to raise million-man armies in Germany, France, and Russia, was frowned upon. This 'new' volunteer British Army, known as 'Kitchener's Army', lasted through 1915 and into 1916 when, by that time, its ranks had been depleted and another 'new' army was required. By now, however, there were fewer and fewer volunteers, and fewer and fewer of them were deemed fit for service. And so, in early 1916, Parliament passed the Conscription Act, which forced men to accept military service. This formed the next 'new' army, consisting again of roughly one million soldiers fighting on the Western Front. It was this army, plus the remnants of the original armies, that was to fight in 1917 at the Battles of Arras, Messines, and Passchendaele. Passchendaele alone would account for roughly 300,000 casualties and would necessitate the raising of yet another million-man army to fight the German offensives of 1918 and the final British march to victory in the summer and autumn of 1918. During the Great War, roughly 5,700,000 men would pass through the British Army. Of these, according to the final British statistics, and always subject to interpretation and dispute, by war's end roughly 673,000 were dead or missing and 1,600,000 wounded. As a nation that only reluctantly entered the war, and whose national interests in fighting that war are still debated, the effort to defeat Germany became one of total commitment when more than one in five, or twenty-two per cent of the adult male population of the United Kingdom, ended up serving in the British Army.[1]

At the conclusion of the Somme campaign in 1916, the allied British and French commands were searching for a location to engage and defeat Germany. As the British Army had grown in number, so too had its share of the responsibility. At the Battle of Arras in April-May of 1917, the British attacked along a 25-mile front in north western France with roughly 25 divisions. This was in support of the French Nivelle offensive at Chemin des Dames in north central France. It was this series of French attacks, and the ensuing disaster in both casualties and morale, that led to the mutinies that were to plague the French army for most of the remainder of 1917. This mutiny encouraged the British, at French urging, to continue to attack at Arras long after any gain could be envisioned or realised, and to embark upon the Battle of Passchendaele. General Haig already had his heart set on the Flanders (Passchendaele) offensive and even without the French dilemma, it was this willingness to go it alone in Flanders, without corresponding French attacks of equal strength, that so worried Prime Minister David Lloyd George. It was under similar circumstances that the British Army under Haig had begun their Somme offensive in 1916 and carried on with it for four months in the face of rising casualties and dreadful weather.[2] The upcoming result for Haig's Passchendaele campaign became almost exactly what Lloyd George had feared, as another British Army was to expire on the battlefield for no apparent gain other than Haig's familiar claim to be achieving and winning the 'war of attrition'.

The British Soldier

The British soldier, or 'Tommy' (the slang name for a British soldier and short for 'Tommy Atkins'), whether conscript or volunteer, was a quality soldier with a willingness to fight. By 1917, the British Army was large, experienced, and well trained. They were well provided for in terms of equipment, food, and medical service. Most came from a working background, either farm or urban, and were accustomed to hard work and the social structure of command and authority. Unlike the French army, there was never a hint of a British Army mutiny or mass disobeying of orders. The British soldier may have complained of his lot, as all soldiers do, but he generally accepted his role and responsibility to serve 'king and country'. The conditions of Flanders during the Battle of Passchendaele, in terms of both fighting the Germans and enduring the horrific conditions of rain and mud, would have taxed any army, but somehow the British soldier, with great courage and endurance, valiantly persevered.

The British soldier's personal equipment usually consisted of the SMLE ('short magazine Lee Enfield') rifle, an extremely dependable bolt action rifle that used a clip of ten .303 rounds; an extra 120 rounds in a waist belt or cloth bandoliers around his shoulder; at least one gas mask in a satchel; a canteen with two pints of water; a bayonet with a 17 inch blade; some rations – usually a tin of bully beef and biscuits; and field dressing for wounds. In all, he carried about sixty pounds of gear. He wore a steel helmet weighing 1.3 lbs., heavy boots with steel studded soles, and a khaki-coloured service uniform. An officer would usually carry a pistol instead of a rifle, but sometimes both. Patches were sewn onto sleeves to identify the rank and unit of the soldier, and he also wore a pair of identification tags. One tag was taken from the body of a dead soldier to the rear to record and account for his loss and the other remained with the body to identify him at burial.

The rotation period in and out of the front line trenches depended upon circumstances. Ideally, it was divided into thirds: a period of time on the front line, a reserve second line (ready reserve) time of duty, and a full back-line period to clean equipment, rest, bathe, and relax. The back-line period could include leave to a French or Belgian village or town, or a cross-channel leave back to England. During the Battle of Passchendaele, both British and German units, if possible, seldom spent more than three days on the front line. Due to the intensity of the combat, anything longer risked heavy fatigue, both physical and emotional. Certain groups, such as artillery and medical units, frequently had much longer front line duration. It should be emphasized, however, that due to the confines of the Flanders sector, anyone with even the most rudimentary responsibilities was in a highly dangerous area. The reach of the opposing artillery, be it for the Germans or the British, exposed one and all to a violent death or wound at *any* given moment. Anyone going near the front for whatever reason – transport, communication, messenger, engineer, road layer, rail repair or even observer – any job or duty, for even limited duration, was under the constant shadow of threat from the opposing big guns. One did not have to be a frontline infantryman going 'over the top' to be targeted randomly, or specifically, and blown to bits without warning or even a chance to take cover. Rotation of troops was all well and good, but at all times and in all places, countless thousands of men and animals were continually at extreme risk. There was no safe zone in the Salient, yet British discipline and morale throughout the war remained strong. Penalties and punishment could be severe for desertion, sleeping during sentry watch on the front trench line, routine indiscretions of insubordination, or failure to properly maintain equipment. According to historian Keith Simpson, the average British soldier, 'obeyed his officers and military authority out of a combination of habit, social deference, the fear of consequences of disobedience, and personal loyalty and respect.'[3]

During the Great War, more than 3,000 British officers and men were sentenced to death for either desertion or other assorted crimes. Most sentences were commuted and reduced to hard labour or punishment by the commander-in-chief. Official statistics now reveal about 300 to have been executed for various degrees of desertion and military crimes. A blanket pardon was issued these soldiers in 2006, declaring them as much a victim of war's cruelty as action in combat.

Following both the Somme and Passchendaele campaigns, there was an atmosphere of discouragement caused by the arduous conditions, horrific casualties, and lack of an achieved goal but, by and large, the morale of the British Army remained at worst indifferent and generally positive. Most British soldiers believed in the cause for which they were fighting and were willing to make sacrifices for the good of their comrades who shared in their experience. This devotion to one's mates, and the shared dedication and responsibility for the man next to you, was what carried a soldier through difficult engagements such as at the Somme and Passchendaele.

Much has been written concerning the leadership of the British high command, but on a personal level toward the ordinary soldier, most lower ranking officers had a deep and sincere compassion and understanding of the needs of the 'other ranks'. A case could, and has, been levelled against the insensitivity of the upper echelon officers who often seemed to disregard the lives of those ordered to repeatedly 'go over the top', but that debate has never been fully settled. Certainly, Prime Minister David Lloyd George was highly suspicious of Haig's apparently wanton waste of British numbers in the pursuit of a war of attrition. Arguments and statistics have been forcefully lodged both ways, but it is difficult to ignore the extended length of the Haig campaigns without any gain other than satisfying the needs of an attrition strategy. The length of time, futility, and numbers of casualties certainly make up a powerful accusation of callousness that is difficult to defend.

The location where soldiers fought on the Western Front had much to do with their survival. On most days, in most sectors, for most soldiers operating at the front and within the front line trenches, there was generally a quiet routine, with occasional small unit trench raids. A 'live and let live' attitude usually prevailed, although some officers found this condition harmful to morale and at odds with the purpose for which they were there. Some officers, to the disgruntlement of their units, encouraged keeping an edge on their front with frequent trench raids to glean intelligence, bring back prisoners for interrogation, or just to keep the other side nervous, and their own troops from becoming complacent. Trench raids, especially at night, kept everyone on both sides alert and anxious.

The trench could be eight to ten feet in depth, although in Flanders, due to the high water table, trenches were shallower. Wooden duckboards provided flooring and allowed some degree of drainage. Wooden wicker branches formed a reinforcing sidewall revetment, and sandbags piled onto the top lip of the trench provided some protection from the stray bullet or piece of shrapnel. Dugouts for sleeping and storage were usually reinforced with corrugated steel and covered with dirt and sod. Rear unit dugouts used for medical dressing stations, headquarters, storage and ammunition were usually concrete bunkers layered over with dirt and sod. At Passchendaele it was necessary to use duckboards to allow the men to walk between the trenches and shell holes and avoid falling into the swampy lakes of mud and water. In the Flanders sector, duckboards were also laid between the forward and back lines and were under constant repair. Duckboards were also were used for the trench floors to provide drainage. But due to rain and the high water table of Flanders, the Passchendaele front was probably the most challenging, as men frequently had to endure water and mud nearly up to their waist while walking through and over their positions. Routine chores such as bringing meals and rations, supplies, ammunition, and reinforcements to and from the front lines required maximum physical effort – besides the nightmare of the constant shelling.

Supplying the British Army

Before his death in the spring of 1916, General Lord Horatio Kitchener had been the de facto commander-in-chief of Britain's Great War effort. Kitchener had advocated a two-million-man British Army in order to provide a serious contribution to the defeat of Germany. At the time of his death, Britain was entering the Somme campaign with roughly that number of soldiers. It would maintain that level through volunteer and conscription until the end of the war in November 1918. A two-million-man army is roughly what both France and Germany had possessed going into the war, and what Kitchener believed would eventually be required by Britain in a lengthy war. Many people scoffed at this notion: the prediction for the length of the war, the size of an army that such a war would require, and the practicality of supplying such a huge force. An army of this size would have massive requirements in terms of food, material, logistics, and administration. British high command might be faulted for many shortcomings during the war, but with the exception of the 'shell shortage' in 1915, the providing of the staples for the two-million-man army and associated transport was a dramatic success.

The British Army on the Western Front required tons of meat, bread, fruit and vegetables every day. Even fresh water had to be delivered in adequate amounts. The staples just for feeding two million people every day are a considerable undertaking. The British Army was a 'city' of soldiers stretching from the North Sea to the Alps, snaking its way through Belgium and France. Behind the trenches was a web of roads, railroads, depots, warehouses, and docks to receive, store, and transport the mountain of food and equipment demanded daily.

Raw food had to be prepared and served, and that involved the cooking apparatus and accompanying fuels and equipment to disperse the equivalent of six million meals a day. None of the raw materials, from bacon to tobacco, could reach the soldier without vehicles to provide transport on roads, rails and waters. Trucks, carts, ships, and railroad equipment were all essential movers of the material. Plus animals – tens of thousands of horses and mules that were employed to help in the delivery – had to be provided with fodder. The requirement for these animals saw 5,438,603 tons of fodder shipped to France over the course of the war.[5] The colossal quantities needed for both man and beast were all shipped across the English Channel from ports in Britain and around the world, to the receiving ports in France. The administrative bookkeeping to service such a 'city of soldiers' was enormous, so too was the organisation, planning and cost.

All of the above has yet to take into consideration the functional spearhead necessities of the fighting man at the front: his weapons, ammunition and military equipment. During the Great War, bullets, shells, and gun powder to the tune of 5,253,538 tons were shipped to France; strangely close to the amount of fodder.[6] Trenches alone, for example, had their own material requirements. For the building of just one mile of trench the British used 900 miles of barbed wire; six million sandbags; one million cubic feet of timber and 369,000 feet of corrugated iron. They also smoked and chewed their way through almost 3,000 cubic feet of tobacco.[7] Over 70 million Mills bombs (hand grenades) were manufactured during the war and the use of 70,000 a day was not uncommon.[8] Over ten million artillery shells were fired by the British guns at Passchendaele alone, numerous days saw half a million, and days of a million or more shells were not uncommon.[9]

Transport/Logistics

The British line of supply began in the factories, farms and ports of Great Britain. Tens of thousands of tons of imported food and war material arrived daily from the United States, Canada and Britain's other Commonwealth outposts. This was the danger posed by the German submarine offensive – cutting off the supply lines of the Allies. Raw supplies, 500,000 tons' worth, arrived daily in the British harbours and much of this was bound for the Western Front. British manufactured goods and imported material had to be shipped across the English Channel, unloaded, and shipped by either rail or truck to the front. Heavy-duty trucks required roads, and railways obviously required rails. The construction and maintenance of these transportation networks, along with the complex administration, was a gigantic managerial operation in itself. By 1917, the British Army was using 6 million gallons of petrol a day to fuel its transport vehicles – fuel that also had to be imported and shipped to France.[10]

France had introduced significant motorised transport early in the war and eventually employed 25,000 trucks and lorries. Upon entering the war in 1917, the United States produced 118,000 all-purpose trucks able to carry three to five ton loads and capable of negotiating the rutted roads of the Western Front. By the war's end, 51,000 of these had reached France.[11]

Even more important was the use of rail transport for the movement of troops, food and material. Hundreds of miles of light rail lines were constructed to link the port facilities to the rear depots behind the front. The rails were built as close as possible to the front and in many instances actually connected at the rear of the back line trench fortifications. In fact, at the outset of the war, it was the rail transportation system and precise railway timetables that Germany depended upon to rapidly mobilise its army and launch the Schlieffen Plan into Belgium, which threatened to win the war. In 1916, the British Army appointed Sir Eric Geddes, a veteran railway expert and administrator, to be Director-General of Transportation in France. Through the Flanders campaign of 1917 and into 1918, the British Army was using 900 locomotives, travelling an average of 9 million miles every month, while carrying 800,000 tons of equipment and 260,000 tons of ammunition.[12]

The movement of supplies went on day and night, around the clock, rain or shine, summer and winter. The two-million-man army was literally a city that had to be fed and watered and supplied. Logistics were more than just a key to victory; they were necessary for survival. Soldiers must eat. But modern rail systems and highways were not sufficient, or indeed practical, to negotiate the last few thousand yards to the actual front line. For heavy guns, ammunition, and rations, soldiers had to use raw muscle to complete the journey. Most of that muscle was provided by several million horses and mules pulling carts, wagons and limbers to the front. Animals remained the predominant source of power and it was not uncommon for soldiers to man-haul equipment and material the last few hundred yards of the journey. Foul weather, mud, wrecked roads and paths, and of course enemy shellfire, all made the final segment of the trip the most difficult and the most hazardous. Over 8 million packhorses were estimated to have been used in the Great War. Most suffered as badly, if not worse, than the soldiers they served. The British Army had nearly 450,000 pack animals at its peak in 1917.[13] Most of those animals did not survive the war, falling victim to fatigue, exhaustion and injury from either the demands of work or combat. They suffered wounds and death just as the soldiers around them did. Sadly, those that did survive the war were often worn out, ill, or unable to return to domestic activity. Many were simply destroyed or shipped to slaughterhouses.

Horses and mules, like soldiers, all have to be fed whether in use or not. Therefore, due to their efficiency, the motorised systems of transport became increasingly recognised and assumed greater responsibility wherever possible. The killing of horses and mules near the front by gunfire was prolific since the proximity of their activity exposed these pack animals to constant danger. Teams of horses and mules pulled every sort of vehicular device (including broken down motorised transport), and carried or hauled everything from food, to ammunition, to the big artillery pieces. Their task was not only demanding, but also essential; without the tens of thousands of draft animals, the day-to-day existence of the fighting soldier would have been impossible. Unfortunately for the poor creatures, the same dangers experienced by the soldiers – exhaustion, disease, poison gas, and gunfire – extracted a terrible toll on them.

By weight, a packhorse generally needed ten times the food of a man and supplying the tens of thousands of animals was one of the largest demands on the armies at the front. Cannon needed shells, but heavy cannon required teams of horses to move those cannon into position before they could fire those shells. Teams of horses and mules brought forward the countless shells that would then be fired by the thousand during the frequent bombardments. There were veterinary hospitals for the treatment of sick and wounded animals, and the importance of the animals for the war effort cannot be ignored or underestimated. Nor can its tragic consequences. The Germans had grossly underestimated both the amount of feed required for their war effort and length of the war. Running short of fodder, they resorted to mixing sawdust into their animal feed in order to sate the appetites of their draft animals. Unfortunately, it also reduced their work capacity, health and lifespan.

There are numerous accounts of soldiers, under the cover of darkness, liberating otherwise doomed horses trapped in the endless mud of the Western Front, and in particular the Passchendaele swamps of rutted roads and paths. Rescuing horses stuck in mud holes up to their shoulders and unable to free themselves, soldiers risked their own lives to save not only their beloved animals, but also to maintain their means for hauling essentials back and forth to the trench lines. There are numerous memorials along the Western Front that commemorate the effort and sacrifice of these animals and the love and respect that the soldiers felt for them.

The German Army

The Germans, of course, had been famous for their professional military system and their Prussian discipline going back to Frederick the Great in the 18th century. The creation of the modern German state by Otto von Bismarck in the late 19th century had been built on the efficiency of the Prussian military machine. That emphasis had only continued in the conscripting, training and arming of the modern nation of Germany under Kaiser Wilhelm II. The German Army featured an officer corps that prided itself on the study of war, strategy, and tactics. The German soldier reflected this commitment to a martial heritage.

Like his British Tommy counterpart, the ordinary German soldier carried a rifle, the highly accurate and well-made Gew (Gewehr) 98 Mauser rifle that used a five round clip and also carried a bayonet. The Mauser was accurate up to 2,000 metres, although 200 metres would be its best effective range for the average soldier. It was slightly longer, and at nearly 9 lbs. was slightly heavier than its British counterpart. The Mauser's smaller clip of bullets and slightly slower bolt action meant a slower firing rate than the British SMLE rifle. The German soldier also wore a steel helmet and by 1916 the spiked 'picklehaub' helmet had been discarded for the coal scuttle (bucket) model; in fact, the coal scuttle model with its improved design gave better protection to the neck and side of the head than the British model. He also carried a gas mask in a pouch, a hand grenade (nicknamed the 'potato masher') that featured a stick handle for better throwing, a sack for rations, a small canteen for water, extra clips of bullets (120) stored in pouches on a belt, and heavy boots. It was quite similar to the British kit. He too wore patches on his uniform to identify his unit and rank.

The German trench positions were considerably different from those of the British. For one thing, on most of the Western Front the Germans were defending positions that they had captured at the beginning of the war, whereas the Allies were usually attacking and trying to win back land that had been lost. This meant that the Germans were willing to invest in heavily fortified trench and bunker systems that used steel and concrete. They were usually, if possible, deeper and better equipped for permanent occupation. Most were almost impregnable unless dealt a direct hit of heavy artillery. German soldiers remained safe and cosy, deep in their bunkered enclosures during the long artillery barrages, and often emerged unharmed, excepting the nerve-racking fright and fear that the bombardment also inflicted. At the Somme, some of these bunkers were thirty and forty feet in depth, but due to the high water table, that was not possible in Flanders.

In Belgium during the Passchendaele campaign, the Germans built hundreds of concrete pillboxes, bunkers, and machine gun nests. These self-contained boxes of concrete could house individual machine gun crews, or larger platoons of soldiers, anchoring key positions in a chain of defensively linked outposts. They also served as command bunkers, dressing stations, and rallying points as the German defenders moved from strong point to strong point according to their mobile and flexible defensive strategy. These bunkers provided a strong network of defensive positions but, as with everything in the waterlogged Flanders/Ypres front, there were also dangerous disadvantages.

Kapitan Kalepsky of Infanterie Regiment 86 describes this danger:

The bunkers were reasonably strong and could withstand even direct hits from some of the heavy enemy shells, but owing to the ground conditions in the Flanders area they could not be erected over a strong foundation. When a couple of heavy shells opened a crater close to them, they would lean over, sometimes with the entrance down, and with the soldiers trapped inside. There was no way of rescuing them, of course, and we suffered a rather heavy number of fatalities in this way – and the thought of the painfully slow death of those entombed haunted us all.[14]

The early German defensive tactic, as was the Allies', was to defend the front line. The Germans, however, abandoned this system as it allowed too many frontline soldiers to become casualties in the initial bombardment and assault. Their revised tactic was to scatter their front line with lightly held outposts, and allow the attackers to enter a killing zone between their first and second line defences. As the attackers drove deeper into the defensive web, the defensive positions would become stronger, inflicting heavier and heavier casualties on the attacking units that became more and more vulnerable. This would be followed up by strenuous counter-attacks that would, in theory, annihilate the attacking units. The counter-attacks would then drive the attacking units back across the original front line German positions, and force the attackers back across no man's land, from where they had started. It was a system that required intensive training, discipline and confidence to be effective. It was an extremely flexible system, relying on the judgement and responses of forward units and their junior officers and non-commissioned officers (NCOs).

Passchendaele proved that the British could continue to grind out incremental forward gains against this system, but the Germans proved that the gains would be of an extremely limited nature and at *very* high cost in casualties. Much of the German military strength came from this frontline organisational command that relied heavily upon experienced junior officers and NCOs exercising the ability and authority to recognise battlefield conditions and issue independent and necessary deployments. This reliance on independent decision-making provided the Germans with frontline flexibility to exert maximum effectiveness on an immediate situation. The German high command created an overall tactical philosophy that incorporated and emphasised this operational confidence. The German defenders also paid an extreme price for this intensive set of tactics, absorbing casualties at a rate often as high as the attacking units. It also depended on the experienced quality of their NCOs, and when that group became depleted through battle, the entire organisation suffered.

Initially as well fed as the Allies were (excepting the Russians), the Germans suffered deteriorating supplies of food as the war progressed. German supplies in food and material were increasingly problematic as the war lengthened due to the increased effectiveness of the British naval blockade of the German ports. The food shortage was particularly acute on the German home front, as the military was designated to receive the major share of foodstuffs. German political and domestic decisions were being determined more and more by the strong authority and influence of the military commanders, namely Hindenburg and Ludendorff. The main diet, at home and at the front, consisted of potatoes and adulterated bread. Meat of any kind was at a premium, but so too was coal and other fuels for heating, cooking and transport. The privations of reduction in nutrition to soldiers, civilians, and animals alike was diminishing the Germans' chances for victory as the war lengthened and in this sense, the war of attrition was indeed being won by the Allies. Lack of food also reduced the morale of both German soldier and civilian, and eventually, the war of logistics would figure heavily in the final defeat of Germany.

4

COMMAND

The command structure of the Great War combatants had much to do with both their entrance and their conduct of the war. Once the war began, those individuals controlling the various levels of political and military priority had an enormous impact on the character and the result of the war that ensued. The debate over both the pre-war decisions and the actual fighting of the war has gone on ever since. Germany's willingness to treat Russia's military mobilisation as an act of war certainly led to the German eagerness to initiate their mobilisation and the activation of the Schlieffen Plan, steering Europe into a full-fledged continental war. The relationship between political leaders and their battlefield commanders was frequently strained, invariably confused and, at times, in total opposition to each other. The resulting actions and decisions deeply emphasised the frustration felt not only by combating soldiers but also by ordinary citizens. Who these leaders were, and the determinations they made, would literally have life and death repercussions, then, and for the future.

Often blamed for the start of the Great War, German Kaiser Wilhelm II was the emperor of the German Empire and therefore frequently condemned as the leader ultimately responsible for the outbreak of the First World War. He was the grandson of Wilhelm I, who had become the first emperor of the newly formed German empire in 1871. A Prussian militarist in mood and temperament, the young Wilhelm II, upon assuming the throne in 1888, quickly relieved his leading adviser, Otto von Bismarck, the true architect of the new German Empire. Ignoring Bismarck's sage advice, Wilhelm II insisted on building a powerful navy to challenge Great Britain and abandoned traditional allies such as Russia and England. Wilhelm's bellicosity in foreign relations was exceeded only by his ignorance of potentially harmful consequences. Worse was Wilhelm's willingness to concede political and military jurisdiction to his generals, which would contribute to igniting Europe into the Great War. This lack of vision, along with his gradual concession of policy to the military during the war, would prevent any pragmatic opportunity for a negotiated armistice during Germany's period of superior bargaining position, early in the conflict. More fatal to German success, and Wilhelm's political future, was the failure to reject his generals' use of unrestricted submarine warfare, thereby bringing the United States into the war and insuring Germany's defeat. Wilhelm abdicated in late 1918, abruptly ending the German Empire, which was not yet fifty years old. Wilhelm died in 1941, while living in exile in the Netherlands. His oldest son and heir, Crown Prince Wilhelm, commanded the German Fifth Army at Verdun. Not an incompetent military officer, Wilhelm was the nominal head of the Verdun campaign but acceded to the requirement of relying on an experienced professional soldier to act in concert with any strategic and tactical decisions. He flirted with Hitler and the Nazis, but basically remained aloof during the Second World War while living in Potsdam, Germany. He died in 1951.

Alfred von Schlieffen, the author of Germany's strategy to defeat France and Russia simultaneously, had died in 1905, but his programme for a rapid victory through the expedient of invading Belgium failed, both tactically and strategically. Invading Belgium risked the potential consequence of convincing Belgium's ally, Great Britain, to enter the war on the side of the Allies. Great Britain would eventually raise a two-million-man army and confront Germany head-on in major land battles. Worse than the tactical failure, this strategic error introduced a stalemated four-year war that would prove to be totally beyond Germany's capacity to endure. With regard to a prolonged war, the Allies clearly possessed a greater advantage in terms of population, resources, and control of overseas trade. To offset these disadvantages, the Central Powers relied on a combination of offensive and defensive gambits that eventually succeeded in defeating the Russian Empire and temporarily occupying captured French and Belgium territory. The strategic and tactical masterminds of this challenging 'two front war' strategy were Generals Paul von Hindenburg and Eric Ludendorff, who became the virtual leaders of Germany during the second half of the Great War from 1916 until the armistice of November 1918.

Hindenburg was a Prussian, aristocratic by birth, and career soldier by occupation. It was Hindenburg, assisted by the non-aristocratically connected Ludendorff, who conducted the victorious battles early in the war on the Eastern Front versus Russia. Hindenburg assumed overall command when he replaced General Eric von Falkenhayn in mid-1916 during the battles of Verdun and the Somme. Neither of these battles brought Germany any closer to victory and both came at costs in casualty that Hindenburg and Ludendorff felt Germany could not sustain and still win the war. Falkenhayn fully understood Germany's predicament in the stalemated war, but his attempt to win the war by 'bleeding' France to death failed. Although inflicting huge losses on the French, it also produced the same murderous consequences on Germany.

Hindenburg was a competent commander but much of his success stemmed from his close association with his partner Eric Ludendorff. Due to the German Empire's strict adherence to aristocratic heritage, Ludendorff could only be officially elevated to a junior command position and given rank accordingly. The senior rank had to be held by a title-holding member of the aristocracy, hence Hindenburg's higher rank and superior status in the eyes of the political and military establishment. It was Ludendorff who devised the almost impenetrable defences that thwarted the Allied attacks in 1916 and 1917, and who planned the devastating series of spring offensives in 1918 that nearly won the war for Germany, before sputtering into defeat.

Between the wars, Hindenburg became the last democratically elected President of the German Republic, before the German government was turned over to Hitler and the Nazis. Hindenburg died in 1934. Ludendorff was initially a co-conspirator with Hitler and the Nazis in the early 1920s, but he soon fell out of favour and played little or no role in politics or the military again. He died in 1937.

There were also several members of the high nobility in command positions in the German Army. Crown Prince Rupprecht of Bavaria was undoubtedly the best of the Great War generals of noble birth. Rupprecht was the son of the former King of Bavaria. Trained and educated in the military, Rupprecht was a respected soldier and officer and was taken seriously by the military establishment during the First World War. Serving in the Lorraine sector of eastern France early in the war, he became the overall commander of the German Western Front and was heavily involved with tactical and strategic decisions at both the Somme and Passchendaele battles. He left Germany during the Second World War, returned after the war, and died in 1955.

Ludendorff and Hindenburg relied heavily on their subordinate commanders and among the best were the Generals Friedrich von Armin and Fritz von Lossberg, who both played significant roles at the battle of Passchendaele. Von Armin was the front line commander of the Fourth German Army, the units that defended against the Passchendaele attacks in 1917. He was known for his rugged defence of a position and his willingness to experiment and adopt Ludendorff's flexible defence tactics. Von Lossberg was Ludendorff's premier defensive tactician and von Armin's chief of staff at Passchendaele. Von Lossberg served on many fronts where he observed and installed the tactics prescribed and developed by himself and Ludendorff.

Great Britain was led by its Prime Minister, David Lloyd George, who had succeeded Herbert Asquith in December of 1916 at the conclusion of the Battle of the Somme. Asquith, the great Liberal leader for the eight previous years, had brought sweeping social changes to Great Britain, but had struggled in the role of war leader during the first three years of the Great War. Asquith was thought to be less than enthusiastic about the war, erratic in his decision making, and generally worn out from nearly a decade of continuous leadership that had now reached a point of exhaustion over the gravity of his wartime decisions. Furthermore, his son had been killed at the Somme, dealing Asquith a crushing personal blow.[1] His ranking political supporters gradually abandoned him and his distaste for the endless casualties, coupled with the bitter disappointments of strategy and disagreements with his generals and fellow Allied leaders, turned the formerly dynamic and optimistic leader into a depressed and alcohol-ridden shell of his former self. In late 1916, beset by the appalling casualties of the Somme campaign, including the death of his son, Asquith resigned as PM. Perhaps he believed he would be retained in a coalition government, but he refused to serve under Conservatives Arthur Balfour or Andrew Bonar Law and in the process, David Lloyd George assumed the reins as leader of a coalition war cabinet and became PM.

In many ways Lloyd George was a logical choice as wartime PM. Asquith's appointment of Lloyd George, one of his most trusted and distinguished advisors, to the post of Director of Munitions in 1915, had been an excellent selection. Lloyd George had reorganised production of weapons and equipment and installed greater efficiency and performance. Factories producing shells, guns and other assorted sinews of war reflected Lloyd George's gift as a most efficient administrator. As PM, he intended to maintain Asquith's Liberal Party domestic policies, while acquiring the enhanced support of a coalition government to lead a more aggressive wartime policy. He reorganised a compacted War Cabinet that administered major decisions for military commands, policy, business and industrial war production. It was an all-encompassing combination of power that was deemed necessary to bring England into a full-scale wartime footing – if the war was to be won. Like Asquith before him, Lloyd George was shocked and dismayed by the enormous casualties and deeply troubled by the independent nature of the British military high command with regard to the decision making process for British wartime strategy.

Lloyd George also took a greater interest in foreign policy and became more deeply engaged in the Allied relationship with the French. He strongly supported a unified command and did not resent that command going to a French general. His avowed goal was to defeat Germany and win the war. Lloyd George would finish the war as Prime Minister and represent Great Britain after the war at the Versailles Peace Conference. Lloyd George would be the last Liberal Party PM.

As Lloyd George took over, it became increasingly clear that Britain was taking on a larger and larger role in the Great War. Its army and responsibilities had dramatically increased in size and presence. Britain was becoming the most important element in the Allied alliance as Italy faltered, Russia suffered revolt and withdrawal, and France wavered. The entire 1916 experience of the Battle of the Somme was an indication of just how deeply Britain had engaged its population, economy and future in the Great War; Passchendaele would now underscore the depth of that engagement.

Lloyd George brought several positive qualities to the leadership of Great Britain: he was energetic and enthusiastic in his desire to defeat Germany and win the war; he was tempered in his expenditure of soldiers and anxious to at least try to rein in the more wasteful methods of Douglas Haig's war of attrition; and Lloyd George was determined to consult with his French allies in negotiations and strategy. Lloyd George was willing to allow the French to command, since he honestly believed the a single command of the allied forces would be beneficial, and he was confident that the French probably had a better feel for the ground war, or at least as strong if not better than the wasteful and distant Haig. Lloyd George would be proved correct on the need for a unified command, but the French were soon to demonstrate that they too had a penchant for wasting soldiers' lives during the failed Nivelle offensive.

Lloyd George never favoured Haig, or his generalship, and had he had anyone else with whom to replace Haig, he would have done so. He called Haig a 'dunce' on numerous occasions, wrote disparagingly of him after the war, and did all he could to contain Haig's profligate spending of soldiers on big battles for little or no reward.[2] Lloyd George certainly possessed a clearer and wider world view than Asquith, which served him well at the Versailles peace conference in 1919. Lloyd George also tended to consider overall war strategy on a greater panorama than Haig's seemingly less than far-sighted vision that rarely encompassed anything beyond endless battles of attrition. He was eventually successful in persuading British commanders into accepting Ferdinand Foch as Supreme Allied Commander-in-Chief in 1918, a unified command structure having been desperately lacking since the start of the war.

Domestically, Lloyd George appointed administrators who were in agreement with him concerning the belief that it would take an all-out effort to defeat Germany. In respect of waging a war versus Germany, Lloyd George proved himself to be a more than adequate wartime leader, certainly more energetic and aggressive than Asquith, and a shrewd negotiator at the war's end.

Only two commanders led Britain's army on the Western Front, Generals Sir John French and Sir Douglas Haig. French commanded the British Expeditionary Force (BEF) from its arrival in France in the summer of 1914 until his removal in December 1915. Haig had been one of French's corps commanders and a leading critic concerning French's tactics, operations and ability to lead a war-winning army. Like Lloyd George, Haig was more aggressively minded to vigorously pursue the war against Germany and defeat the Germans on the battlefield. The question, of course, becomes – were Haig's methods and tactics the most efficient and economical way to win that war? Was Haig the person to lead Great Britain's army to victory, and at what cost in lives?

General Sir Douglas Haig remains one of the most controversial commanders of the Great War. He was not the overall commander-in-chief of all British military forces; he was, however, the commander of British forces on the Western Front in Belgium and France. And it was in Belgium and France, against the German army, that the Great War would come to be won or lost. Haig was fifty-five when he was given command of the British Western Front armies. The Germans considered him industrious, but unintelligent and ambitious – implementing a simple-minded strategy of attacking until the enemy is worn down.[3] This straight ahead approach of wearing down an enemy was responsible for Haig's oft-repeated belief that espoused the benefits of a war of attrition, which he regularly asserted to deflect the accusation that he was wasteful in regard to soldiers' lives. He was trained, as many Great War British officers were, as a cavalry officer and his faith in cavalry never wavered. Haig never lost confidence in the strength of cavalry in the face of modern weaponry, or in the potential for cavalry to exploit an enemy's weakness or to capitalise on a battlefield breakthrough. His cavalry division was at all times primed and ready to be thrust into battle. Unfortunately, throughout Haig's many First World War battles, that opportunity never arrived. His primary battlefield philosophy promoted an initial probing by blunt pounding to identify an enemy's weak point, followed by a rapid penetration. To this end, the months' long campaigns of the Somme and Passchendaele became testaments to his dogged determination, if not success.

Haig did show a willingness to introduce and use new weapons, even if it frequently was a reluctant or belated acceptance. The tank, aeroplane and the creeping barrage by the artillery were eventually accepted and promoted by Haig. He was not, however, open or receptive to disagreement or even suggestions that went contrary to his wisdom. This flaw, in particular, was to plague his command since it did not allow for the free flow of ideas to formulate a better method of fighting the war. Most subordinate commanders would dutifully agree and go along with Haig rather than challenge him, and those that didn't agree were soon not holding a command position. It was not the healthiest of promotional channels for younger officers, or for those veteran officers who felt that new and different approaches were required to fight the stalemate trench war.

Hubert Gough was chosen by Haig to command the opening of the Flanders Offensive (the Battle of Passchendaele). At age 47, he was the youngest British Army commander in the Great War. At the Battle of the Somme in the previous summer of 1916, Gough had commanded the Fifth Army that was held in reserve. The Fifth Army later fully participated in the Somme campaign, but not as Haig had envisioned. Trained as a cavalry officer, as so many of Haig's commanders were, including Haig himself, Gough was considered a master of offense. He was to be responsible for leading, or following up, the great breakthrough that Haig had envisioned on the Somme. Of course, it never happened. The selection of Gough to now lead the Flanders campaign can be seen in two ways. The first is that Haig wanted to break through and Gough was considered the ideal man to plan the attack and conduct the breakthrough. This is what Gough contended Haig had instructed him to do at the time, and he held to this view the rest of his life. The other view is that Haig chose Gough and his Fifth Army to lead the Flanders offensive to gain the greatest forward momentum possible, but that it was *not* intended to be an attempt at an all-out breakthrough effort. Either way, Gough planned the attack on a broad front with the idea that he would pierce the German lines and proceed immediately to capitalise on the breakthrough.

Later, Gough repeatedly commented on his understanding of Haig's orders for the planning of the 31 July attack:

I have a very clear and distinct recollection of Haig's personal explanations to me and his instructions were when I was appointed to undertake this operation. He quite clearly told me that the plan was to capture Passchendaele ridge and to advance as rapidly as possible on Roulers ... I was then to advance on Ostend. By the time I reached and had taken Roulers, Haig considered that the Fourth Army [under General Rawlinson] on the coast would have advanced sufficiently to cover my left, and combine with me in clearing the coast. This was very definitely viewing the battle as an attempt to break through and moreover Haig never altered this opinion till the attack was launched ... He confirmed this general idea on several occasions.[4]

In the event, Gough's attacks were blunted, casualties were enormous, and Gough requested Haig to suspend the offensive, especially in the face of the incessant rains that made the fighting, let alone advancing, almost impossible. Instead, Haig called upon General Herbert Plumer to revise and pursue the offensive with the Second Army, with Gough's Fifth Army being relegated to assisting. Plumer fared somewhat better than Gough with his 'bite and hold' tactics, although casualties remained high and gains limited. The following year, during the German spring 1918 offensive, the Germans would pour through Gough's sector of the Flanders defences and almost completely defeat the British and French in a nearly war-winning effort before being halted at the Second Battle of the Marne. Gough was held responsible by Haig, blamed for the defeat, and removed from command. Gough claimed he was not provided with either enough men or intelligence to properly defend the position. He would spend many years pleading his case and defending his role both at Passchendaele and during the 1918 German offensive.

At sixty years of age, Herbert Plumer was one of the older British generals remaining on active front line command. He also proved to be one the best. Famous for his walrus moustache, Plumer's background was as an infantry officer and his many victories reflect his more careful and methodical approach to tactics, especially when attacking a position. Many British high commanders, such as Haig and Gough, were cavalry officers, and their tactics and philosophies tended to be bolder and more inclined to attempt the sweeping strike to victory – a method that repeatedly failed to gain any traction during the artillery-dominated stalemate of trench warfare.

Plumer's techniques during the Messines operation that culminated in the victory of June 1917 are a classic example of his emphasis on methodical, advance preparation. The same approach was employed by Plumer and his Second Army when they were given the lead during the second phase of the Passchendaele offensive. Plumer's design employed his determined faith in the 'bite and hold' form of attack. 'Bite and hold' required limited goals followed by a halt in the advance to fully secure the captured ground. Plumer's tactics also required a programme to fully train and familiarise his army with the objective. Ordinary soldiers, non-commissioned officers (NCOs), and upper echelon officers, all received instruction as to exactly what the attack would entail and the responsibilities for each individual. Finally, there was a period of physical preparation that at Messines included a year of tunnelling 20 mine shafts under the German position. At Passchendaele it would be a thunderously powerful opening barrage that demanded appropriate timing with the infantry to escort them to their objectives, and then to shield them upon completing their seizure of the position. This worked extremely well for three separate 'bite and hold' engagements that were part of the Battle of Passchendaele: Menin Road, Polygon Wood, and Broodseinde. Each of these victories was followed by a pause of several days to bring up the big guns, reinforce the attacking units, and prepare the logistics before the next 'bite and hold' was attempted. It was a method of attack for which the Germans never really found an answer, even with their vaunted flexible defence in depth and counterattacks. As the campaign progressed, Haig became anxious and encouraged Plumer to push on in terrible weather and without sufficient preparation, leading to the setbacks at Poelcappelle and

First Passchendaele. Plumer's exhausted Second Army then gave way to Lieutenant General Arthur Currie's Canadian Corps, and the final capture of the Passchendaele heights and village. Currie, a Canadian, will be examined more closely in Chapter Nine.

Many commanders dealt almost exclusively with politicians and the 'home front' administration of the war effort. Stationed in London, and in theory the official conduit between the Prime Minister and the 'Chief of the Western Front' Douglas Haig, was Lieutenant General William Robertson. He headed the British armed forces from 1914 to 1917 as Commander in Chief of General Staff (CIGS). As chief of the general staff, Robertson assumed full responsibility for military decisions and appointments following the untimely death of Lord Horatio Kitchener. Kitchener was killed sailing to Russia, when the cruiser he was aboard struck a German mine. It was Robertson who assumed the chief administrative position and became responsible for maintaining a functional relationship with the politicians in London, such as Asquith and Lloyd George, and the Western Front generals such as Haig. It was a difficult balancing act. In early 1918, following the Passchendaele campaign, Robertson resigned and was replaced by Lieutenant General Henry Wilson, who had formerly been Lloyd George's personal military adviser.

Chief of British intelligence, and a loyal supporter of Haig, was Brigadier General William Charteris. It was Charteris who repeatedly invoked the belief that Germany was on the ropes and ready to collapse. Charteris touted this rather unfounded sentiment to the London government, the military leadership, and to Haig in particular. Charteris' optimistic appraisal of the British being close to knocking out the Germans with a 'big push' offensive helped to lead Haig to believe that the endless attacks at the Somme in 1916 and Passchendaele in 1917 would eventually succeed, if given enough time and effort. This, of course, proved to be false. Charteris was removed in early 1918, just before the surprise German spring attack, resulting in the nearly successful German spring offensive.

The French in 1917, as in 1916 at the Somme, were again desperately in need of British support, this time to cover the effects of the French army's mutiny following General Nivelle's disastrous spring offensive. Called upon to restore the French army's confidence was General Philippe Petain, the hero of the battle of Verdun in 1916. Petain had taken command of a nearly defeated army and restored their strength and resolve while preventing the German capture of the French fortress area of Verdun. He was a strong believer in massive amounts of heavy artillery, establishing an efficient and robust supply system and the frequent rotation of soldiers in and out of difficult combat zones such as the 'meat grinder' of Verdun. When the Nivelle offensive deteriorated into disaster and mutiny, it was Petain who was again called upon. Petain restored order, morale, and discipline to the French army, and rehabilitated the fighting capability of the French forces.

Unfortunately, the hero of Verdun became the shame of France during the Second World War when he caved in to Nazi occupation and became the puppet head of the Nazi-controlled Vichy French government. After the war, and by then an elderly man, he was placed on trial for treason and lived out his days under arrest. He died in 1951.

Petain's fellow general in the recovery of the French army after the 1917 mutiny was Ferdinand Foch. Foch had earlier been the architect of the French offensives that believed spirit or élan would win victories. This practically suicidal doctrine in the face of modern weapons was hopelessly outdated, but Foch was capable of adapting to the changing times of modern military firepower. His career suffered setbacks during the war as he was shuffled in and out of command positions, but after the Nivelle failures and the French mutinies, he was reassigned as chief of staff to assist Petain. Together, Petain and Foch rebuilt the confidence of the French army. It was Foch who was later selected by the Allied governments to become the Supreme Commander of Allied armies following the near defeat of the Allies during the German offensive in the spring of 1918. Foch went on to successfully lead the Allies to victory, employing a dazzling summer and autumn offensive that led to Germany's defeat, collapse, and surrender.

For his part, French General Robert Nivelle had demonstrated brilliance in his use of heavy artillery to drive the Germans out of the captured French forts and territory that they had temporarily captured in the opening months of the year-long struggle at Verdun. In 1916, Petain's declaration, 'they shall not pass' and the accompanying alteration of tactics had proven to be a life-saver at Verdun. Petain strengthened the artillery, improved logistical support, and installed a shorter and more frequent rotation of soldiers through the maelstrom of the Verdun fighting. It worked wonders. When Nivelle relieved Petain, it was with the vigorous enthusiasm of a supremely confident commander who effectively transitioned Petain's rejuvenation efforts into an offensive spirit that drove back the Germans and earned for Nivelle the opportunity to command the next big French offensive in 1917.

Nivelle spoke excellent English, was open and sociable, and got along well with the British commanders who enjoyed his personality and confidence. Nivelle, widely and loudly, predicted a breakthrough for 1917 at Chemin des Dames along the Aisne River. He would use overwhelming artillery to support a massive French attack and win the war in a single swoop. He was energetic, confident, and very public as to his intentions and tactics. When the French attacked in the spring of 1917, this tactic met some early success before disintegrating into a calamity of huge losses, with little or no gain, and a deflated French spirit within the army that soon degenerated into the widespread mutiny. Petain was called in to remedy the situation, which he was able to do, and Nivelle was sacked and sent to a North African command for the duration of the war. But the damage had been done and, as in 1916 at the Somme, the British Army was called upon to fight a brutal and costly offensive action to tie down German troops. The British cooperated with continued attacks at Arras, where they had already been blocked at great loss. This resulted in another month of fruitless action and at huge cost – actually the highest daily British casualty losses of the war.

The French mutinies would then impinge upon the British in two more ways: they would not have adequate or complete French support for their own scheduled offensive in Flanders, and the British would have to endure losses beyond what they might have expected since they were encouraged to continue the Flanders offensive well beyond what most considered a reasonable duration for some of the most bitter and difficult fighting of the war.

The French did participate in the 1917 Flanders campaign, but due to the mutiny crisis of 1917 their contribution was limited. Sandwiched between Gough's Fifth Army and the Belgian First Army entrenched along the Belgian coast, the French First Army under General Francois Anthoine conducted several attacks north of Gough's main front. Anthoine's participation featured the usual French competency in artillery preparation and minor gains were accomplished. But the effort was a secondary one to Haig's overall offensive. As in 1916, the British were left to take on the brunt of the German army virtually by themselves. Make no mistake, for better or worse, Haig was willing to accept the challenge and the opportunity. With the French reorganising and virtually impotent, the British chose not only to attack and fight, but to pursue the attack to an almost diabolical end.

This, then, was the result of Germany's failure to properly anticipate not only the entrance of the United Kingdom into the Great War, but Britain's ruthless motivation to see it through to a conclusion. The British, a dominant world naval power, had morphed into an world land power. British artillery, infantry, and determination, had increased to such an extent as to threaten the existence of the ferocious German defence. British command and operational decisions can be argued about and faulted, but the pressure placed on the German army in both 1916 and 1917 was almost unsustainable. As strong, imaginative, and resilient as the Germans were, they were almost overwhelmed by the British willingness to attack repeatedly, under all conditions, and at the tragically sacrificial expense of their manpower. Such, according to your point of view, was either the failure, or the success, of Haig's 'war of attrition' and the commanders and soldiers who bravely fought the brutal battles of 1917.

5

EQUIPMENT

The soldier of any army remains the basic ingredient of warfare. However, the soldier is sometimes only as good as his equipment and his leadership will allow. Leadership involves human emotion, discipline, and determination, blended with imagination and action. There are no guarantees for success no matter how creative, brilliant, or determined the leadership might be. The same can be said of equipment – it is necessary but, again, there are no guarantees. Much of the equipment used by the World War One soldier was being newly introduced to the battlefield or was in an experimental stage. Many of these innovations, commonplace today, completely altered the way war was waged. Although new and inventive equipment can be essential, or even revolutionary, it is the soldier behind the technology that allows survival and produces victory. And so it was during the Great War.

Rifle

The basic weapon of the Great War soldier was, of course, the rifle and this weapon had seen outstanding development over the previous fifty years. Portable, accurate and lethal, it was a weapon carried by the majority of the millions who were engaged in the course of more than four years of the Great War. Both the German and British soldiers had effective and practical rifles.

The Germans relied on the bolt action Gew Mauser 98 that weighed about nine pounds, and used a five round clip of 7.92 mm bullets. About four feet in length, it had a detachable bayonet and for the average soldier, an accurate range of over 200 metres. It required the bolt to be pulled back and re-slotted after each shot, thereby engaging the next round in the firing chamber. It was a durable and dependable weapon. The British SMLE (short magazine Lee Enfield) was similar. Being 6 inches shorter, it was slightly handier in a tight situation, such as a trench. It was roughly a quarter pound lighter, carried a magazine of ten .303-inch rounds, and had a faster rate of fire. A trained 'Tommy' could accurately fire 15 rounds per minute with its short bolt action. Like the Mauser, it used bolt action to reload the rifle after every shot, necessitating manual re-bolting after each firing. The SMLE could also have a bayonet attached to it. Like the Mauser, it was durable and dependable and extremely accurate at 300–500 yards. The French had a similar rifle, the Lebel, the first modern rifle to use smokeless powder. It was the main rifle of the French 'poilu' (soldier), carried a magazine of ten rounds of 8 mm bullets, and was the heavier and longer of the three main infantry rifles. It, too, was bolt action and capable of accuracy at 400 metres.

All three of these weapons were produced in vast quantities, were dependable and durable, and were highly accurate and devastatingly lethal.

Machine Gun

Rapid firing automatic weapons had come of age at the end of the 19th century. Multiple barrel weapons, such as the Gatling gun, had been developed and used by several armies under wartime conditions but it was not until the late 1880s that American inventor Hiram Maxim designed a fully functional rapid firing weapon that used the recoil force of the exploding shell to eject one shell and insert another. With that revolutionary development, the machine gun came of age.

So rapidly did the gun fire, up to 600 rounds per minute, that a jacket of water around the barrel was required to cool the weapon. Even then, barrels had to be frequently changed to prevent heat damage. An ordinary Maxim heavy machine gun contained almost two gallons of water (7.5 pints) and could reach boiling point in one minute of continuous fire.[1] The effective range of the heavy machine gun was 2,000 yards, well over a mile, and could reach greater distances with indirect fire. Great War commanders at first failed to fully realise that a machine gun could sweep a battlefield with continuous fire, destroying any exposed attacking columns. In April of 1915, Sir Douglas Haig, then a corps commander, pessimistically stated: 'The machine gun is a much over-rated weapon and two per battalion is more than sufficient.'

This would, of course, change over the course of the war, both in recognition and implementation by Haig and other commanders as the machine gun came to dominate the observable front of a battlefield. So devastating was this concept, along with the additional firepower of artillery, that soldiers were soon forced to dig in and the stalemate war of the trenches, dominated by the defence, took root.

Unable to obtain a suitable market in the United States, Hiram Maxim relocated to Great Britain where he was joined and supported by Albert Vickers. The Maxim-Vickers machine gun was manufactured in Britain by the Vickers Company becoming, through numerous adaptations, the Vickers machine gun. It was also produced in various versions by several European nations, including the dominant military powers of Germany, France, and Russia. Hiram Maxim became a British citizen, and was later knighted.

The basic Maxim-Vickers heavy machine gun used the same .303-inch bullet as a rifle, was belt fed, and could fire for as long as bullets were fed into it. The gun weighed at least 40–50 pounds, depending on model and carriage, and a crew of several soldiers was required to carry, mount and operate the gun effectively. One soldier fired and another fed the ammunition belt. The other members provided relief, observation and supplied extra ammunition, water, and barrels for the gun. By the end of the Great War, the machine gun was acknowledged for its ferocious capacity to dominate a battlefield front. It gave a handful of soldiers the firepower of many more riflemen. The 'machine' gun was the perfect symbol of the dark side of the Machine Age. It personified the industrialised nature of the Great War. It was made of metal, had interlocking parts and operated by the explosive recoil power of an exploding bullet that then automatically inserted the next bullet into the chamber to repeat the process. A soldier operated the machine gun as any factory worker would operate a machine in any shop mass-producing a product. It was a fully industrialised weapon in an industrialised war. The British disaster on the first day of the Somme in July 1916, when the British Army suffered nearly 60,000 casualties and 20,000 killed in a single day's action, epitomised the power of the machine gun as it mowed down wave after wave of attacking Tommies crossing no man's land. Charging across a field into the teeth of mass machine gun fire proved to be nearly suicidal, and the figures from battles such as the Somme only reinforce this fact. By the war's end, the heavy machine gun was being produced and used by all nations and in huge numbers.

Besides the heavy machine gun, such as the Maxim-Vickers, there were a number of light machine guns that were more mobile and portable. The Lewis gun was a superb lightweight rapid firing weapon, under 30 pounds, less than half the weight of a Maxim heavy machine gun. The Lewis gun could be carried by one man, with his accompanying partner carrying extra ammunition cases. The economically designed gun used circular pan-shaped trays for quick loading and firing, even when moving from position to position across the battlefield. It could fire at a similar 500–600 rounds per minute rate as the Maxim but was limited by the size of the pan tray, roughly 50 rounds, that fed the gun before another pan had to be inserted. What it lacked in continuous fire, it more than made up for with its mobility. Like the Maxim, the Lewis was invented by an American, Isaac Lewis, only to have his gun idea rejected in the US for political and personal reasons. Like Maxim, Lewis took his weapon to Europe to have it promptly adopted by the British Army.

In a battle such as Passchendaele, where soldiers were moving from one muddy shell hole to another to avoid the relentlessly blanketing machine gun and artillery fire, the mobile Lewis gun was invaluable in providing portable firepower while negotiating difficult positions during attacks. The Lewis gun was also employed on lighter reconnaissance aircraft and as a secondary weapon on tanks. It was a versatile weapon, and like the Maxim, was dependable and ruggedly built.

Poison Gas

Poison gas had been introduced in the Great War by the Germans at the Second Battle of Ypres in 1915. The first massive gas attack had used chlorine gas against the French. The gas was released from canisters and allowed to drift across the battlefield. The gas produced potentially fatal effects on the lungs and respiratory system. It wasn't long before the Allies too were using gas. Gas masks were soon designed and issued, becoming standard equipment in a soldier's kit.

The British released 150 tons of chlorine gas at the Battle of Loos in September of 1915. Released from over 5,000 cylinders, much of the gas proved ineffectual, or worse, dangerous to the British themselves, as a shift in the wind direction blew much of the gas back into the British positions and trenches.[2] The use of chlorine gas was followed by phosgene gas, another gas that affected breathing and the lungs. First used by the French, and more lethal than chlorine gas, phosgene has less odour and colour than chlorine gas. It is also a slower, although deadlier, killing agent. Therefore, for combat purposes, it lacked the knockout quality commanders sought. Soldiers could continue to fight back, even if they did not realise they were doomed to die the next day when the gas finally took hold.

Gas dispensed from canisters in a cloud was highly unpredictable as to where it would end up. The chance of a wind shift could blow the gas back upon those releasing the gas and deny the user the planned benefits of the attack. Therefore, the most efficient way of launching a gas attack was to insert the gas into artillery shells and blanket a desired area with gas. This was especially effective for putting distant gun crews and back line reinforcements out of action, even if only temporarily. Firing the gas in artillery shells also reduced the risk of the gas affecting one's own troops. The British used 2,000 tons of poison gas during the Passchendaele campaign, mainly fired from artillery into the German back line positions.[3]

At Passchendaele, the Germans unveiled a new poison, mustard gas, and with it, a new horror to the Great War battlefield. Besides rain, mud, filth, death, and the fear of horrible wounds, was added the new terror of mustard gas, something that the Germans had been holding back for the propitious moment. That moment arrived during the brutal and savage fighting at Passchendaele. A gas mask is basically a breathing apparatus and does not allow for complete protection; mustard gas burns hideous blisters on whatever part of the skin it touches. If inhaled it can burn out the lungs; it can also burn out the eyes, blinding those who come into facial contact with it. Unlike the previous gases used, mustard retains its lethality within clothing, the soil, and in underground pockets such as dugouts. If the living hell of the battlefield was not bad enough, rent with artillery shrapnel and machine gun bullets, now the terror of poison gas lurked hidden in the remnants of previous gas attacks, increasing the agony and fear for the ordinary soldiers who were forced to endure this new nightmare of an often-unseen horror. Soldiers on both sides feared the silent killer that could be lurking anywhere and at any time, trapped in bunkers or in the depressions of shell holes. It wore no face and showed no mercy.

Mustard gas has the nasty habit of not chemically dissolving or dispersing as easily as chlorine and phosgene. Water, rain, and dilution will eradicate those two other poisonous vapour agents.

But mustard gas lingers in the ground, in trench dugouts, in the clothes of the dead and wounded, just waiting for an opportunity to inflict its hideous consequences on the unsuspecting. Even if not fatal, its burning of blisters on the skin will instantly incapacitate a soldier with painful burns wherever the chemical touches the skin.

The dreaded *fear* of attacks by poisonous gas was often as devastating as a real attack. From 1915 onward, every soldier was required to carry a gas mask in his personal kit. As gruesome as gas attacks were, they did not provide the magic spear to break through an enemy's defences; instead they became just another dangerous form of death and pain to be feared on the Great War battlefield.

Aircraft

Heavier than air aviation began in 1903, when the first successful flight of the Wright Brothers' aeroplane took place at Kitty Hawk, North Carolina. The growth and development of the aeroplane had then been rapid. Corresponding with the improved output of the gasoline-powered engine and a better understanding of the dynamics of flight and flight control, the plane entered the Great War capable of flying at almost 100 miles per hour and able to reach altitudes of 10,000 feet while carrying the weight of several passengers.[4] From the beginning of the war, the aircraft was seen as a way to 'see over the hill' at what the enemy was up to. The first role of the aircraft was, therefore, observation. Bad weather, cloud cover, or superior enemy air strength, all hindered an army's ability to see what the other side was doing and to prevent their observation of enemy positions and installations. It did not take long for one pilot and his observer to begin shooting a pistol, a rifle, or light machine gun at an opposing aircraft, or taking a primitive small bomb up into the air and attempting to drop it on an unsuspecting opponent. The air war had begun.

From the very opening of the Western Front battles in 1914, it was aerial observation that identified the exposed flank of the German advance, leading to the Allied attack and victory at the First Battle of the Marne. Because the observation of enemy positions was so important, it was not long before the *prevention* of enemy observation became of paramount importance. Aircraft quickly became an essential factor in the artillery duels in which the Great War soon became enmeshed. Seeing where your targets were located, and identifying the results of your shelling, was a huge advantage before launching an infantry attack. Aircraft soon adopted roles as spotters, or as fighters either to protect your own spotters or to shoot down an opponent's spotters. Photography from the air, that could be later studied and analysed, became a necessary branch of the service. So too grew the unique ability of pilots to engage opponents' aircraft and successfully shoot them down – thus giving birth to the 'aces' of the air.

A major breakthrough came when Anthony Fokker (among others) developed the interrupter gear for German single seat aircraft, allowing a pilot to shoot through his own forward propeller and fire at targets directly in front of him. The French and British soon followed with their own versions of this mechanical work of genius and the daily 'dog fights' in the air over the trenches soon involved dozens, then hundreds, of aircraft.

By 1917, at the Battle of Passchendaele, aircraft had advanced in speed, range, altitude, and firepower. Aircraft equipped with heavy machine guns, and loaded with a few hundred pounds of bombs, could now fly at 150 miles per hour and begin seriously threatening an enemy trench or dugout position. Although aiming, delivery, and accuracy were primitive and unsure, the science and technology were advancing. So too were the *numbers* of airplanes increasing; the original few hundred spotters had now blossomed into air squadrons of several thousand planes. Air superiority became one of the most vitally important operations of the Western Front. Gradually commanders came to understand the value of air superiority, and also the tactical effect of using aircraft to strafe and bomb enemy positions, either pinning them down or destroying them. Suppressing reinforcements of troops and material became especially important during or preceding an attack. The blending of air and ground forces would contribute to the breaking out of the stalemate condition and, by the end of the war, the combination would be grasped and perfected as a war-winning offensive to contribute to the victory by the allies.

With the initial development by Anthony Fokker of the interrupter gear to fire a nose forward machine gun through the propeller, the Germans dominated the early air war. The Allies, however, soon caught up in technology, drawing even, and then pulling ahead in the air war with superior aircraft that were faster, more manoeuvrable, and possessed higher ceilings. Most importantly, the Allies had the capacity to produce more of them. Numbers do count, and the Allies had the numbers to control the skies. Unfortunately, nature did not always cooperate, and when weather dictated the aircraft to stand down, the Allies lost much of their *ground* superiority due their inability to take advantage of their *air* superiority. By 1917, individual bouts of air combat continued but the strength of the air was now in numbers. Air squadrons possessing 50–60 warplanes by early 1917 increased to vast fleets of over 1,500 planes on daily missions by the time of the great Allied offensives of late 1918.[5] During the Passchendaele campaign, due to the atrociously bad weather of storms, rain, and clouds, the inability to take advantage of its air superiority was a serious drawback to the British attacks.

Tanks

During the Great War numerous ideas, stratagems and solutions to breaking the stalemate of the Western Front were suggested, tested, and found wanting. The idea of a mobile vehicle with tractor treads and an armoured box had been around for several years. The British Army had sent Lt Col. Ernest Swinton to France to inspect the battle conditions, only to be appalled by the mud-sodden stalemate.[6] Swinton believed an armoured vehicle with farm-style tractor treads and heavily armed with either cannon, or machine guns, or both, could be a method to attack or penetrate the German lines of defence. At the same time the First Lord of the Admiralty, Winston Churchill, was proposing a similar idea to the War Office and under the auspices of the Navy, formed the Landships Committee.[7] The result was a rhomboid shaped box of armoured steel, driven by a powerful engine and using tractor-style caterpillar tracks. After experimenting with it in fields, ditches, and muddy roads, the vehicle was found to be capable of crossing a field at several miles per hour while carrying a crew equipped with a small cannon and machine guns. Several prototypes were investigated. General Douglas Haig attended a trial, declaring it to be potentially useful and ordered 60 of them for the upcoming Somme offensive of 1916. They made their first appearance at the battle Flers on the Somme front in September of 1916; 49 tanks were available, 32 began the operation, and nine were able to successfully escort infantry and reach the target village of Flers. The tank had arrived.

Going into the Battle of Passchendaele, the tank had been modified and improved from the initial design and the result was the Mark IV, the first truly serviceable and fairly dependable tank produced in large numbers. Seventy-six Mark IV tanks were available at the battle of Messines in June, shortly before the big push at Ypres in July 1917. Unfortunately, due to the heavy rains, the sea of mud, and the overall destruction of the battlefield at Passchendaele, the tank did not have an opportunity to prove its worth in the ocean of goo that was Flanders. It bogged down repeatedly in the mud, failed to negotiate the shell holes of the destroyed and torn apart battlefield, and often ended up ditched in a shell hole, as a sitting duck for German gunners with armour piercing bullets. The tank would not begin to come into its own until the Battle of Cambrai, in northern France, in late November of 1917 – after the Battle of Passchendaele had been concluded.

The Mark IV tank, produced in such large quantities, had the makings of an important tactical weapon, but needed further refinement in design and to be produced in even more significant numbers. So, too, the use of tanks in conjunction with other ground forces demanded rethinking; commanders would need more imagination in the tactics of small arms warfare, joined with artillery, air, and mobile armoured power. Such would be the winning combination in the summer to autumn of 1918 when the Allies would storm to victory, defeat the Germans, and end the war.

The capability of the Mark IV can be viewed in terms of what we take for granted today in an armoured vehicle. Any tank designer must decide how much emphasis is to be placed on thickness of armour, which weighs down the vehicle; how powerful an engine, which will determine its speed and ability to navigate across open or broken terrain; and the firepower of its guns, which, by definition, will add weight and volume to the vehicle, thereby affecting the other two requirements. So it is a compromise.

The Mark IV came in two varieties, both of which were used at Passchendaele. They featured a six-cylinder petrol engine generating 105 horsepower, were shielded with a half-inch of steel armour, and carried a crew of eight. On a level, evenly graded road, it could travel at a speed of 4 mph. The 'male' version was equipped with two 6-pounder cannon and three Lewis machine guns, and weighed 29 tons. The 'female' version was similar in size, weighed slightly less, and had an armament of five .303 machine guns.

The British invested over two hundred tanks in the Passchendaele campaign but only a handful survived in serviceable condition, and most remained either broken down in the mud or destroyed by German guns. The Menin Road became an infamous tank graveyard, littering the landscape. Their struggle through the mud and slime of the Passchendaele swamp of shell holes and flooded ditches produced some of the most enduring images of the difficulty for *any* object to move about over the wreck of the mud-choked Flanders fields.

Numerous explanations of how and why tanks received their name abound. The most common, and sensible, is that being a secretly developed weapon, it was important to maintain their secrecy until arrival in France and their use on the battlefield. What then could a crate contain of this immense size and weight? The only containers of similar size and content were the huge water storage tanks, so the crates were labelled and classified as 'tanks'. When the vehicles were rolled out, the name stuck and they have been tanks ever since. It is as good an explanation as any other, and probably at least close to being accurate.

Flame-thrower

The flame-thrower was used to flush out and incinerate soldiers holed up in bunkers, trenches, and pillboxes, stubbornly refusing to give up or surrender. A flammable fluid, such as petrol, was forced out under pressure. The petrol was carried in a backpack tank, connected to a hose and nozzle, and ignited at the nozzle end to shoot a sheet of flame at a target. The Germans were the first to experiment with the concept and, on first using it in the trenches, were not surprised that British soldiers were quick to surrender. The pressurised flame could easily be thrown upwards of 50–100 feet, depending on the type. Carrying the tanks was extremely dangerous and flame-thrower operators were prime targets of any defenders. One well-placed shot and the man would go up in a ball of flame himself. Both the French and British adopted flame-throwers of their own design. The British also developed a longer-range flame-throwing weapon that could be shot from tanks.

Mills Bomb (Hand Grenade)

Two types of grenades were used in the Great War: a hand thrown bomb that would explode on impact and a timed bomb that, when thrown, also released a timer before detonating. These timers were usually spring loaded, and were set to explode within several seconds of releasing the fuse. William Mills of the Mills Munitions Company in Birmingham, England, developed the most commonly used British hand grenade, hence the name 'Mills Bomb'. Grenades could be thrown, or actually lofted or tossed, by hand, or shot from a specially adapted rifle. The Mills bombs were famous for their distinctive pineapple design on the metal containment vessel, providing thinner weak points the better to split and shatter the metallic outer shell, which produced lethal metal fragments on detonation.

All grenades were basically a compact metal vessel containing explosive material, designed to disintegrate into numerous pieces of shrapnel when detonated. If not sufficiently distanced or shielded, the bomb could be as dangerous to the thrower as to the target. The German grenades featured a wooden shaft for easier throwing and were known as 'stick bombs' or 'potato mashers' due to their distinctive shape.

Grenades were extremely useful for close-in fighting, such as in confined trenches, bunkers, shell holes, and during any type of raiding attack in small groups. A soldier would often carry a half-dozen with him when on a trench raid or during an attack. Follow-up waves would frequently carry sacks of fresh grenades to replenish those that had been used. It is estimated that 75 million grenades were produced during the Great War.[8]

Individually, none of the newer weapons would be a game breaker. As important as they would be in the future, tanks and aircraft could not, by themselves, win the war. What most of these new and devastating devices did was to further paralyse movement, as troops remained hopelessly pinned down in their trench positions. The relentless pounding of the cannon, the spraying hail of bullets from the machine guns, and the observation of every troop movement from the sky, all contributed to further enforce the need for cover to survive. To be exposed was to risk certain death. In fair weather, airplanes and aerial photography would increasingly record every movement and preparation, coinciding with the greater emphasis on analysing what the photos revealed. Sheer numbers in attacking, be it soldiers, tanks, artillery, aircraft, or exotic weapons such as flame-throwers and poison gas, could not, in four years, break the stalemate. The key to breaking the standoff was to be in the creative use of tactical combined arms: the new weapons mated to a more independent and imaginative way of tactically probing for weak spots and following up with support in strength. Massed attacks, even when supported by overwhelming artillery, were clearly not the answer, although they would be repeatedly, and futilely, attempted, again and again, at Passchendaele.

Small arms and heavy artillery, backed up by accompanying tanks under the cover of superior air cover, would be the method to finally break the stalemated Western Front.

Besides the development and success of mixed arms and the adjusted tactics to take advantage of these weapons, the need for a corresponding assault on the reinforcing capacity of the opponent became more and more apparent. Reducing or denying an opponent the reinforcements in manpower and the ability to re-supply food, ammunition and materials that are the backbone of industrialised warfare, was to be the path to victory. At the same time, it was imperative that each side continued to be reinforced in massive numbers, resupplied with adequate amounts of food, equipment and ammunition, and then persevere both on the battlefield and on the home front. The war would be fought in the factories and farms as well as in the trenches. Such were the conditions for victory as the Great War endured its fourth year of a seemingly endless round of attacks and counter-attacks to no apparent conclusion.

6

ARTILLERY

Modern weapons had a revolutionary impact on the formation of tactics and strategy. Generals of the warring nations would be haunted by the frustrations that limited their opportunity to manoeuvre on the battlefield. Conscription would provide never before imagined manpower and the size of the armies, coupled with the lethality of the weapons, brought unforeseen and unrehearsed challenges for leaders and commanders. There seemed to be unlimited numbers of both men and machines, and the necessary reduction of each would take years of industrialised warfare. Machine guns, poison gas, aircraft and most deadly and dominating of all, artillery, were to hamstring the movement and coordination of these million-man armies and lead to the brutal strategy of attrition. Suffering an obscene number of casualties while conducting a fruitless 'non-winning' offensive could be counted as *progress* if an opponent was being decimated and worn down. Therefore, if absorbing outrageous casualties was determined to have hastened the process of subduing and defeating the enemy, then the human cost could be considered justified. Such became the strategy and, increasingly, the justification of tactics.

Although the machine gun swept the battlefield clear of attacking soldiers, it was artillery that became the thundering killer of the Great War. Guns had never possessed such power, size and numbers in any prior war. All sizes and varieties contributed to the massive barrages that devastated the battlefields into featureless, treeless, moonscapes, Passchendaele being a notorious example. German, French, and British artillery continually evolved during the course of the war not only in number, but also in range, accuracy, and dependable explosive power. As the war progressed, the weight and influence of artillery became heavier and more devastating. Verdun, the Somme, and Passchendaele all saw larger and larger expenditures of artillery. More than fifty per cent of all Great War casualties were due to artillery – far and away the deadliest and most consistent killer on the battlefield. At Passchendaele, the number and potency of the artillery would reach unprecedented levels. The technical and numerical development of artillery was continuous but usually lagging somewhere close behind was recognition by the commanders that these powerful weapons posed unresolved challenges to tactics of defence and attack. At times, the lag seemed to be a chasm or desert devoid of common sense, as men were hurled to their deaths in a wantonly wasteful series of suicidal attacks. A learning curve that continued through the length of the war included advancements in ranging, aiming, training, and positioning. Successful barrage techniques depended on dependable weapons, experienced gun crews, disciplined timing, and predictable shell placement that was gradually perfected as the war progressed.

Background

In the fifty years leading up to the Great War, tremendous advances had been made in all aspects of artillery. Both the cannon itself and the propellants to discharge the shells had seen constant and revolutionary improvement. The sheer size of the cannon and weight of the projectile had grown to such an extent that when the Great War began, the Belgian fortresses at Liège, considered impregnable to bombardment, were within days reduced to rubble by the big German siege guns. Shell size had expanded and they could now weigh over a ton. In little over a half century, due to the greater potency of improved explosive compounds such as cordite, melinite, lyddite, and trinitroluene (TNT), the one-ton shells were capable of easily reaching ranges up to 10 miles and with a bursting power able to destroy steel-reinforced concrete emplacements several feet thick. Huge howitzers such as a 'Big Bertha,' the awesomely powerful German siege weapon produced by the famous Krupp armaments factory, were making any reinforced fortresses obsolete. Not only were the guns bigger and better at lofting heavier and heavier shells, but due to rifling in the barrel, the range and accuracy was dramatically increased. Again, in less than fifty years, the ordinary effective range of long barrelled guns (cannon) had advanced from 3,000 metres to 25,000 metres. Not only in range and shell weight, but also in accuracy, the long guns continued to rapidly evolve during the 19th century's industrial revolution in metallurgy and manufacture. Rifled barrels, breech loading, and more stable and controlled propellants were influencing the advancement of artillery and shell. This, in turn, enhanced the accuracy and therefore the efficiency of the weapon. Observation reports from forward spotters would note the placement of a shell, plotting the range and accuracy. Adjusted shots could then be expected to increasingly 'zero in' on the target.

Several factors contributed to this exponential growth in firepower and lethality. There were many types of artillery used throughout the Great War, but all benefitted from advancements in industrial technology, precision engineering and chemistry. Names and designations can be confusing, but long-barrelled guns firing at lower arcs with high muzzle velocities are termed 'guns' and are capable of reaching greater distances. Howitzers fire at higher arcs and shorter ranges, using slower muzzle velocities, and carrying heavier shells; they are effective at firing 'up and over' to reach a target. Mortars fire at the steepest arcs and therefore they reach the shortest distance, which is very effective at hitting a nearby target. Shorter range meant a heavier projectile, and shorter range allowed nearby positions, such as an opponent's neighbouring trench position, to be engaged with an artillery-weight projectile.

The specific weight of shell, length of barrel and mobility of the weapon would be determined by the requirements and demands of the individual battlefield. The assortment of Great War battlefields required a variety of sizes, shapes, and types of artillery to fit the need of the operation. Passchendaele featured many of these various types of artillery pieces and in high numbers.

Field guns

For centuries artillery had typically been loaded through the muzzle using separate shell, propellant, and primer. The advent of the 'quick-firing' (QF) field gun was dependent on a breech-loading gun, equipped with finely tooled mechanisms to load and seal a single piece of fixed ammunition containing shell, propellant and primer within a single casing – similar to a rifle round. The inception of breech loading allowed for faster and more efficient loading by the gun crews. Two other devices combined to enhance a 'QF': shock absorbers, termed 'buffers' to absorb the recoil of the cannon, and a 'recuperator' mechanism to automatically return the barrel to its prior firing position without re-aiming. This combination, which was first fully incorporated in the famous French .75 field gun, became the standard for all armies employing mobile field guns. A weapon such as the French .75, or the equivalent British 18 pounder, could fire up to thirty rounds a minute, but in actuality would normally use a rate of four to six rounds per minute to conserve barrel life and crew stamina, achieve accuracy, and maintain a supply of ammunition. By definition, field guns were lighter, more mobile, and faster to load, fire, and re-position. Field guns were the descendants of a mobile form of artillery designed to advance with cavalry and infantry in unison and quickly produce an accurate stream of firepower.

Howitzers

The value of the howitzer became more apparent as the Great War developed. Early in the war, the French had not felt the need for howitzers, so great was their faith in the 'French .75'

QF. The Germans, however, soon reaped significant benefits from large howitzers such as 'Big Bertha', a fortress-destroying weapon that could lob a nearly one-ton shell almost eight miles with devastating destructive power. The angle of penetration for these powerful howitzers was nearer to vertical, as opposed to the flatter trajectory of the long guns, giving the howitzers and their heavier shells even greater explosive power on impact. As the war staggered on and armies began digging ever deeper and stronger bunkers, the necessity for cannon with shorter range, higher arc, and more powerful shell potential became apparent. Due to the proximity of the opposing lines of trenches and the relative nearness of the enemy artillery batteries, it was essential to be able deliver a heavy curtain of high explosive (HE) and shrapnel on a nearby target. The howitzer, with its higher arc and greater shell weight, could achieve this. Though needing a stronger working platform and requiring more time and muscle to reposition than a field gun, it provided much heavier firepower both to the forward positions and to rear echelon targets.

Heavy Artillery

Using a flatter trajectory, the long-range heavy artillery pieces were awesome in their size and capability. These guns could weigh 200 tons and frequently had to be moved on railways. Often termed 'rail' guns, the devastating power of these weapons was legendary. The British 18-inch rail gun could hurl a 2,500-pound shell 13 miles. The benefits were the ability to reach deep into the rear of the enemy's front lines to hit transport, communication, supplies and reinforcement collection areas. Because of their great range, these guns were also of course more deeply in the rear and therefore less exposed to counter battery (artillery) fire.

The trade-off was in spotting targets and recording the accuracy of where the shells were falling, what damage they were doing and what re-aiming was required. Even so, the sheer raw force of these long-range weapons was impressive and frequently essential in reducing an enemy position, or pinning down reinforcing units.

Mortars

Mortars come in all sizes and shapes, but their one common trait is the ability to loft a shell at a very high arc and reach a very close target. Mortars frequently are designed to fire virtually straight up into the air to land on a target only a few hundred yards, or even a few hundred feet, away. It is the ultimate 'up and over' weapon. With the two sides deeply entrenched and separated by a no man's land that could be as narrow as 100 yards, the mortar was the preferred method to lob an explosive device on an entrenched enemy who was very close. An opponent, dug-in beneath sight lines, could avoid being vulnerable to straightforward rifle, machine gun, or field gun fire, as the projectiles would only go over their heads. With its high arc and steeper angle, a mortar could achieve both the short distance and the vertical penetration that was desired, falling directly into an entrenched position. Mortars could be light enough to be operated by a two-man crew and heave shells as light as a few pounds, or be quite large and require teams to operate such as the heavy-duty German 14-in 'minenwerfer', or bomb thrower. Smooth- or rifled-barrelled, in light and heavy varieties, and usually muzzle loaded, the mortar was an extremely effective weapon that was highly suited to trench warfare.

Ammunition

Gun crews had many responsibilities concerning their artillery pieces. Artillery was no longer just for blasting great holes in the ranks of advancing soldiers. Artillery was now capable, and was *required*, to reduce buildings, bunkers and fortresses. It was essential for the disruption, if not destruction, of back line transport routes, supply dumps and reinforcing units. It was responsible for suppressing the enemy's artillery, known as counter battery fire, to prevent the opponent from using his own artillery to disrupt and destroy your positions, your troops, and your supplies. And it was a killing instrument, reducing enemy soldiers, whether in attack or defence mode. And kill it did. As previously mentioned, artillery accounted for over fifty per cent of all casualties during the First World War and produced the tens of thousands of unidentifiable bodies whose names line the numerous memorials. No one could move on the open battlefield under its shroud of iron. And nothing could survive when its shells were on target. A man could hide in a hole to avoid rifle or machine gun fire, he could dodge an opponent's bayonet, he could wear a gas mask; but when the big shells went off directly in his vicinity, he was fortunate to only be wounded and not killed outright. Men became 'shell shocked' not from rifle fire but from the endless booming of the big guns and the never-ending bursting of the big shells sent over in relentlessly violent and thunderous barrages. It was a fearsome hammer of death.

The gun crews were responsible for a multitude of tasks: to position, aim, and maintain the guns, plus tend to the mules and horses that provided much of the transporting of the guns and ammunition. The shells themselves had to be properly fused to achieve maximum effectiveness. This involved coordination, with officers in charge of supervising the placement and timing of the barrage, and the ability of the crew to properly process and execute that information.

Not only the gun itself, but the projectile and its content had undergone recent, radical development. With the technological advances in artillery engineering, there were also advances in the chemical compounds of the explosive material that was both hurling the projectiles and detonating the shells as they reached their target. Larger and larger shells, using smokeless powder and chemical compounds of much greater explosive power, had not just changed the killing power on the battlefield but removed the clouds of smoke that had formerly obscured visibility. For centuries, black powder had been the chief explosive component in weapons and blasting devices. Once again, the mid- and late 19th century had produced revolutionary changes in the chemical composition of gunpowder. Black powder produced clouds of smoke, masking the battlefield and making observation difficult. More importantly, it lacked the bursting power of the newer propellants such as cordite, lyddite, melinite, and the more practical trinitrolucene (TNT). These improvements in chemical propellants were able to not only throw a shell farther, but also provide greater explosive power to the shell on reaching its target. It was these heavy-duty shells fired from the powerful Krupp cannon, and using powerfully explosive projectiles, that destroyed the Belgian fortresses at Liège at the outset of the war.

The combination of improved loading from the breech, greater explosive power in the shells, and the modern employment of recoil absorbing mechanisms that allowed the barrel of the cannon to fire its shot and return to its pre-firing position, contributed to a remarkably potent weapon. Coupled with the manipulation of targeting by forward observers, shells could be redirected to accurately hit a target.

These shells contained their own fusing mechanism that predetermined when the shell would burst. At the same time, the type of the shell's explosive content could also be pre-determined and adjusted to suit the range and type of target: high explosive (HE) to destroy buried or fortified targets and shrapnel shells that dispersed hundreds of tiny balls of lead, as in a shotgun shell, to obliterate soldiers in the field.

The destruction of barbed wire in front of defending trenches was a primary need for an attacking unit, and a difficult responsibility for artillery. The failure to completely destroy barbed wire during the Somme offensive had caused considerable alarm for the commanders of the British Army but, more to the point, resulted in enormous casualty rates for advancing soldiers who were caught on the wire and became easy targets for defenders. The introduction of the '#106 fuze' helped resolve that problem. The French and British developed an artillery fuse that would only detonate on contact with an object, such as barbed wire or bunker housing. This advance reduced the percentage of shells that had been detonating either too early or too late to effectively destroy barbed wire. It became a highly valuable solution to the responsibility of artillery and increased the reliability of gun crews to properly fuse their shells prior to an attack.

The science behind artillery technology had progressed to integrate these features to the weapon but also necessary was the training of the gun crews to efficiently and accurately operate these steel behemoths. As thousands and thousands more cannon were required, and millions and millions more shells to feed them, so too was the improvement in the manufacture of the weapons and their projectiles. Early in the war, the British produced an insufficient number of cannon and shells to feed the voracious appetite of the battlefield artillery batteries. Worse, the shells that were manufactured, or imported, were often 'duds' and incapable of performing properly programmed settings, or just ploughed into the ground. Today, the farms around the Passchendaele battlefield, as at the Somme, contain literally tons of unexploded ordnance. Every year, another one-and-a-half tons of metal is unearthed from the Passchendaele area alone.[1]

Artillery production clearly went beyond the mere manufacture of a steel barrel and a gun carriage to support and transport it. The cannon and shells had to be precisely made to narrow tolerances, and the number of shells and barrels had to be made in great quantity. There was always a greater and greater demand for more cannon, more shells, and better quality of each.

Command

Trying to catch up with the industrial and scientific advancements in weaponry, and thus their potential for maximum tactical deployment (killing power), was a major hurdle for many Great War commanders. The use of mixed arms and coordination of the new weapon systems was a complex study in operations and for the commanders, employing these weapons was as difficult a process as the engineering and technical obstacles had posed for the manufacturers. Many in the military leadership struggled: both under the obstinate reluctance to accept the *use* of these weapons, and the unacknowledged ignorance of the *potency* of such weapons, such as the machine gun and modern artillery. Commanders were often lacking in practical operational knowledge and failed to use, or even understand, the full potential of artillery. The same was true with regard to a commander's lack of understanding about how well a soldier could perform under such intense firepower. Early in the war there was clearly a lack of respect for the lethality of the rapid firing weapons that could repeatedly clear a battlefield of any living soldiers. Spirit, élan and desire could not compensate for the sheer wall of metal encountered by attacking units. Six months into the war, both sides resigned themselves to digging-in and the system of trenches from the English Channel to the Swiss Alps was established. The next question for the commanders was how to alter the balance that was so heavily tilted in favour of defence. The rapid firing machine guns and artillery pieces swept a field clear of soldiers, retarding mobility and any opportunity for a war of manoeuvre. This was to be a daunting challenge and one that would cost the lives of tens of thousands as the generals sought to find an answer to the overwhelming firepower of the dug-in defensive positions that dominated the battlefield.

The command problem was two-fold: how to disrupt the opponent's guns to allow your units to manoeuvre and attack, and how to best maximize your guns to achieve that solution. The stalemate of the Great War testified to the difficulty of accomplishing this, and the attempts to use brute and blunt force to penetrate a well-designed defence proved not only ineffective but murderously costly. Artillery, with its terrible firepower, seemed the simple solution; just disgorge an overwhelming barrage of shells until the enemy is demolished. That idea, however, was found wanting.

Firepower

The initial response was to inundate a defensive position with a curtain of shellfire that would precede an attack. In other words, outgun your opponent's gunners and the defenders. The Germans and French at Verdun would both simultaneously attempt this approach. Nothing would be gained by either side in nearly a year's fighting, at the cost of nearly a million casualties in the attempt. The stalemate conditions remained the same. At the Somme in 1916, the British would take their turn and over one million shells would be fired at the German line in a little over a week before the launch of the initial 1 July attack. But the majority of the shells failed to do their job. Shells failed to explode, or exploded at incorrect heights, thereby negating their power. Barbed wire, which should have been destroyed, remained intact. German bunkers placed deep underground and reinforced with steel and concrete were impervious to anything but a direct hit. And accuracy and ranging over the course of the four-month battle was found to be woefully lacking in the inexperienced British gun crews of the newly formed Kitchener army. At the Somme, the British day one attack produced the greatest one day casualty total in all of British military history. The next four months devoured nearly one million British, French, and German casualties for barely a few miles of gain. In terms of attrition, the Somme was considered by some to have been a success but it certainly did not produce a breakthrough on the Western Front. It also demonstrated that artillery alone, no matter how powerful and abundant, could not produce a victory.

Commanders all too frequently considered artillery, if in great enough number and strength, to be the easy solution for safely escorting an advance – to the detriment of their attacking armies. Improperly aimed or targeted artillery, even at the great shell expenditure by the British at the Somme, demonstrated that it took more than just sheer numbers of guns and shells to pierce an enemy defence for an offensive. A disciplined plan of attack that featured coordinated units of infantry and artillery working in unison, coupled with overwhelmingly massive amounts of well-targeted and dependable firepower, would be required for a successful offensive.

When Generals Herbert Plumer and Arthur Currie were placed in command at Passchendaele, to rejuvenate the offensive in

Flanders, the *first* request was inevitably for more artillery. Both demanded more guns and bigger guns, with greater accuracy in the form of creeping and protecting barrages. Their tactic was to 'bite and hold' a limited section of targeted territory, using an intense artillery barrage to precede the attack, and then to protect and maintain it with equally concentrated artillery fire. Artillery was to escort the attacking infantry and then provide a shield to resist counter-attacking German units. It proved a very successful tactic when well coordinated and executed. The Germans had no answer for the method when properly conducted.

So, artillery was clearly more than just producing a steel barrel and firing off tons of loud and colourful fireworks of explosive metal. It required the top to bottom skill of manufacture, engineering, manning, and ultimately tactical usage. Anything less would ultimately fail to both protect and properly escort an advancing soldier who was called upon to secure a position.

As great as the advances in the chemistry, metallurgy and engineering of the modern artillery weapon had become, well into the war there remained a considerable lack of knowledge and experience regarding how to effectively apply this increased firepower. Commanders readily conceded the destructive force of the *big* guns, but often were ignorant of what practical application of artillery could, and could not, do on the battlefield, and thus were frequently inclined to relegate the big guns to the chore of merely assisting an operation.

Napoleon had been an artillery commander first, then a field commander and is supposed to have commented, 'God fights on the side with the best artillery.' British generals such as French, Haig and Gough were all cavalry officers first, trained to manoeuvre and thrust with speed and spirit, seeking the swift, *arme blanche* charge to achieve a victory or seize a position. Since limbers and weapons were drawn by horses and mules, it was only natural for officers of artillery to be horsemen first and artillery experts second. The transport and movement of the animal-drawn weapons was of primary importance, especially when the guns were only firing at straight ahead targets chosen by line of sight. Innovative ideas for the targeting and plotting of unseen targets, as well as the scientific principles involved in accurate firing, would have to be significantly improved. Everything from maps, to gun sights, to the grid location of targets, was to witness a sea change in both attitude and implementation. As the Great War progressed, it became increasingly apparent that not only would the number and quality of the guns need to be increased but, more importantly, the *method* of using the devastating firepower to either defend or to attack an adversary would need to be enhanced. If the war was destined to be an artillery war, then the grasp of the importance of all aspects of artillery would have to be revolutionised.

The week-long shelling of the German positions before the opening attack of 31 July 1917 at Passchendaele was the largest single artillery expenditure up to that time in the war: 3,100 guns, firing three-and-a-half-million shells during the weeklong preparation. The bombardment featured every calibre of cannon, from the mobile 18-pounder field guns to the mammoth fifteen-inch naval rail guns. Both high explosive and shrapnel shells were used to destroy the German positions preceding the advance. The larger failures of the Passchendaele campaign, in particular the Battles of Poelcappelle and First Passchendaele, were mainly attributed to the lack of adequate artillery fire to escort and protect the attacking infantry. Likewise, the successes experienced by Generals Herbert Plumer and Arthur Currie were contingent on their insistence on overwhelming artillery firepower in preparation for their offensives, and the precise placement of a protecting barrage to shield their infantry upon the occupation of their attacking targets.

Currie in particular, with his background training in artillery, was adamant about the availability of heavy artillery before an advance, and the use of artillery to prevent the Germans from successfully counter-attacking newly won and held positions. Both Plumer and Currie also insisted upon bringing the guns forward to the newly taken positions *before* proceeding with the next set of advances.

The Adversaries

Examining some of the guns employed by both Anglo-French and German artillery, it is clear both sides took similar approaches to field and siege weapons. Early in the war when the Germans were attacking the great Belgian forts at Liège, the emphasis was on heavy duty howitzers and mortars, whereas the French and British concentrated on more mobile field weapons such as the British 18-pounder and the French .75. As the war progressed and the Germans dug in to protect their captured territory, it was the French and British employing the monstrous siege weapons to drive the Germans out of their defensive lairs, while the Germans relied more on shorter range howitzers and trench mortars. The Germans did develop the 50–75 mile 'Paris gun' that they would use to hurl shells into downtown Paris between March and August 1918, but it was more a terror weapon than a true tactical weapon of any strategic value.

During the 1917 campaign at Ypres, between 15 July and 2 August alone, the British employed at least 280 pieces of heavy artillery, 718 pieces of medium artillery, and 2,092 pieces of field artillery firing a combined total of over 4,283,550 rounds of ammunition. The most frequently fired British artillery piece was the 18-pounder, expending over 2,239,608 rounds.[2] These figures do not include the three-and-a-half-million shells fired the week before the 31 July campaign began, or the multiple millions of shells fired during the rest of summer and only ending with the conclusion of the offensive in mid-November. Of these millions of shells it must be remembered that many were duds and many ploughed into the soggy muddy fields where they remain to this day – undetonated. Others were gas shells, loaded with poisonous gas to suppress troops, particularly in the back lines where artillery batteries and reinforcement counter-attacking (Eingreif) groups were stationed. It was understood that a gas shell exploding anywhere in the vicinity of an artillery battery was particularly useful in quieting that unit. Due to the terror and confusion of a poison gas detonation, the need for precise, direct hits on a gun position to put it out of commission was eliminated. The Germans, of course, used similar tactics, doubling down on the bet with the employment of newly developed mustard gas. Used for the first time at Flanders in the summer of 1917, mustard gas was particularly effective, since it blistered the skin of any exposed area and it was difficult to dissipate as it hung over and became absorbed into the soil of the battlefield. Mustard gas could seal off an area with its pervasive qualities that remained in the earth, in dugouts, even on garments and equipment. Its toxic dangers could linger for days or even weeks in an exposed area. Artillery became the primary delivery method for the use of poison gas. It was the optimal expedient for the saturation of a distant area with little or no danger of it rebounding on those using it.

Finally, the Germans clung to their faith in large mortars, the 'minenwerfers', as a mobile form of artillery. Certainly powerful, and well suited to the demands of the short ranges of trench action, they had drawbacks. Heavy and difficult to move around, they required large crews to move, load and fire, and their low rate of fire was not fully compensated by their acknowledged punch.

The Barrage

Any discussion of artillery must include the method of placing the barrage. When the war began, the typical barrage featured an intense blanketing of a forward target, and usually preceded an offensive attack. Infantry could not go forward until the barrage was lifted, which then exposed the attacking infantry to the enemy's machine gun and rifle fire. As the war progressed, a greater sophistication of barrage lifting was developed and employed. The creeping barrage was a curtain of artillery fire that would move forward across the battlefield at a certain speed, providing a shield of explosive steel to lead the advancing infantry across no man's land'. From time to time, the barrage would lift and move forward to curtain the advance, the advancing infantry following in its path from lift to lift. To be effective, it took perfect coordination between the advancing infantry and the batteries of the gun crews of the distant guns. The infantry had to have complete faith in the artillery curtain, routinely advancing only 100 yards behind the barrage and sometimes advancing as close as only 50 yards behind the exploding shells. Casualties routinely occurred due to friendly fire from poor timing either by gun crews or infantry, faulty timers on the artillery shells, or inexperience by either group. Even though 'friendly fire' casualties were quite common, the overall benefits for a successful attack far outweighed the risk. The French calculated, and accepted, that an extraordinary ten per cent of their attacking casualties could be attributed to friendly artillery.

By war's end, the level of artillery precision had reached such a confident level that attacking groups could expect not only immediate protection in front of them, but also expect a barrage to conduct intricate patterns of lifting sweeps. Such manoeuvres of the barrage included swinging forward, left to right, as a swinging door; pushing forward to clear enemy reinforcing soldiers, followed by a return to the previous position; and moving at adjusted speeds, which would anticipate the predicted speed of troops crossing the battlefield. Also used were box barrages, which literally boxed off an area of the battlefield, allowing a limited penetration of a selected sector of the battlefield that would be temporarily isolated for attacking ground troops to carry out a specific mission while protected from counter-attacks.

Once again, however, this type of barrage involved training, experience and the complete dependability of the weapons and ammunition involved. It also required precision maps that included accurately labelled grids of the battlefield into definable sectors for the gun crews to reference in their targeting. At the Somme in 1916, the moving barrage was being developed and experimented with, but by the time of the Passchendaele campaign of 1917, the method had been fairly well perfected, relying on implementation of the interacting groups in concert. By 1918, and the Great War winning offensive, the moving barrage had developed into a highly sophisticated and predictable tactical tool that helped push forward the surging Anglo-Franco-American offensive that brought victory on the Western Front.

Observation

In order to place a shell on a target, it is essential that the gun crew knows where the shell is landing. The fire from a short-range gun can be observed by the gun crew from their firing post, which is how cannon operated for centuries. And since the early cannon remained basically straight line in their firing, it was not difficult to point and aim at advancing infantry and cavalry. This is known as direct fire – where the target is clearly visible. But as ranges increased, the placement of the shell soon left the line of sight, and the accuracy became unknown. The early answer was to have a soldier climb a tree or a pole to elevate his field of vision, but it soon became necessary to have forward observers reporting back the accuracy of the shot through some sort of signalling device or medium. This became known as indirect fire, the firing of the cannon without the gun crew able to visibly sight its target. This was all supposing that the gun crew had the technical capacity to mechanically adjust the gun for the placement of the shell, thereby affording the correct result. Assuming this ability on the part of the gun crews, it then soon became more and more difficult to observe where the shells were falling, miles away, as gun ranges began to reach deep into enemy territory. This science of indirect fire required an entirely new scheme of aiming.

During the Great War, the ability to put an observer into the air added a new dimension to his ability. Balloons and aircraft soon became an integral part of the observer's work. Mapping and plotting also became essential for the spotters and plotters. A map with coordinates would be set in a grid of sectors, with each gun crew responsible for a sector. Distance was set and plotted for where each shell was expected to fall. Next, an observer in a balloon or aircraft would locate the enemy target and plot the target on the map. This would be for either immediate, or later, use. Once the basic grid was established, it was just a question of aiming and setting the fuse for the time it would require for the shell to reach its target. Charts were then composed that calculated what type of shells and precise amounts of propellant would be required to hurl the shell a particular distance. Timed fuses on the shell would then, hopefully, detonate and explode at a desired time and place. Eventually airplanes would be equipped with a telegraph device, and through wireless connection; the gun crews on the ground could immediately alter the range and direction of the shell fall. Contact fuses would only detonate on contact with an object, such as a bunker or barbed wire.

Lacking observation, another method was to bracket a sector of a zone and blanket that sector. This method would ensure the desired placement of gunfire to suppress reinforcement, block a transport route, or seek and hit suspected gun batteries. The suppressing of gun batteries, known as counter battery fire, was essential to allowing advancing infantry a better chance to cross no mans' land and occupy captured positions. The enemy, of course, was doing likewise and the battle of fire versus counter fire was never-ending. Defenders were always in fear of being overrun by attacking infantry and losing not only their position and their guns, but also of course their lives. As aircraft achieved greater numbers and efficiency, the strafing of back line gun batteries became an additional function for the increasingly important air arm.

In order to better pinpoint the enemy gun positions for counter battery fire, several new scientific technologies were developed. Sound, shock and flash observation were all experimented with and eventually became important methods to pinpoint enemy gun positions. Sound observation required the use of sound receivers placed at different locations and through triangulation, a location could be identified from where a particular sound originated. In this case, a certain gun or group of guns (gun battery) would be sound detected and then plotted to determine an otherwise unseen target for counter battery fire.

If visible to observers, flash spotting used a similar technique to identify the source of a gun firing and, again through triangulation, it could pinpoint the location of the flash of a single big gun or gun battery. Measuring the shock waves of the gun explosions was another method of identifying the location of a given point and source for the origin of the explosive shock, which then sent a following wave. Tracing the intensity, speed and decay of the shock wave proved an invaluable source for spotting and plotting, since it could be used in all weather and without reliance on visual spotting.

After the war, this technique of tracing a shock wave became an import tool for geologists to trace the composition of the earth. Exploding a charge beneath the surface sent a variety of shock waves to a receiving device, thereby revealing different layers of rock and sediment. It was therefore a very useful tool in the geological identification of potential resource locations such as petroleum.

All three of these methods – sound, flash and shock – became essential means of identifying and plotting targets of indirect gunfire and the suppression of enemy gun batteries. They also required the accurate drawing of grid maps of every area on the Western Front to profit from the information. However, many of these ideas and disciplines needed to be accepted and encouraged by the commanding officers for any benefits to accrue. As mentioned earlier, many officers were hidebound and against any scientific technology and very reluctant to experiment or employ innovation.

The Great War recognised artillery as not just a powerful blast of explosive but an essential and vital arm of the entire military and civilian operation that required extensive discipline, science, manufacture and innovation in order to respond to the conditions of the battlefield and enemy modifications.

Transport

One last consideration of artillery concerns the demands of physically moving the iron monsters. Horse and mule teams of four to eight animals were needed to transport the guns from one position to another. Many guns were so enormous they required being positioned and transported on railway flat cars. Rail guns were the giants of the Great War's battlefield. All guns involved extremely heavy work in mounting, moving, and loading. At Passchendaele, there were further problems in the sodden, muddy terrain that demanded added bolstering to hold the weight and the recoil from the gun. Manhandling the guns into position and man-hauling shells to the gun emplacements was not uncommon. Not just the guns but the individual shells frequently had to be physically carried the last few hundred yards to the forward gun positions. This was especially difficult at Passchendaele since the roads were so utterly destroyed by the incessant shelling, or already flooded. Then too there was the extreme danger, as every area was also well plotted by the German gunners. Many positions, such as the appropriately named 'hell fire corner' just east of Ypres and a major intersection leading to the front, had been thoroughly zeroed in on and were dangerous to cross at any time, day or night.

The battlefield at the Salient was relatively cramped: roughly twenty miles in width at the base, which narrowed to only a few hundred yards at the tip as the battle continued, and barely four to five miles in depth. This meant shells were constantly falling within less than a mere 100 square miles of territory. And this area was only marginally advanced over the course of the four months' heavy shelling. Every inch of the battlefield was registered for the guns and shelled repeatedly. The photographs of Passchendaele's bleak craters are testament to the constant pummelling that it endured. Animals and men alike continuously suffered from the shellfire; avoiding exposure to German observers, or from British spotters if you were German, dictated *every* movement. Transport and re-supply was generally conducted only at night and was, at all times, extremely dangerous. Even under the cover of darkness any detected movement along the narrow roads and duckboards was sure to draw immediate and intense shellfire.

Maintenance

The firing of thousands of shells exacted a toll on not only men and animals but on the equipment itself. Constant maintenance was required to prevent the gun barrels from deteriorating and thereby risking the gun exploding within the gun battery, an occurrence that was not all that infrequent. Gun crews kept charts and logged how many shells were fired so barrels could be replaced, and either re-bored or scrapped. Gun sights had to be recalibrated, shells had to be cleaned and inspected, and the entire gun and carriage apparatus had to be serviced and lubricated if the guns were to perform the desired tasks at levels of optimum efficiency and dependability. At Passchendaele, this was particularly important owing to the rain and mud.

Back in Britain, the manufacture of shells had undergone a complete revision – both in production and in quality. The great shell shortage earlier in the war had been a scandal the ramifications of which on the battlefield had prompted reorganisation of not only factories but of the government administration itself.

As with so many of the Great War's other enterprises, artillery occupied a footprint of mammoth scale. Artillery truly dominated, its importance reaching to every aspect of the war effort, from command, to innovation, to science, to delivery, to mobility – all were intrinsically interconnected and all required cooperation and a fully integrated system. The big guns tyrannised the battlefields and meant life and death to everything within their long and terrifying shadow and no sector typified that fact more than the narrow confines of Passchendaele.

7

THE FOUR-MONTH CAMPAIGN OF THIRD YPRES / PASSCHENDAELE IS INITIATED

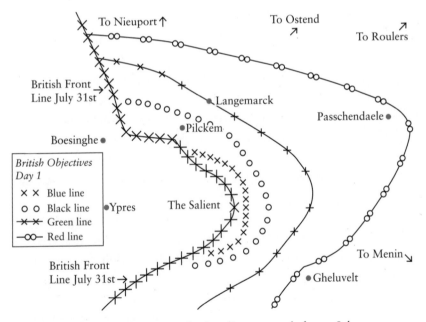

The Salient. Objectives, Day One, the four lines are goals for 31 July.

The official go-ahead from Prime Minister Lloyd George and his War Cabinet to allow Haig and his command to embark on a fully fledged Flanders offensive came on 18 July 1917 and was submitted to Haig by the Chief of the General Imperial Staff (CIGS) General

Sir William Robertson. This was very late in July and planning had already gone far ahead, but there had also been numerous delays as requested by both the French and British generals, Anthione and Gough, for further time to prepare. Even so, the decision from Lloyd George came with great reluctance:

> The decision to undertake the Flanders offensive was taken by Lloyd George and by most of his colleagues with reluctance and misgiving. No one believed that a strategical result could be achieved, and all shrank from the terrible losses, which they knew it must involve. But the consensus of naval and military opinion was so overwhelming that the War Cabinet could not take the responsibility of rejecting the advice thrust upon them with so much cogency. It is true that that they adopted the Italian plan as a reserve plan in case the Flanders attack failed or degenerated in to a mere slogging match. They went so far as to order that staff officers should be sent to Italy, railway timetables worked out, and that ammunition dumps should be built up for an eventual force of heavy guns. With this in view the progress of the Flanders attack was to be kept under constant review by the War Cabinet.

This was related by the Secretary of Prime Minister Lloyd George's War cabinet, Maurice Hankey.[1]

Even with this dread and hesitation, no one really believed Lloyd George and the War Cabinet would abandon the Western Front and redirect major operations into Italy. Help for the Italian Front – yes, and maybe, but change strategic course and shift the concentration of the British Army – no.

Such was the fear and lack of optimism on the part of Lloyd George and the political establishment going into the offensive. The tragedy of another Somme campaign involving tens of thousands of casualties for little or no return was dreaded by all. However, the early results from Flanders were encouraging. The capture of the Messines Ridge in the southern area of the Flanders region brought renewed optimism, and became the true launch of the Flanders offensive. Its success was welcomed, both politically in London, desperate for something positive to crow about; and by Haig's command, also desperate for a victory to hoist up the military pole.

The introductory engagement of the third Battle of Ypres, which became the Battle of Passchendaele, was this successful British attack at Messines Ridge in June of 1917, nearly two months before the main Passchendaele campaign commenced. Under the direction of General Herbert Plumer, the British Second Army had spent over a year digging twenty-two tunnels underneath the German defensive positions and planting 450 tons of ammonal high explosive. The Germans had been suspicious of a potential British tunnelling programme and were alert to the threat. Countering with their own mining crew, the Germans conducted a virtual underground 'tunnel war' beneath the area that fronted the ridge and directly under the Messines Ridge. The Germans were able to disable one of the mines and two more were never detonated during this subterranean war-within-a-war. The inventive Plumer had identified within his units 30,000 qualified mining engineers and former miners, who were able to carve out galleries of tunnels that burrowed directly underneath the German front line positions on Messines Ridge, many reaching depths of 200 feet. Tunnelling and detonating huge mines under German positions had been successfully accomplished before, including several large ones. The enormous Lochnager Crater from the Battle of the Somme in 1916 can still be seen to this day. But the extent and number of mines that had been created during Plumer's patient yearlong excavation at Messines Ridge was quite unique. The entire attack was to feature more than just the mines going off; Plumer had planned a well executed attack that included a well timed creeping barrage, accurately placed and plotted in-depth artillery fire to suppress the German counter battery fire, and well trained and rehearsed infantry units to quickly seize the ridge and hold it.

Plumer's preparation also incorporated more than just mines, lots of guns and training. His logistical design laid new water pipelines to the front areas that could supply each of his corps with 150,000 gallons of fresh water a day. Also added was construction of new light railway lines to advance the tons of food and ammunition to the forward areas, which included 144,000 tons of ammunition stockpiled in dumps for the attack. Artillery was increased, and in the big and medium gun sizes in particular: 2,266 guns, 756 of them heavy or medium, with an average of 1,000 rounds for each 18-pounder, and stacked in readiness. Three-and-a-half-million shells were fired in support of the attack before and during the first day of the battle. The artillery barrage would both precede and follow the blowing of the mines.[2]

Concerning the upcoming Messines action and the size of the mining operation, General Plumer's chief of staff General Tim Harrington was reported to have said (others attribute it to Plumer himself), 'Gentlemen, I do not know if we will change history tomorrow, but we shall certainly change the geography.'[3]

On 7 June at 03:10, the nineteen mines were detonated, and the attack got underway. The mines went off with an explosion that could be heard in southern England. Supposedly, Lloyd George heard it at No. 10 Downing Street in London. Up to 10,000 German defenders were instantly killed along the Messines Ridge front line, some with no visible wounds other than the convulsively fatal shock of the explosions. As the attacking British infantry arrived at the former German positions, they discovered the remains of dead German soldiers scattered within the enormous craters, completely obliterated German defences, and German survivors who were entirely disoriented and dazed from the shock of the fearsome explosions, and more than willing to quickly and quietly surrender. The attack was a complete triumph and the Messines Ridge, the first step in Haig's move to drive to the North Sea coast, had succeeded.

Many observers believed that a follow-up attack to take advantage of the initiative could have immediately been engaged. But so confused was the overall strategy for the Flanders campaign that Haig had not contemplated what course would be advisable if the situation presented itself; nor how to inaugurate such an extension, even with the potential for his much dreamed of breakthrough staring him right in the face.[4] In truth, the ground was so completely mangled that it would be weeks before anything could be transported across it.

The German commanders were surprised at the British delay in following up their victory at Messines Ridge. Crown Prince Rupprecht, Western Front commander, commented that the Germans had been badly shaken by the violence and rapidity of the Messines attack and were anxiously concerned that the British would immediately launch attacks on the next ridge in line to the north, the Gheluvelt plateau. That attack would not take place for another six weeks, as the British consolidated their Messines position and Haig dealt with the government in London, which was then considering Haig's proposal for a full-blown Flanders operation.[5]

Part of the problem was that Haig was still in the planning stages of his great Flanders offensive and had not yet fully concluded an agreement with the government in London as to the parameters of the plan.[6] There remained confusion as to the type of offensive the Flanders operation was to be. Was it to be small steps with limited objectives, or another attempt at a breakthrough? On this issue there was complete misunderstanding between Haig and his own selected commander for the offensive, General Hubert Gough. Therefore, no appropriate follow-up was in place after the capture of the Messines Ridge and perhaps a real opportunity to achieve some sort of deeper penetration was lost.

The British had captured Messines Ridge, the southern heights of the Flanders/Ypres position, but their punishing use of artillery and mines had so devastated the battlefield that a month was required to restore the destroyed ground to a condition that could support transportation to facilitate the moving forward of the line with its attendant guns, support and communication links.

The instantaneous devastation of the Messines battle was such a violent shock that German commanders felt the impact was a significantly brutal blow in terms not of only casualties and position, but also of morale. Ludendorff concluded: 'The morale effect of the explosions was simply staggering ... 7th June cost us dear, and owing to the success of the enemy attack, the drain on our reserves was very heavy'.[7]

However, some British commanders and commentators saw it as an isolated success. Even as a success, it was again costly, as another 25,000 British casualties were incurred.[8] Six weeks later, the full-scale Flanders offensive would commence.

It should be added that of the two undetonated mines that remained buried over 100 feet below the Flanders farm fields, one detonated during a thunderstorm in 1955, killing a cow. The other mine survives and its location is *probably* identified, although it still possesses over 20 tons of high explosive. It is not known if the HE ammonal retains any volatility, or if it has since been so soaked in moisture and decay by a century of time so as to be neutralised.[9]

When considering the Third Battle of Ypres, it is easy to forget how small an area the battlefield actually covered. The focus of the three-and-a-half-month battle stretched along a front barely 15 miles in width and penetrated to a depth of only four miles. A total of roughly 60–70 square miles witnessed the concentrated activity of over fifty British and French divisions, and over eighty German divisions: more than one million soldiers. In four months of fighting, this compacted area absorbed an average of over 50,000 British artillery shells being fired every day.

Million-shell days, shot by British guns, were not unusual, sometimes even doubling this amount![10] Such a pummelling in so narrow a field not only completely destroyed the terrain but every building within it. Any living thing that dug in or moved, man or beast, was a target and subject to injury or death at any time, day or night, from the incessant shelling. By comparison, the Somme battlefield covered easily five times the area and experienced probably one-tenth of the artillery fire and over a longer period. The intensity, duration and concentration of shellfire at Passchendaele were unlike that of any other battle in history, and by a wide margin.

The network of supplies and reinforcements for soldiers and weapons was prodigious in terms of both amount and method of delivery. Factoring in the condition of the battlefield and the lack of any kind of surviving infrastructure, the task for a soldier fighting there would have been difficult but add in the torrential rainfall and oceans of mud that soon covered the landscape and the endeavour bordered on the maniacal.

Added to the considerable immediate Allied strategic considerations for the Flanders campaign was General Haig's personal belief that Flanders was where he felt he could best beat the Germans. He had pondered plans for this offensive since first being assigned to Belgium as commander of the First Corps when the BEF arrived at the outset of the war. He felt he knew the sector well and was confident in what he believed his army could accomplish there. He had passed on choosing General Herbert Plumer as the lead commander, instead choosing the more aggressive General Hubert Gough to work out the actual plans for the battle. As mentioned, there remains dispute as to what kind of offensive Haig actually desired. Gough was under the impression that Haig desired a strategic breakthrough and planned accordingly. Haig, even though he had selected the younger 'slasher' cavalry officer in Gough, later contended he had urged Gough to plan with a more conservative approach, more in line with Plumer's 'bite and hold' tactics. Whatever the truth, Gough was chosen and Haig accepted his plan.

Gough's Fifth Army attack would be preceded by a seven-day artillery barrage of over four-and-a-half-million shells – the largest and most concentrated preliminary barrage of the war to that date. The Fifth Army would go 'over the top' on 31 July, and attempt to capture the ridges of Pilckem and Gheluvelt that lay forward of the village of Passchendaele, located in the centre of the highest ground in the area, the Passchendaele Ridge. Attacking out of the Salient that extended beyond the Menin Gate in the town of Ypres, the 200-foot Passchendaele Ridge and village was a scant four miles away. If possible, and if the attacks went well, Gough's Fifth Army would smash forward and attempt to reach the railhead of Roulers, a further five miles farther north east and the centre of the German transport system, setting up an opening for a piercing swing to the coast. This was the plan as the Fifth Army prepared to attack.

Gough's Fifth Army was built up during June and July to comprise four corps that included sixteen divisions, with two in reserve. On Gough's left flank was the French First Army, under Francoise Anthoine, composed of six divisions. Protecting Gough's right flank would be Plumer's Second Army. This would give Gough an opening attacking weight of twenty-two British and French divisions, with two in reserve. Besides the Fifth Army's own considerable stable of artillery, the attack would be augmented by an extra allotment of 752 heavy howitzers, and 1,422 field guns and howitzers. Gough could also call upon 216 tanks of the new Mark IV model. North of the French First Army was General Rawlinson's Fourth Army, designated to move up the coast and junction with Haig's merging offensive thrust, and six Belgian divisions that were limited to defensive participation in the protection of Belgian soil.

In preparation for this attack, the element of surprise would be abandoned in favour of overwhelming superiority by artillery. This was spelled out by Western Front artilleryman Mark Severn, who later wrote:

Contrary to the teachings of the great military commanders of the past, it was accepted as an axiom at this stage of the war that achievement of the element of surprise in the delivery of an attack was out of the question. The stereotyped method of advertising the part of the line on which the impending assault would fall by a lengthy preliminary bombardment reached its climax at Ypres in 1917. From the middle of June to the end of July, the process of packing the base of the historic Salient with guns went on without cessation. Abandoning all hope of secrecy, the higher command crammed guns behind every hedge and wall, and into every field and street. In any case, every possible battery position in that small area was already known to the enemy. They had been occupied by a succession of British batteries during the past two-and-a-half years, and the German artillery had had ample opportunity to verify and re-verify their exact line and range. A large number of siege batteries had been told off to engage the hostile artillery, which, owing to the open nature of British preparations, had been concentrated in almost equal numbers by the opposing army. There developed, in consequence, throughout the month of July an artillery duel which exceeded, in magnitude and intensity, anything that had ever before been experienced on any front.[11]

The primary objectives for day one were designated by four sets of coloured lines on the attack map. The first advance aimed to reach and hold the 'blue' line 1,000 yards beyond the British jump-off point. The next position was labelled the 'black' line, a progression of a further 1,000 yards. Next would be the 'green' line, a full 3,500 yards from the original starting point. If the attacks reached the 'green' line in strength, a decision would be made whether to proceed in an attempt to go for the 'red' line, another 1,000–1,500 yards beyond the 'green'.[12] The attack would, of course, have been prepared by the week-long, four-million shell bombardment, but a crescendo of shellfire lasting six minutes would signal the actual 'over the top' at 03:30 on 31 July. The attacking soldiers would be escorted by a creeping barrage that would lay a curtain of steel roughly 100 yards in front of the advancing soldiers, but sometimes as close as 50 yards, pausing to 'lift' every four minutes and move another 100 yards further across 'no man's land'. From behind this shield of shrapnel and high explosive, the advance would hope to penetrate, occupy, and rapidly reinforce the captured German positions. Within the newly won trenches, and protected by a rain of shellfire calculated to prevent German counter-attacks, the infantry would pause, ascertain their situation, consider their options, and evaluate their opportunity to go forward. If possible, forward officers would signal or communicate with rear echelon officers and decide if and when to proceed to the next level of target colour. Reinforcements would be sent forward to establish a defensive posture or to pour through and push forward the attack. In the meantime, a further artillery barrage would do a shifting dance to pin down and confuse the enemy.

According to Brigadier General Sir James Edmonds, all of this would be conducted,

> ... to teach the enemy to lie at the bottom of his shell holes or dugouts whenever barrages are going on. After one barrage has passed over him he must always expect others. In doing this, cause as many casualties as possible to reduce his morale. This will be affected by working a succession of deep creeping barrages of every nature of gun and howitzer over the whole area to a depth of 2,000 yards beyond the last objective.[13]

As the date for the Flanders offensive approached, there still remained considerable disarray concerning the overall target goals, and methods to achieve those objectives. This disarray was shared by British leaders within both the military and governmental sectors. What *was* certain was the launch of a week-long prelude to the largest artillery preparation yet unleashed in the Great War. This overture of artillery would expel a concert of murderous metal into a narrow cauldron of targeted area – the Ypres Salient.

The Germans on the receiving end probably described it best when General Ludendorff recorded:

> On 31 July the English, assisted by a few French divisions on their left, had attacked on a front of 31 kilometres (less than

20 miles). They had employed such quantities of artillery and ammunition as had been rare, even in the West ... But, besides a loss of from two to four kilometres of ground along the whole front, it caused us very considerable losses in prisoners and stores, and a heavy expenditure of reserves.[14]

General Hermann von Kuhl of the German General Staff and chief historian was even more vivid in his description of the British opening artillery maelstrom:

In the early morning of 31 July a storm of fire broke out the like of which had never been experienced before. The whole Flanders earth moved and appeared to be in flames. It was no drum fire [*trommelfeuer*] any longer; it was as if Hell itself had opened. What were the horrors of Verdun and the Somme in comparison with this great expenditure of power? Deep into the farthest corners of Belgium one could hear the mighty thundering of battle. It was as if the enemy wanted to announce to the whole world, 'We are coming and we shall overcome.' At 6:30 in the morning the British and French troops rose from their trenches, following the heaviest drum fire, and moved into the attack.[15]

And of course it was true. The barrage of artillery fire was the heaviest single shower of steel onto a defended position to this date. The narrowness of the German defensive position magnified the concentration of explosive iron being poured on the target area. As the British launched their offensive across the Salient, the Battle of Passchendaele commenced.

8

BATTLE OF PILCKEM RIDGE, 31 JULY–2 AUGUST 1917

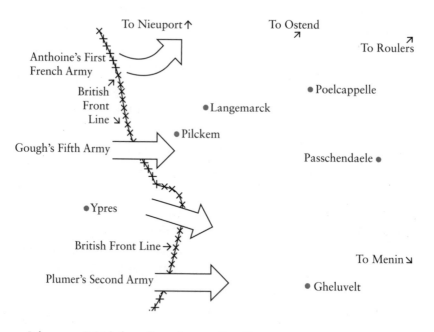

31 July 1917, British front line advances Day Two.

The opening round of the Third Battle of Ypres, the battle for Pilckem Ridge, began on 31 July 1917. In this action the combined British and French forces would achieve some varied success and were optimistic about more gains. The struggle would take three days of ferocious fighting, attain some limited objectives, but fail to secure the vital and heavily defended Gheluvelt Ridge heights, key to the Ypres Salient position. Once again, as in so many British offensives of the past three years, enormous casualties would be incurred on the first day alone, a harbinger for the next three months of the intense and ghastly fighting – that would include almost a daily deluge of rainfall that turned the battlefield into a frightening moonscape of mud and a charnel house of death.

The first day's operation encompassed frontal attacks that would envelop Gheluvelt Ridge, the highest ground in the vicinity and arrayed with German artillery that could otherwise command the Ypres Salient. The goal was to secure the high ground of Pilckem Ridge and beyond, sweep forward across the Steenbeek Creek, through the destroyed Flanders villages that were by now only piles of rubble, and hopefully, overrun the area from Langemarck in the north, Passchendaele Ridge in the centre, and on to Gheluvelt Ridge in the southern sector. The projected corresponding amphibious landings along the English Channel would seize the port of Ostend and link up with the main Flanders assault, and then proceed to pivot across northern Belgium. After seizing the German railhead of Roulers behind the Passchendaele Ridge, the Allied armies would be poised either to outflank the German army to the south or, if possible, break through the main German lines – the Holy Grail for Allied dreams of victory. It was an ambitious plan and, as we have seen, one that Haig had favoured from the beginning of his command.

From the start of the operational planning, there had been confusion about the overall designs for the offensive in the Ypres Salient. British Commander-in-Chief General Sir Douglas Haig and his designated tactical commander for the offensive, Fifth Army commander Hubert Gough, believed that the other was of the same frame of mind when, in fact, there was considerable variance in their perceived methods and goals for the offensive. Was the goal to be a deep penetration and possible 'breakthrough' of German lines, or a more conservative 'bite and hold' strategy for the gradual reduction of the German position? Gough was firmly of the opinion that it was the former and planned appropriately. As previously quoted, Gough stated that Haig's instructions were

> ...very definitely viewing the battle as an attempt to break through, and Haig never altered his opinion till the attack was launched, as far as I know.[1]

The finalised plans called for fourteen British divisions (Gough's Fifth Army and units of General Sir Herbert Plumer's Second Army) and two French divisions (part of the French First Army under General Francoise Anthoine) to attack the Germans across a broad front. The attack would be along a 14,000-yard front, extending from the Messines Ridge (now controlled by the British) in the south, to the northern Ypres-Staden rail line north east of the town of Ypres, with the French attacking the northern region, north of the rail line. This region of Flanders formed a notorious salient that protruded into the German defensive line. East of the town of Ypres was the low (less than 150 foot) Pilckem Ridge. Running perpendicular to the ridge was the Steenbeek Creek, and beyond that, 4,500 yards away from the British frontline and further east of Ypres, sat the main goal of the Gheluvelt Ridge that dominated the Ypres Salient. North of the Gheluvelt Plateau ran Passchendaele Ridge and beyond that, the key railroad junction of Roulers. The capture of the Gheluvelt Ridge was the primary initial objective; anything attained up to and beyond that point, this early in the offensive, would determine the course of the follow-up tactics in the days to follow. Such was the optimism of General Gough and his staff.

North of the French position were the semi-aquatic fields of northern Flanders that had been intentionally flooded by the Belgians early in the war to prevent further German penetration of Belgian territory. It had succeeded up to a point – that point being the coastline of Belgium, south of the town of Ostend. The flooded Belgian farm fields were indicative of the terrain that both armies were confronted with in all of Flanders: flat, featureless, and with an extremely high water table. Centuries of careful draining, damming, diverting, and constructing canals had allowed the region to produce abundant crops, but with intense military action of the past three years came the pulverisation of these water-controlling methods. The low ground was now prone to flooding at the slightest amount of rain. The flat, low terrain also increased the importance of any elevated area, no matter how slight, hence the desire to control any ridges. These ridges provided essential reconnaissance for artillery and placed opposing trenches and transport routes in constant danger. The Ypres Salient, dominated by the Gheluvelt Plateau, had plagued the British since the beginning of the war in 1914, and the chore of eliminating the threat from this heavily defended German position was a prime consideration for the British Army.

After the weeklong bombardment of shells from more than 3,000 cannon of various calibres, the 'over the top' command was preceded by an unprecedented hurricane of artillery fire. On 31 July, at 03:50, which normally constitutes daybreak in the summer at this latitude, over 75,000 British and French soldiers climbed out of their trenches and began crossing no man's land to assault the German positions. Instead of daylight however, the morning was dark, with very low-level clouds hanging in the warm, muggy mid-summer air. In front of the attacking formations crept a curtain of flaming steel that would provide an escort of diabolical destruction, spewing from hundreds of cannon well trained in the art of sheltering the advancing soldiers. At a pace of 100 yards for every four minutes, the troops crossed the deserted and cratered fields and assumed the takeover of the forward German line of trenches – designated line 'blue'. Awaiting reinforcements, and in some instances not lingering, the assaulting army began advancing to capture more German-held lines labelled 'black' and 'green'. Still shepherded by the protective cover of the creeping barrage, the attack proceeded. Ultimately, if fortunate enough, the attack would proceed to a fourth line – the 'red' line. As the advance continued, it became increasingly difficult to communicate the position of the infantry in relation to their position on the battlefield and therefore more difficult for the artillery to concentrate its fire where needed. This artillery curtain was critical to the success of the assault.

Artillery, of course, was the hammer and shield that provided the infantry the protection required to cross 'no man's land', and after securing a position, to possibly advance again. The thunderous bombardments that lasted days before a major offensive were spectacular displays of murderous firepower that can only be imagined. We do, however, have vivid descriptions of what these fantastic explosive demonstrations were like as a personal experience, to witness and to endure. Lieutenant Edmund Blunden of the 11th Royal Sussex Regiment wrote:

A flooded Amazon of steel flowed roaring, immensely fast, over our heads and the machine-gun bullets made a pattern of sharper purpose and maniac language against that diluvian rush. Flaring lights, small ones, great ones, flew up and went spinning sideways in the cloud of night; one's eyes seemed not quick enough; one heard nothing from one's shouting neighbour.[2]

And to be on the receiving end must have been a terrorising hell as German gunners attempted to return fire against the advancing attackers. Gerhard Gurtler, of the German artillery, recounts his experience:

Darkness alternates with light as bright as day. The earth trembles and shakes like jelly. Flares illumine the darkness with their white, yellow, green, and red lights and cause the tall stumps of the poplars to throw weird shadows. And we crouch between mountains of ammunition (some of us up to our knees in water) and fire and fire, while all around us shells upon shells plunge into the mire, shatter our emplacement, root up trees, flatten the house behind us to the level of the ground, and scatter wet dirt all over us so that we look as if we had come out of a mud-bath. We sweat like stokers on a ship; the barrel is red-hot; the cases [shell cases] are still burning hot when we take them out of the breech; and still the one and only order is, 'Fire! Fire! Fire!' until one is quite dazed.[3]

At least Gurtler could feel like he was hitting back, keeping busy, participating in the action, and wearing himself out with the physical exertion. But for many, assuming they survived the agony of the barrage, there was only the waiting for the inevitable direct hit to end it all. It must have been sheer horror as it was endured in both the physical and mental realm. To only wait and endure the seemingly endless bombardment must have been worse than actually manning an actively firing gun pit. Even more obscenely frightening was to cower in concrete bunkers and pillboxes with nothing to do but wait out the barrage, all the while praying that a shell did not make a direct hit. German Lieutenant Colonel Freiherr von Forstner, of the 164th Infantry Regiment, describes that horrific experience:

The fire increased to an intensity that was simply beyond our power to comprehend. Our blockhouse and a nearby mortar battery received more than a thousand large calibre shells. The earth trembled, the air shimmered. My pillbox heaved and rocked as though it was going to collapse. Almost by a miracle it received no direct hits. Everyone who dared to go out was wounded. At 6:00 am there was a gas alarm. I went outside and watched as a cloud of gas ten metres thick drifted slowly by. The entire pillbox stank of it. I had every tiny gap wedged up with wet cloths. At 7:00 am the firing reached a peak intensity. It was simply ghastly. The men in the outer room were wounded or died of gas poisoning. The small reserve of gas masks was exhausted because many men needed replacements for masks which had been shot through. The enemy followed up behind the gas cloud.[4]

On the British right flank, the II Corps had succeeded in reaching the shattered village of Westhoek and the Sherwood Forest (a forest in name only, as it and all other wooded areas had been reduced to nothing but stumps by the withering artillery barrage of the last few weeks).

Along with the XIX Corps to its left, it was progressing on the Gheluvelt Plateau. Farther north, the British XVIII and XIV Corps undertook the securing of the village of Pilckem and crossing the Steenbeek Creek, as the offensive seemed to be making headway. Progress continued until the rain began to fill everything – the slightest depressions, creeks, and shell holes – with waist-deep water. For all their early success in the advance, the XVIII and XIV Corps soon bore the brunt of the German counterattacks and a ferocious bombardment of return fire that forced their withdrawal.[5]

As groups of attacking soldiers advanced, the methods for communicating their positions soon deteriorated. Telephone lines – now all virtually destroyed by the constant German artillery barrages of return fire – along with message-carrying carrier pigeons, and human 'runners' – personnel who would be charged with verbal or written messages to be delivered to rear echelon commanders by personal contact – were all failing to connect with command control stations. All of these methods would prove inadequate to correctly pinpoint where targets were being met and to what extent the infantry gains were achieved. Vital communication, therefore, failed and those messages that did get through would be sparse, confused, and often inaccurate by the time they finally did reach the rear lines. Aircraft reconnaissance was difficult due to the low clouds and would become impossible with the ensuing rainfall that was about to shower the battlefield with a torrent. It soon became almost impossible to determine on a map where units actually were in order to assist them. Equally difficult was the determination of which attacks were failing and falling back. Confusion from the fog of battle reigned supreme and by early in the morning of 31 July, the attack, though progressing in many points, was about to bog down and receive increasingly intense counter-attacks from both German artillery and infantry. Soon the inevitable German counter-attacks overwhelmed the short-lived gains of the first six hours. The corresponding fallback of the unreinforced and un-resupplied British soldiers caused them to relinquish the hard-earned gains of the initial attack.

As predictable as the inevitable German counter-attacks were to both the soldier on the ground and the commanders in their rear positions, there now began a new threat, one that was to overwhelm the battle, the battlefield, and the outcome of the next three months. Torrential rains. The downpour began around mid-morning, as the ominous low-level clouds released at first a steady set of showers, followed by a deluge that would continue almost unabated for the next three days, and nearly unremittingly for the next three months. Soldiers would now be forced to endure the volcanic shower of steel and explosives while wading through waist-deep quagmires of mud.

Many British units were able to reach their initial targets, including the capture of Pilckem Ridge. These units now attempted to forge ahead to the greater task of acquiring the Gheluvelt Ridge that dominated the entire Ypres Salient and was thereby the key to flanking the German position. To this end, the German defences were not about to surrender easily. As the British began to occupy these former German positions, the German artillery zeroed in to the exact locations of their abandoned areas, able not only to thwart further British advances but to hit the newly held British positions with complete accuracy. Attacks could no longer go forward, resulting in a desperate attempt to hold on to what had been taken. Shells from German artillery rained death down upon the British Tommies clinging to their newly occupied positions, while the incessant downpour unleashed buckets of the liquid variety, combining to churn up the ground into a vast brown sea of deep mud.

Lieutenant J. Annan of the 1st/9th Btn., Royal Scots, explained how and why an attack would cease going forward:

Our objective was as far as we could go. The Gordons (Scots regiment) were doing well. They were advancing away ahead of us, so we only got stray 5.9" shells on the way across. We didn't have a single casualty until we got to Minty's Farm. It was a strongpoint, an outpost, fortified by the Germans and bristling with machine guns, but the Gordons had taken it. They took it with bayonet, like wild things, and when we got to it the dead were lying all around. Germans, grey against the mud, all mixed up with the dead Gordons lying there in their kilts ... they'd even set up Battalion Headquarters there, and moved a way on ahead. Of course the Germans had every one of their own positions marked on the map and registered by their artillery, so that if they had to get out of them and give them up they'd have the guns on them right away. So, just as we were coming up to Minty's Farm, the shells started falling all around. We got a slashing there all right.[6]

Unfortunately for the forward attacking elements, these gains were mere German outposts, as the Germans chose to defend in depth, with their positions becoming stronger as the penetration deepened. Later attacking units met heavier and heavier resistance as they probed more deeply into the German lines. German artillery fire, counter-attacks, and fresh units were soon chewing up the advancing British and recapturing positions at great cost to the attackers. Beyond Pilckem Ridge, further advances became impossible due to the withering counter artillery fire that was relentless. Consolidating Pilckem Ridge became the new objective as the attempt to gain Gheluvelt Ridge, the true main goal, became, for the moment, obviously futile.

With the pouring rain, shell holes and battlefield craters soon filled with water. Soldiers who sought cover in these basins were soon waist-high in slippery slime. Wounded soldiers were quickly submerged and drowned by the score. Weapons encased in mud became useless. Through it all was the continuous bursting of German artillery shells and the deadly spray of shrapnel. German machine-gun fire from unsilenced concrete pillboxes spelled a quick death to anything that moved or crawled above ground. A total of 136 British tanks had been designated to support the attack but failed to have any influence due to their inability to negotiate the ground, soon becoming immobilised from enemy gunfire or simply stuck in the mud. The Anglo-French air superiority was meaningless due to the low cloud cover and appalling rainfall that prevented any type of meaningful aerial operation.

It was impossible to ignore either the amount, duration, and consequences of this continuous downpour of rain. Officers and soldiers alike reeled and suffered. Concerning the first day's events, even Haig had to comment honestly in his Fourth Dispatch, written almost four months later – perhaps to defend the exorbitant cost in lives that was to go on for the next three months – about the problem that the deluge had provided.

War correspondent John Buchan later recorded:

The weather had been threatening throughout the day, and rendered the work of our aeroplanes very difficult from the commencement of the battle. During the afternoon, while fighting was still in progress, rain began, and fell steadily all night. Thereafter for four days, the rain continued without cessation, and for several days afterwards the weather remained stormy and unsettled. The low-lying, clayey soil, torn by shells and sodden with rain, turned to a succession of vast muddy pools. The valleys of the choked and overflowing streams were speedily transformed into long stretches of bog, impassable except by a few well-defined tracks, which became marks for the enemy's artillery. To leave these tracks was to risk death by drowning, and in the course of the subsequent fighting on several occasions both men and pack animals were lost in this way.[7]

Typical of the situation for those who had to cope with the rain and mud, and also fight very determined Germans, was this report from Pvt. W. Lockey, 1st Btn. Notts & Derbyshire Regiment as he and his comrades completed their journey across no man's land and occupied the captured first (blue line) German trenches:

> The barrage lifted and on we went, those that were left of us ... But as we got further into their lines there was more and more machine-gun fire, not just from their (forward) positions ahead of us but coming from outposts all around about ... But the fellows coming up behind us had a really rough time. We got into our position on the Westhoek Ridge, took over some trenches and dug-outs, and another division was supposed to pass through and carry on the advance. While we were waiting it began to rain. The battalion that was to pass through our line were the Royal Irish Rifles and when they reached us they were in a bad way. The majority were either knocked out or wounded by the German machine-guns. Three or four stumbled into our part of the trench and every one had bullet wounds in the arms and legs. They were dragging along another boy, young lad, only about eighteen. He'd been hit by an explosive bullet that passed straight his right cheek and blew away the whole of his left cheek. It was a terrible sight. His tongue was sticking out through this great hole in his face. He kept calling out for water. It ran out through the hole in his face as fast as we gave it to him...We couldn't get the wounded away...They (Germans) were pasting us with shells and machine-gun fire and the rain kept pouring down. The trench began to fill up with water.[8]

Near the end of 31 July, General Gough decided to call off the continued attacks due to the incessant rain and lack of progress. He reported to General Haig that so far the operation had been 'a great success', even though only Pilckem Ridge had been secured. Gough believed the rains would subside and ordered the guns to be moved forward in order to continue the following day.

A battery commander of British artillery, the future Lord Belhaven, summed up the foolish optimism of this approach as the rainfall soon dominated all activity:

> ...simply awful ... The ground is churned up to a depth of ten feet and is the consistency of porridge ... the middle of the shell craters are so soft that one might sink out of sight ... there must be hundreds of German dead buried here, and now their own shells are re-ploughing the area and turning them up.[9]

Moving up the guns to support and continue the assault presented a formidable task when the weather was clear and dry. Subjected to enemy gunfire while hauling heavy equipment was a perilous chore under the best of circumstances and heavy work at all times for man and beast alike. Underscoring the frightening task involved by the orders to 'bring up the guns' and prepare for the next stage of attack is the description by Subaltern R. B. Talbot-Kelly while under fire:

> I received orders to move the guns further under the lee of what had been Sanctuary Wood ... And the weather worsened and it rained and rained, and the whole area became a great morass and ammunition could no longer be brought up in a wagon but had to be carried, eight rounds at a time, on a led packhorse. All night and all day the German artillery pounded the gun lines and quite early on we had two guns damaged by shell fire, one badly. We had had no time to dig gun pits and, even if we had had time, we could not have done it in the flooded and boggy ground in which we stood. The best we could do for ourselves was to make a little scrape about one foot deep and try to get what shelter we could in that when it was our turn to sleep. I remember waking up in the morning and feeling water squelching between my shoulder blades.

Many of our men had ague from the damp and could hardly talk for the chattering of their teeth or keep their hands still.[10]

On the first day, 30,000 British soldiers became casualties, over 3,000 of whom were killed. That, however, was actually not as bad as the first day on the Somme, when twice that number became casualties and over six times that number were killed. The Germans had also suffered an estimated 30,000 casualties, including the loss of over 6,000 prisoners. Yet this was just 'day one', and the rain and the battle for Pilckem Ridge would continue for two more days without any further gains. The goal of taking the prize of Gheluvelt Ridge was postponed until the weather dried out – which it wasn't about to do.

For the next three days in August the attacks continued along the front in attempts to secure the Gheluvelt Ridge. So too did the torrential rains. The necessary re-supply of forward lines had to continue through these appalling conditions. A mile of swamp and deadly terrain had to be crossed in the darkness of night to provide an army under fire the sinews of war. Ammunition, food rations, fresh water and spare equipment to replace that which had been lost or destroyed – all needed to be brought forward through the remnants of the now flooded British trenches, then transported across the former no man's land of broken and flooded shell holes, and finally carried to the re-entrenching forward lines, which were digging into the wreck of the newly captured former German trenches. Everywhere German shells rained down, and to cross this nightmare landscape took incredible fortitude, strength, and valour.

Following the attacking brigades of infantry, and the units of the quartermasters in charge of re-supply, came the engineering battalions. Their job was to lay new light gauge railway track, improve roads and help reinforce or dig new trenches, all under the German artillery fire and the relentless rainfall. Through this cauldron of mud and shellfire came all the necessary re-supply units with their essential material that was so vital to the forward units who were either holding on to newly won territory or preparing to go forward in the next round of attacks.

After renewing their attacks on 2 and 3 August, the British were unable to achieve the gains of the first day's attack. German counter-attacks were continuous, not only preventing the British from gaining new ground, but forcing the British back across previously gained territory. Ernst Junger, who wrote extensively after the war, was a twenty-two-year-old German lieutenant at Passchendaele and recorded in his diary the circumstances of the British attacks and the violent and frequent German counter-attacks, which rocked the British back on their heels:

> At six in the morning, the dense Flanders fog lifted, and permitted us to view our situation in its full hideousness … Half-an-hour later, the shelling commenced, washing over our little refuge like a typhoon. The forest of explosions gradually thickened into a solid whirling wall. We squatted together, every second expecting the annihilating hit that would blow us and our concrete blocks away.[11]

Describing the counter-attack, Junger writes: 'Quickly I clipped four hand-grenades on to my belt … the attack was to be carried out by two battalions; ours and one battalion from the regiment next to ours. Our orders were short and sharp. British units who had got across the canal were to be repulsed.'[12]

It was just that simple and direct, violent and immediate.

Junger continues, 'Everyone threw themselves to the ground … The force of the barrage was terrific; I confess it exceeded my wildest notions. It was a wall of yellow flame flickering in front of us; a hail of clods of earth, bricks, and iron splinters that battered down our heads, striking sparks from our steel helmets. I had the sensation that it had become harder to breathe, and that whatever air was left in this iron-charged atmosphere was no longer quite sufficient for my lungs.'[13]

The British gains were often limited to the capturing of a German pillbox: one less set of German machine guns to contend with, and a sturdy concrete haven in which to regroup and pause before pushing on to the next objective. Many of these pillboxes were already full of dead Germans, but others held on and fought bitterly to the end. The Tommy was not happy to expend so much energy and blood on a surrounded pillbox and expected the German contingent to surrender; when they did not, they frequently paid the price, as explained by Lieutenant Harold Ridsdale of 76 Field Company RE, The Guards Division, following the assaults of 2, 3 and 4 August:

8/2 Raining hard again. The men went out to clean up some of the concrete MG [machine gun] emplacements of the Boche. We started in one in Hey Wood, a beauty, intact, concrete 6 feet thick, but in a dirty state. We cleaned it up and built a sandbag parapet in front of the door as it faced the wrong way ... In the 'Blue Line' there were dozens, full of water and wreckage. Some were sound, one had been shifted bodily by one of our big shells. This trench was in an awful state; we saw several dead Germans ... We looked at several farms; the concrete in these was completely wiped out. The heavy shelling on this part and the heavy rain made the ground awful, up to your waist in mud.

8/3 Finished the dugout at Hey Wood ... other concrete dugouts; nearly all were smashed. One we found full of dead Germans, dead for many days too. In another dugout, evidently an officers' mess, a shell had penetrated right through and killed the lot. There was a third instance of a dugout which evidently refused to surrender and, as the occupants came out, they were clubbed. There were 30 dead Huns outside this, all with their heads smashed in.

8/4 The section was repairing the footbridges across the canal, all of which had been smashed. We made 2 good ones and just at the end lost 2 men, Turner and Rossiter, Turner being seriously hit. The sun came out and it stopped raining, the first time for a week.[14]

The renewed offensive of 2 and 3 August became fruitless attempts through the quagmire and it became clear that no new gains were going to be made, and that the rain was not about to subside. Generals Haig and Gough decided to call a halt to the attack, regroup, reinforce, and wait for the battlefield to dry out. The immediate offensive, to become known as the battle for Pilckem Ridge, was ending. The larger goal of capturing Gheluvelt Ridge had fallen short and the greater goal of Passchendaele Ridge was considerably farther beyond in both yards and effort.

9

RENEWED BATTLE FOR GHELUVELT PLATEAU AND THE BATTLE FOR HILL 70, AUGUST 1917

A week later, the British would renew their general attacks along the Ypres Salient. Again, the design was to be the control of the commanding Gheluvelt Ridge in order to continue the assault and capture of the high ground of Passchendaele Ridge, and then to proceed on to the rail junction of Roulers. Simultaneously, the scheme for the amphibious attack on the English Channel seaport of Ostend was placed temporarily on hold, since the junction between the two British armies, Rawlinson's Fourth and Gough's Fifth could not be immediately affected. The planned swing across northern Belgium and up to the Dutch border of the Netherlands by Gough's Fifth Army now seemed decidedly remote. It was time to step back and reassess the situation rather than continue headlong with an unprepared renewal.

The delay, however, gave the Germans more time to reinforce their own positions. So strong was their primary position that their main reserve counterattacking units (Eingreif Divisions) had not yet been required for action. Not only were the British faced with the potent German defences, but they were also confronting the daunting task of organising their next push forward while contending with the abominable weather conditions. British Brigadier General John Davidson of General Headquarters described the situation with acuity:

> We know from experience, however, that in these subsidiary operations [the post D-Day attempts to renew the stalled offensive], hurried preparations and the use of part-worn troops are generally the cause of failure, and that failure involves waste of valuable time and personnel. In this particular case we want to make absolutely certain of the artillery preparation, which will require very careful control and accurate shooting and one or two more days of good flying weather prior to the attack. To ensure success, which is all-important at this stage, the corps ought really to attack with three fresh divisions.[1]

The scheduled date, weather permitting, was to be 10 August, a week after the opening attacks that had gained Pilckem Ridge but had then dissolved into futility due to the rain, mud, and stubborn German resistance. The Germans, suspecting renewed attacks and fully aware of the importance of the Gheluvelt Ridge, began a continuous artillery bombardment of the British lines in front of the ridge, thus further weakening the already worn-out British ranks. Reluctantly, Gough replaced these units with fresh reserve units. And so the next round began after a thoroughly and carefully prepared programme. Fresh troops were brought up and, when the weather finally co-operated, the attacks on Gheluvelt Ridge were renewed and the offensive re-commenced. These attacks temporarily succeeded in taking Westhoek Ridge but, once again, under fierce German counter-attacks, the ground was regained by the Germans with both sides incurring heavy casualties. A small foothold was maintained on Westhoek Ridge, but further operations on 16 and 22 August proved futile, the British suffering large losses with no gains on either date. Gough commented:

The state of the ground was by this time frightful. The labour of bringing up supplies and ammunition, of moving or firing the guns, which often sunk up to their axles, was a fearful strain on the officers and men, even during the daily task of maintaining the battle front. When it came to the advance of infantry for an attack, across the water-logged shell holes, movement was so slow and so fatiguing that only the shortest advances could be contemplated. In consequence I informed the Commander in Chief that tactical success was not possible, or would be too costly, under such conditions, and advised that the attack should be abandoned. I had many talks with Haig during these days and repeated this opinion frequently, but he told me that attack must be continued.[2]

In concert with the early August renewal of the effort to finally capture Gheluvelt Ridge, the British decided on a simultaneous diversionary attack further south near the French town of Lens. The operation would not only attempt to take Lens, an important German rail junction, but also divert German forces from relieving the Ypres front. Therefore, roughly two weeks after the renewed attempts on the Gheluvelt Ridge, the Battle for Hill 70 commenced outside Lens. Hopefully, this show of force to the south would relieve pressure at Ypres by preventing the Germans from being able to transfer fresh troops from the Lens sector to the relief of the Ypres Salient. For this task, General Haig chose the Canadian Corps under Lieutenant General Sir Arthur Currie, who had risen to prominence along with his immediate superior and now British Third Army commander, Lieutenant General Sir Julian Byng. Together they had conceived and conducted the successful spring 1917 attack at Vimy Ridge, a strategically important and redoubtable German position in north-western France, which had previously resisted all attempts to capture it.

While this secondary operation for the capture of Hill 70 was taking place, the main British Army on the Ypres Salient began preparing for the next big push – a flanking attack centred on the village of Langemarck, north of the Gheluvelt Ridge. The capture of Hill 70 and the preparation for the upcoming push at Langemarck went on concurrently, while fighting within the Salient remained constant, with heavy casualties continuing. The Battle for Hill 70, although outside the Flanders theatre, was to affect the Third Battle of Ypres in two ways. It was to provide diversionary cover for the upcoming British push at Langemarck as intended; and its success would later lead to General Currie and the Canadian Corps being chosen by Haig for the final drive that would capture Passchendaele and complete the offensive.

Located outside the French coal-mining town of Lens, Hill 70 dominated the nearby area, including the German-controlled railhead centre of Lens. As at Vimy Ridge, the Canadians, under General Currie, would rely on meticulous planning and rehearsal, heavy artillery in a narrow range of frontal attack, and the invitation to local commanders to go forward, where possible, on their own initiative. 'Bite and hold' would be the goal, rather than deep penetrations. Each soldier would carry a map of his designated area, and have a firm grasp of the design and geography of it. Each soldier would be prepared to take over his platoon or accompanying assault group in case his fellow non-commissioned officers should fall or be wounded.

Currie, and the entire Canadian force for that matter, believed in the economical use of manpower. Trained in artillery, Currie believed in the 'shells not soldiers' school of a massed concentration of artillery to do the preliminary work on the battlefield prior to an assault. Currie's was a progressive doctrine in approach and preparation. He encouraged his fellow officers to offer competing points of view and was readily willing to alter his plans if better ones were presented. Currie was the first Canadian to command the Canadian Corps, and both he and the Corps had proven their competence during previous actions. Haig had great faith in both. Currie, and his fellow Canadians, assumed a sense of independence in their actions and would not hesitate to insist on such methods in their contact with their superiors, frequently challenging accepted practices, even with the Commander-in-Chief Haig. For these reasons, the Canadian Corps was often the most competent and dependable of all the British and Commonwealth armies. Currie himself was a marginal type who had worked his way up through the ranks of the Canadian militia, and was anything but a traditionally groomed public school British officer. After the war, it was hinted by Prime Minister David Lloyd George that had the war continued on for another year, Currie would have been considered for promotion to Commander-in-Chief, replacing Haig.

Lloyd George was certainly prepared to dismiss Haig but whether or not the position would have been offered to Currie is purely post-war chatter from the PM, and perhaps not entirely accurate. Certainly the candidates from whom Lloyd George would have had to choose were limited. Currie, though a successful commander at the brigade, division, and corps level, had no experience commanding anything as large as an army group, let alone an entire army. But it does point to the high esteem that Currie had earned.[3]

Attacking at 04:50 on 15 August, and following a withering pre-attack barrage of heavy artillery, the Canadians were able to quickly rout the Germans from Hill 70 and proceeded to attack the town of Lens. Indicative of the tenacity exhibited by the Canadian Corps, six Victoria Crosses were awarded in the engagement, the highest British military award. War diary entries from the official daily reports, though often brought up to date a day or two later if the unit was actively engaged, trace the rapidity of battlefield movement. Action was acutely dangerous at all times. Units were relieved whenever necessary, or possible, during heavy engagements. This sequence is from the week of the Canadian Corps' successful capture of Hill 70 in the battalion field diary:

August 12: numerous gas shell in the evening ... August 13: Our artillery very active all day, very heavy retaliation in the evening ... August 14: Runners warned for duty for impending offensive ... rations arrived by light railway ... Brigade Major McCollum badly wounded whilst reconnoitering the front [died the following day] ... August 15: Sudden orders received to go into the lines again to reinforce the 87th Battalion who had been badly cut up ... Later we were ordered to relieve the 87th altogether. We found matters terribly disorganized ... fighting patrols were sent forward to re-establish advanced posts ... did not complete relief till midnight ... August 16: Operation Order 63 was issued containing instructions for an offensive to be undertaken on the following [follow-up on successful assaults] in conjunction with the 4th Brigade on our left ... August 17: 4:32 am Barrage opened ... immediately received from 'D' Company to the effect that a good start had been made ... 5:30 am runner reported that advance had been held up by wire in the (German) trench coupled with heavy machine-gun fire ... 5:55 am Word was accordingly sent ... to the (attacking) companies warning them to be careful ... 6:55 German prisoners captured ... 8:30 'C' Company had been sustaining heavy shell fire and was now reinforced ... from Company 'A' ... remainder of the day was spent in maintaining original positions ... Lieutenant G. G. Callum, battalion Bombing Officer, wounded in legs whilst superintending the sending of supplies to Front Line, 16 Other Ranks wounded ... August 18: 2:30 am ... men began coming in as relieved; a hot meal was in readiness after which the men turned in and rested all day.[4]

Although in the next few days of fighting the Canadians were unable to capture Lens, they did withstand the furious counter-attacks of the Germans to regain Hill 70. This capture accomplished two goals for the British: acquiring the high ground to maintain a constant threat on Lens, and preventing the Germans from transferring rested troops from Lens to replace the exhausted troops defending the Ypres Salient, which they had been prepared to do.

The Canadian Corps had once again shown its effectiveness and, more importantly, it demonstrated the leadership and preparation of Currie and his staff. Their thorough planning, training, and the faith in the ability of well-trained soldiers to initiate actions themselves proved to be a better method than the wasteful methods of mass attacks previously insisted on by British High Command. The 'bite and hold' system, the use of the 'creeping barrage', and the elimination of enemy artillery with pinpoint accuracy to prevent devastating counter-fire on newly held positions would all become essential in breaking the stalemate. Currie, and the Canadian Corps, would be the important component in the eventual capture of Passchendaele Ridge in the autumn of 1917. Currie was at all times meticulous in his preparation for an attack, and invariably willing to resist the pervading stubbornness of the British High Command, right up to and including Haig. In this instance, Haig had ordered the capture of Lens as the priority and Currie had stubbornly resisted, insisting that the attack would be costly in lives and probably unsuccessful. Better, he argued, to take the adjacent Hill 70 that controlled the Lens area. Hill 70, said Currie, could be taken, held, and used to dominate Lens at a much smaller cost and with a greater impact on the Germans. There was a pleasing bonus: the Germans would do all in their power to regain Hill 70, and the Canadians could then zero in on these attempts and smash the German counter-attacks.

The capture of Hill 70, along with the victories at Vimy Ridge and Messines Ridge, demonstrated that British and Commonwealth troops could succeed in the offensive mode if properly trained and prepared. Although a subsidiary campaign, and frequently neglected in many accounts of Passchendaele, the achievement at Hill 70 reminded the Germans that, in a war of attrition, they were doomed to come out second best. This may explain why Haig again and again took refuge in this strategy, to defend his seemingly unimaginative tactics. Equally lacking in sufficient manpower and material resources in comparison with the Allies, the Germans were hard-pressed to defend every foot of soil in this prohibitively costly method of defence – holding to the theory of continually counter-attacking to hold every and all positions. The war would not, and could not, be won on the defensive. It was becoming more and more apparent to many that Germany must either sue for a negotiated peace settlement, or somehow win the war outright with a brilliantly conceived offensive of their own and force the Allies to surrender. By 1917, they were paralysed in their holding position. The choice of place, time and intensity of operation was entirely with the larger and better equipped and supplied Allies. At this point, the German general and de facto Commander-in-Chief, Erich Ludendorff, commented about this phase of the Passchendaele campaign:

> In spite of all the concrete protection, they seemed more or less powerless under the enormous weight of the enemy's artillery. At some points they no longer displayed the firmness which I, in common with the local commanders, had hoped for. The enemy had managed to adapt himself to our methods of employing counter-attack divisions. There were no more attacks with unlimited objectives, such as General Nivelle had made in the Aisne-Champagne Battle. He [the British enemy] was ready for our counter-attacks and prepared for them by exercising restraint in exploitation of success. In other directions, of course, this suited us very well. I myself was being put to a terrible strain. The state of affairs in the West appeared to prevent the execution of our plans elsewhere. Our wastage had been so high as to cause grave misgivings, and had exceeded all expectation.[5]

It is clear that Ludendorff and the Germans were desperately worried about the expenditure of their troops in the defence of their positions. The Germans were relying on the Allies to continue with their wasteful and fruitless assaults of self-annihilation to provide the Germans with status quo outcomes, however, this was incurring a frightful cost to the defenders themselves as they sought to retain their occupied positions in Belgium and France. The Allies seemed committed and willing to make such continued and enormous sacrifices, and the Germans had no recourse except to respond in kind. Starkly apparent was the reality of superior Allied manpower and material resources. The arrival of the United States was clearly on the horizon, and with their seemingly unlimited well of fresh American manpower and supplies, the Germans would be forced to reconsider their course. In the meantime, Germany would continue to count on the British to squander their abundant manpower on endless offensives in hopes of the oft dreamed-of breakthrough on the Western Front.

Therefore, the capture of Hill 70, along with the recent successes at Vimy Ridge and Messines Ridge, proved to be an exception to the usual German ability to successfully defend and to the repeated British and French frustration of gaining little or no ground while causalities mounted. Currie's plan for the capture of Hill 70, as opposed to the originally ordered attack on the German railhead at Lens, demonstrated that there were sensible and achievable options. Currie offered not only a suggested alternative target, but also alternative methods to attack and hold a dominant tactical position and then force the *Germans* to pay with their reckless counter-attacks. He predicted that the Germans would recognise the threat and respond with all-out counter-attacks to regain the position.

This proved to be the case, and in the next two weeks the Germans proceeded to make no fewer than twenty-one costly and unsuccessful counter-attacks on Hill 70. Currie correctly foresaw this opportunity to induce the Germans to expend great quantities of manpower in a predetermined killing zone. According to plan, Hill 70 was taken, reinforced, and immediately fortified to withstand the anticipated German response. The 25,000 German casualties lost in these efforts must be compared to the cost of 9,100 Canadian casualties, as the Germans repeatedly ordered futile attempts to retake the position. These troops were now being denied to the Germans for the reinforcement of their Ypres Salient defence, thereby thwarting them in any attempt to regain lost ground there. Currie's thoughtful methods, shrewd view of the battlefield, and decision to focus on results that could be realistically achieved, brought positive gains and tactical success.

For many reasons, General Sir Arthur Currie's is a fascinating story and he was perhaps the most unusual member of Britain's Great War high command. He was also one of the most successful. Currie was born near Strathroy, Ontario, Canada. His initial enlistment was at the lowest rung of military service as an artillery gunner in the Canadian militia.

His pre-First World War private life was chequered to say the least. Currie experienced mixed results (and debts) in business, while also serving part-time in the Canadian militia. In spite of this pre-war civilian career, or perhaps because of it, Currie's outlook on tactics, the power of artillery, the requirement for adequate training, and his faith in what well-prepared soldiers could accomplish, plus his belief in the economical use of manpower – all set him apart from the majority of the upper echelon British commanders. As mentioned, Currie was the first Canadian to command the entire Canadian Corps, made up of the four Canadian divisions that, until then, had been commanded by British officers.

Of the hundreds of British First World War generals, nearly all were professional British Army commanders and only a handful would rise through the non-commissioned ranks on merit during the course of the war. This resulted in an inbreeding of military strategic and tactical thought. Along with a similar mindset in training and discipline, came the reactionary reluctance to volunteer any original thought and a hesitation about ever questioning one's superior officer as to method or military doctrine. By the same token, commanders were discouraged from seeking opinions that conflicted with their own. This in-bred fraternity had largely been stationed in similar locations, performed similar functions. These parallel careers would only be separated by the relative speed and success of an individual's climb up the command seniority list. This ossification of thinking and action, coupled with the lack of alternative routes to senior responsibility, helped contribute to the tragic examples of repeated failures and disasters on the battlefield. Men such as Currie were few and far between, and even had they been identified, there was no career path for their advancement due to the rigid social and professional status system then employed by the British Army.

While working in Canada, Currie had taken his militia artillery training seriously and spent his time studying artillery and the tactics thereof. He gradually rose in rank as the Canadian militia expanded, becoming an officer and eventually achieving the rank of Lieutenant-Colonel. He also suffered several financial misfortunes, including charges of embezzling from his own military unit's treasury, but was rescued by the outbreak of the Great War. Shipping off to France with his Canadian unit, Currie avoided scandal and dismissal by eventually securing through borrowing from more affluent fellow officers enough money to repay his debts. This, and his talent and success as an innovative officer, helped prevent the taint of scandal from damaging his career arc.

It should be pointed out that being a neophyte was no guarantee of innovative thinking. U.S. General John Pershing, commander of the freshly arriving American Expeditionary Force, notoriously refused advice as to the effective use of his inexperienced troops in offensive action. Rejecting the valuable lessons so painfully learned by the British and French, Pershing stubbornly believed in the priority of spirit and desire of his soldiers in an assault to overcome the lethal realities of 20th-century machine guns and artillery. It was to prove a costly and unnecessary faith in discredited tactics.[6]

Experiencing the panic of the first major German gas attack at the Second Battle of Ypres in 1915, Currie acquitted himself with quick thinking, daring, and a natural feel for leadership under pressure. Although Currie was determined to husband his soldiers from unnecessary mortal waste in fruitless assaults, he was never a favourite among his own troops. Known as 'Guts and Gaiters', Currie was profane in the extreme, aloof, and distant to the ordinary soldier. Yet he was always respected for his dedication to achieve success while conserving his soldiers' lives – a far greater quality than merely being 'one of the boys'.

Currie made a point of visiting the horrific French front at Verdun and interviewing French officers about which artillery tactics succeeded, and which did not. He also interviewed ordinary soldiers concerning battlefield conditions, gleaning important information that would benefit him and his Canadian Corps as they prepared their assaults at Vimy Ridge, Hill 70, and in later engagements. He soon recognised the value of massive artillery preparation before an assault and became a firm follower of the 'bite and hold' tactic of attaining and securing limited offensive goals before pushing on to the next objective.

He and his Second Army group commander, General Sir Julian Byng, were assigned the taking of Vimy Ridge in north-western France. Both Byng and Currie believed in thoroughly training their soldiers before an attack. This preparation included rehearsals using mock-up German positions; giving each and every soldier a map of his intended position; training every soldier to be capable of leading his unit in case of casualties to their NCOs; and positioning assaulting troops as close as possible to their specific targets before an attack, thereby reducing exposure to enemy fire. All these concepts gave the Canadian Corps greater confidence and flexibility to overcome the most daunting of assignments. The Canadian Corps' reputation as one of the British Army's most successful and dependable units also extended to the Germans, as they always desired to know the Canadians' location, calculating that this was where the British were preparing to attack next.

In the 1918 war-winning Allied offensive, Currie's Canadian unit would spearhead the penetration of the German defences and hasten the end of the war. Among the innovations being developed by the British Army in general, and the Currie-led Canadian Corps in particular, was the use of range finding techniques to locate the position of enemy artillery and the source of deadly return fire that was crippling the ability of an offensive effort to secure and reinforce a subdued target.

Two important methods were the spotting of 'flash' from the muzzles of the firing cannon and the tracing of the booming sound-waves to detect the location of the German gun positions (*see* Chapter 6, Artillery). Both would become increasingly accurate tools as a guide for British gunners to direct their fire to silence enemy return fire.

So too were the British gunners gradually becoming better at fusing and aiming their weapons to more accurately place their shells where they would provide the greatest impact, whether suppressing German artillery or supporting attacking infantry with a dependable 'creeping barrage'. Learned through bitter experience, there was now complete agreement, and better availability and reliability, on the use overwhelming artillery concentration to escort an offensive operation.

Alongside the preponderance of artillery favoured by Currie, was the use of combined mixed weapons to achieve tactical success. Advanced training for all ranks, the use of airpower, light and mobile machine guns, and the use of the infant force of tanks in large numbers to develop true combined operations, were methods that would become the standard for success. The victories at Vimy Ridge and Hill 70 were to become the templates of what could now be achieved on the Western Front if enough imagination was applied and diligent preparation was carried out. There certainly were no guarantees but at least there were now tactics that promised a path to potential success and eventual victory.

Unfortunately, for much of the Passchendaele campaign and for those soldiers who had to endure and suffer through it, not enough of these methods were sufficiently explored and employed in time to avoid the savage 'war of attrition' that would inflict such great cost in human life for so little marginal gain. At Passchendaele, that attritional philosophy would continue to be gruesomely implemented.

IO

THE BATTLE OF LANGEMARCK, AUGUST 1917

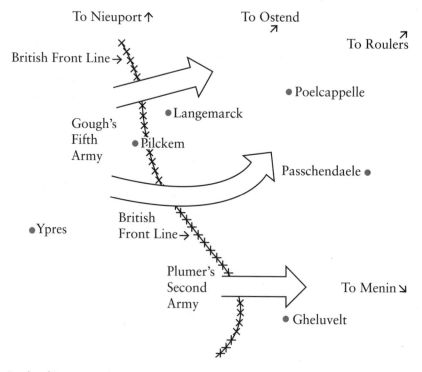

To Nieuport ↑   To Ostend
                          ↗

British Front Line →   To Roulers ↗

                                    ● Poelcappelle

                        ● Langemarck

Gough's
Fifth   ● Pilckem
Army

                              Passchendaele ●

        British
        Front Line →

● Ypres

Plumer's
Second   To Menin ↘
Army
                        ● Gheluvelt

Battle of Langemarck

Aprt from the actual difficulty in attacking and capturing the German-held positions leading to and including Passchendaele Ridge and its commanding heights, British strategy was now being dictated by two critical elements: the atrocious rain that was delaying not only the attacks themselves but also the re-supply of the units involved, and the need to pierce the German lines to the north of Ypres and link up with the anticipated amphibious landings along the English Channel coast near Ostend before the end of August. This last objective, nicknamed 'Operation Hush', demanded completion before the end of that month to take advantage of the high tides that would permit the amphibious landing. These two elements placed enormous pressure upon the commander of the offensive, General Sir Hubert Gough. The capture of Pilckem Ridge and the small area of Westhoek Ridge to the south had been at considerable cost in casualties and the necessary injection of reserve troops. Gough had already committed eight of his Fifth Army reserve divisions into the offensive, plus two more borrowed from General Plumer's Second Army. Some units, manning the forward salient positions, had already endured frontline duty for well over two weeks without relief.[1] These units were already numerically depleted and absorbing constant fire from German artillery. The rain brought the misery and suffering of impossibly swampy conditions to all, but especially to those manning the forward outposts. Re-supply to the front line, always difficult and dangerous, became a nightmare during the offensive. The extent of this rain-soaked lowland, and the depth and exhausting consistency of the glutinous mess covering it, cannot be exaggerated. After the first rains of August, Sergeant-Major J. S. Handley recorded the terror of the conditions, and the frequent, dramatic, and tragic effects:

> In my searchings I had come across a pack-mule sinking in the mud. His load had been removed and he had been left so far submerged when I saw him that only the top of his back, neck, and head were above the mud. I'll never forget the terror on his face with his eyes bulging out of their sockets.

I just could not leave him in his agony, so, putting to his head a Smith and Wesson pistol I had found, I shot him.[2]

One week into August found the British battling both the forces of German resistance and severe weather. The failure to quickly advance and secure more ground toward Passchendaele Ridge, as originally envisioned, led Gough to appeal to Haig to call off the offensive. But Haig was fully determined to follow up on the already achieved limited gains and pursue the attempt to seize the ridge. To accomplish this, however, would first require capturing Gheluvelt Ridge on the south end of the Salient, and that would necessitate securing both of its flanks. The Gheluvelt Ridge provided the Germans with advantages in both the observation of British movements and the superior delivery of well-aimed firepower. The taking of Gheluvelt Ridge would, in turn, only be achieved by seizing the village of Langemarck on the north, and the stoutly defended Glencorse Wood and Polygon Wood on the south. One step would have to be completed before the next could be contemplated. The return to the 'bite and hold' formula was agreed on due to the failure of the continuously anticipated 'breakthrough'. Gough began preparing for these renewed assaults, although all movement of troops, supplies, and equipment was hindered by heavy rains and deep mud. Accomplishing any of these tasks was no easy chore. The renewed assaults amounted to fully securing the Day One goal of the blue, black, green and red line targets that the British had been initially unable to do on 31 July. The Germans were by now fully aware of what the British were doing and began to reinforce the now obvious areas along the Salient that the British would be attacking.

But optimism remained high among British high command, and General Haig's dispatches underscore his enthusiasm for success in this renewed sequence of attacks:

Close upon the heels of this success ... our second attack was launched east and north of Ypres, on a front extending from the north-west corner of Inverness Copse to our junction with the French south of St. Janshoek. On our left the French undertook the task of clearing up the remainder of the Bixshoote peninsula ... the British attack ... reached the southern outskirts of Langemarck.[3]

Preliminary assaults had been scheduled for 13 August but heavy rains prevented any major attack then or on the 14th. The next target date was to be 15 August, and some dry and sunny days allowed for not only re-supply but also the laying of planks, duckboards and pontoon bridges across the swollen Steenbeek Creek that had to be crossed in order to assault the ridges, woods and village of Langemarck. This preparation went on for days under difficult physical conditions and constant sniper fire as the Royal Engineers struggled to prepare the swamped area – much of it now over four feet deep in mud – with suitable crossing areas. Once across the Steenbeek Creek, the infantry would hold the new positions to provide a springboard for further assaults. Failure to rapidly cross the Steenbeek valley would seriously expose attacking groups as easy targets for murderous German artillery, machine guns and snipers firing down from their elevated positions.

The heavy rains had so further delayed the opening of the battle for Langemarck that its commencement was now postponed until the early morning of 16 August. Typical of the difficulty experienced in this attack was that of the 16th Irish and the 36th Ulster divisions. Both divisions had been held in reserve until 4 August and they should have been rested, fresh and primed. However, for almost the past two weeks they had found themselves positioned at the front, poised and waiting for the weather to abate in order to attack. To their grief, all the while they were forced to sustain continuous artillery fire with its accompanying casualties, while also coping with the deluge. When finally charging 'over the top' on the 16 August, their assignment was the penetration of the German third (green) line but, by then, they had already suffered over 3,000 casualties before ever leaving their own trenches, and their attack was therefore blunted from the start. The 36th Ulster Division history recorded:

The story of the attack, alas! is not a long one. The German barrage came down swiftly, but as it was for the most part on the assembly trenches and behind them, it had small effect on the leading waves. But the enemy machine guns all along the front opened fire almost simultaneously with our barrage. The concrete pill-boxes, containing in some cases half a dozen separate compartments, seemed to be entirely unaffected by the pounding of many weeks [of artillery]. Moreover, strong wire entanglements running down obliquely [from the front] were encountered. The lanes cut by artillery fire were covered by machine guns. The ground was a veritable quagmire. The 'mopping up' system was found to be impossible. The concrete works had to be fought for; they could not be passed by and left to 'moppers-up' in rear. The inevitable result was that men quickly lost the barrage. The strength of the attacking force had become inadequate to its frontage of one-thousand-five hundred yards. The foremost wave must have consisted of less than three hundred men, probably reduced to a third within half a minute.[4]

Haig's dispatches reported gains but not total success, due to the creativity and effectiveness of the German defensive system that was elastic, in-depth, and devastating in its lethality:

... the village (Langemarck) had been taken, after sharp fighting. Our troops then proceeded to attack the portion of the Langemarck-Gheluvelt Line which formed their [the British] final objective, and an hour later had gained this also, with the exception of a short length of trench north-east of Langemarck. Two small counter-attacks were repulsed without difficulty.[5]

However, although the village of Langemarck was seized, the rest of the offensive had again ground to a halt, as even Haig admitted:

> In the centre of the British attack the enemy's resistance was more obstinate. The difficulty of making deep mined dug-outs in soil where water lay within a few feet of the surface of the ground had compelled the enemy to construct in the ruins of farms and in other suitable localities a number of strong points or 'pill-boxes' built of reinforced concrete often many feet thick. These forts, distributed in depth all along the front of our advance, offered a serious obstacle to progress. They were heavily armed with machine guns and manned by men determined to hold at all costs ... In addition, weather conditions made aeroplane observation practically impossible, with the result that no warning was received of the enemy's counter-attacks and our infantry obtained little artillery help against them ... therefore, later in the morning a heavy counter-attack developed ... our troops, who had reached their final objectives at many points in this area also, were gradually compelled to fall back.[6]

The reality was that even though the village of Langemarck had been taken, the cost in casualties had again been very high. The weather, German defensive tactics, and a greedy desire for too many objectives, had prevented greater success. The broad advance on too wide and deep a front had prevented consolidation of early gains, let alone the grasp of the Gheluvelt Plateau or the heavily defended flank of Polygon Wood. The results confirmed the obvious, as vividly recorded by those who witnessed and bore the brunt of the operation, in this case, correspondent Phillip Gibbs:

> The two Irish divisions were broken to bits and their brigadiers called it murder. They were violent [in] their denunciation of

the Fifth Army for having put their men into the attack after those thirteen days of heavy shelling, and, after the battle they complained that they were cast aside like old shoes, no care being taken for the comfort of men who had survived. No motor-lorries were sent to meet them and bring them down, but they had to tramp back, exhausted and dazed. The remnants of the 16th Division, the poor despairing remnants, were sent, without rest or baths, straight into the line again, down south. I found a general opinion among officers and men of not only the Irish division, under the command of the Fifth Army ... that they had been victims of atrocious Staff work, tragic in its consequences. From what I saw of some of the Fifth Army staff-officers, I was of the same opinion. Some of these young gentlemen, and some of the elderly officers, were arrogant and supercilious, without revealing any symptoms of intelligence. If they had wisdom it was deeply camouflaged by an air of inefficiency.[7]

The fog of war on the battlefield was obvious to those fighting. Where to go? What to do? How to do it? Communication was limited, the weather conditions were atrocious, and the objectives, although seemingly close on a map, were in reality beyond what human endurance could withstand. Worse was the frustration and inability to reach out to fellow comrades and assist those who were struggling with all of their might against overwhelming adversity. So unforgiving was the environment that, even when able to comprehend the situation and recognise an effective course of action, indiviuals and units were frequently without any power or authority to do anything beyond hang on and hope for the best for themselves, leaving others to their fate.

During the battle for Langemarck, Major R. Macleod DSO, MC, C.241 Battery, Royal Field Artillery, expressed this feeling of helplessness:

We had a tremendous barrage down this morning. All you could see, in front of the German line, were red and yellow flashes of shells bursting. The Germans must have been completely demoralised, because although their artillery was firing back on the infantry as they [he British infantry] tried to get across, there was hardly any machine-gun fire coming from the German trenches. But there was *no* chance of the infantry getting across. I watched them gradually trying to work their way forward, struggling like blazes through this frightful bog to get at the Germans. However, they were up to their knees in mud, and by the time they got half-way across, it was virtually impossible for them to move either forward or back. Then when we lifted the barrage, the machine-guns started to pick them off. ... I learned much later, after the war when I had access to the German unit records, that the Germans were so demoralised that they were prepared in front of our infantry to come out and surrender as soon as our barrage lifted. But when it did, they saw the infantry struggling and realised that they couldn't get to them, so they went back into their shell-holes and started shooting them up. They just went down in the mud. It was a sickening sight. It made me quite ill to watch it.[8]

It was at this point that Gough made his appeal to Haig to call off the attacks; he was told it would be impossible. Gough reported to Haig:

When it came to the advance of infantry for an attack across the waterlogged shell-holes, movement was so slow and so fatiguing that only the shortest advances could be contemplated. In consequence I informed the Commander-in-Chief that tactical success was not possible, or would be too costly, under such conditions, and advised that the attack should now be abandoned.[9]

Haig remained determined and confident that progress was being made at a high, although acceptable, cost. There were other serious strategic considerations to respect. The pressure must be maintained on the Germans in the west to prevent Russia (their government now under Alexander Kerensky) from collapsing in the east. It was also necessary to prevent the Germans from recognising the weakened state of the French armies following the recent mutinies under the blundering leadership of Robert Nivelle. Finally, Haig sought to continue his Flanders offensive becuase he still believed it would result in the elusive strategic breakthrough.

Renewed attempts were therefore ordered. On 27 August the attacks were particularly frustrating and futile. British officer Edwin Vaughan of the 1st/8th Warwickshire Regiment described the difficulty his unit encountered on attacking through the waterlogged shell holes:

> Up the road we staggered, shells bursting around us. A man stopped dead in front of me, and exasperated I cursed him and butted him with my knee. Very gently he said, "I am blind, sir," and turned to show me his eyes and nose torn away by a piece of shell. 'Oh God! I'm sorry, sonny,' I said. 'Keep going on the hard part,' and left him staggering back in his darkness.[10]

Even the British Official History commented on the impossibility of the conditions for the assaulting troops: 'so slippery from the rain and so broken by the water-filled shell holes that the pace was slow and the protection of the creeping barrage was soon lost.' These were units who had marched to the front in the night, waited ten hours to 'go over the top' to encounter a rain of German shell fire and impassable conditions to cross.[11]

Officer Vaughan commented on the confusion and the variety of ways to die:

> ... we sent the 16 [German] prisoners back across the open but they had only gone a hundred yards when a *German* machine gun mowed them down ... From other shell holes from the darkness on all sides came the groans and wails of wounded men; faint,

The toll of the guns, German dead in their pulverised trenches at Passchendaele July 1917. (Courtesy of Jonathan Reeve B119pic10)

Classic image of British infantry silhouetted against the battlefield, men of the 8th Battalion, East Yorkshire Regiment going up to the line near Frezenberg during the battle at Broodseinde, October 1917, part of Passchendaele. Photograph taken by official war photographer Ernest Brooks who took about 10% of all official British war photographs. (Courtesy of Jonathan Reeve B119pic11)

The British 18-pounder, artillery gun in its pit at the remains of Zonnebeke, Belgium, October 1917. This was the single most widely deployed gun on the Western Front by the British. All the other types of artillery pieces together just about equalled the number of 18-pounders used. The municipality of Zonnebeke comprises the villages of Beselare, Gheluvelt, Passchendaele, Zandvoorde and Zonnebeke proper. Situated in the centre of the Ypres Salient, the whole area was finally destroyed during Passchendaele and left abandoned until the early 1920s. (Courtesy of Jonathan Reeve B119pic23)

British machine-gun nest, Poelecappelle 1917. The Battle of Poelcappelle (9th October 1917) marked the end of the string of highly successful British attacks in late September and early October 1917, part of the wider Battle of Passchendaele. (Courtesy of Jonathan Reeve 3d94)

In the firing line at Passchendaele, 1917. This isn't a trench so much as an embankment. digging secure, deep and stable trenches was incredibly difficult in the mud. (Courtesy of Jonathan Reeve 3d96)

Through gas and smoke, British Tommies advance to the final assault of Passchendaele Ridge, 1917. (Courtesy of Jonathan Reeve 3d97)

August 1917, scene at Boesinghe leading to Passchendaele in Belgium. (Courtesy of Jonathan Reeve JRb1001fp222)

Enemy shells bursting in the ruins of Ypres, September 1917, during the battle of Passchendaele. (Courtesy of Jonathan Reeve B119pic5)

Captured German trench near Langemarck, on the Ypres Salient 1917. The Battle of Langemarck from 16 to 18 August 1917 was the second Allied general attack of the Third Battle of Ypres. (Courtesy of Jonathan Reeve B119pic7)

Wounded and prisoners, Lens, France August 1917. They could have been the result of the Battle of Hill 70 fought at Lens 15–25 August 1917 to relieve pressure on the allies at Passchendaele. (Courtesy of Jonathan Reeve B119pic8)

Menin Road, Ypres, September 1917. The Battle of the Menin Road was the third British general attack of the Battle of Passchendaele. The battle took place 20–25 September 1917. (Courtesy of Jonathan Reeve B119pic26)

Pack mule advancing through the mud at Pilckem Ridge, August 1917. The Battle of Pilckem Ridge (31 July–2 August 1917) was the opening attack of the main part of the Battle of Passchendaele. (Courtesy of Jonathan Reeve B119pic37)

British stretcher-bearers carrying wounded in deep mud, Pilckem Ridge, August 1917. (Courtesy of Jonathan Reeve B119pic55)

Men of the 16th Canadian Machine Gun Company hold the line amidst a ruined landscape of water-filled shell holes and mud. (Courtesy of Jonathan Reeve B119pic60)

An abandoned tank, Westhoek Ridge, September 1917, part of the Battle of Passchendaele. (Courtesy of Jonathan Reeve B119pic61)

General Sir Douglas Haig, general-in-chief of the British Army, Western Front. It was Haig who led the British Army from December 1915 until the end of the war in November 1918. Haig believed Germany could be defeated through a war of attrition, even if a breakthrough of the German lines remained impossible. During the first four years of the war, Haig and other generals, continued to attack and attempt a breakthrough. Haig remains one of the most controversial of all First World War generals due to his insistence on attacking in the face of very high casualties for very little gain. (Author's collection)

Red Zone warning of potentially dangerous unexploded bombs and shells. Today, throughout France and Belgium, tons of undetonated shells and projectiles lie beneath the ground. Every spring a fresh tonnage of material surfaces and must be salvaged and destroyed. Most of these shells were duds during the Great War, but some remain dangerous. Some still retain poison gas. (Author's collection)

German 210 mm (8") howitzer. Produced in large numbers by the Krupp Armaments Co., it was a mainstay of German heavy artillery. Labelled a 'morser' or mortar, it was an extremely effective and versatile weapon, able to hurl a 250-pound projectile 9,400 yards (nearly 6 miles). (Author's collection)

Mark IV tank. The tank was introduced at the Battle of the Somme in 1916, as the British were the first to produce an armoured, mechanised, fighting vehicle. Originally known as 'landships', and employing a crew of eight, the Mark IV tank was an improved and more dependable version. There were two variations, curiously deemed 'male' and 'female' depending on their assortment of cannon and machine guns. The British used several hundred at Passchendaele. However, most either broke down or were disabled by German gunfire. Heavy rain, water-filled shell holes, and the deep mud of the Passchendaele terrain limited their effectiveness. (Author's collection)

Replica British trench in Zonnebeke, Belgium. Trenches were typically 8–10 feet in depth and provided with drainage, but the high water table in Flanders made proper trenches very difficult to maintain. Many were frequently flooded, and the Germans relied on their concrete pillboxes and bunkers. (Author's collection)

Essex Farm dressing station and storage bunkers on the Yser Canal. It was here, in 1915, near the Yser canal, that Canadian medical officer Colonel John McCrae wrote his moving and famous poem, 'In Flanders Fields'. Typical of the concrete bunkers used as field hospitals and storage facilities, but very close to the front lines nonetheless. (Author's collection)

The Yser Canal, a frequent boundary and obstacle during the Ypres campaigns. It is an 11-mile river that has been improved as a canal, running through south western Belgium and draining many of the Flanders fields and streams. (Author's collection)

The towns of Langemarck, Zonnebeke, and Passchendaele would be on the horizon in the distance; Passchendaele roughly two-and-a-half miles away from this point. Behind the viewer, another two-and-a-half mile stretch back to the British jumping-off point on 31 July, where the battle commenced. This was the total distance gained by the British army in nearly four months of fighting at the battle of Passchendaele. During the summer of 1917, this area would have been swept repeatedly by machine gun and artillery fire, and have become a sea of water-filled shell holes, mud, and swampy ooze. (Author's Collection)

German soldiers with .30 calibre Maxim machine gun. This was the standard heavy machine gun used by all armies during the Great War. It came in many variations and all could fire 500–600 rounds a minute. The Germans are wearing the coal scuttle (bucket) model helmet. (National Archives)

Lieutenant General Arthur Currie of the Canadian Corps. Trained in artillery from the lower ranks and working his way up through the officer ranks, Currie was instrumental in the massive use of overwhelming artillery on a position and the conservation of soldiers. He believed in the motto 'shells, not soldiers'. It was under his leadership that the Canadian Corps successfully captured the village and ridge of Passchendaele in November of 1917. (Reproduced courtesy of the Canadian National Archives; Canada. Dept. of National Defence/Library and Archives.)

Lieutenant General Hubert Gough. General Sir Douglas Haig place Gough in charge of the planning and execution of the 1917 offensive in Flanders. Trained in the cavalry, as was Haig, Gough envisioned and planned a breakthrough assault on the ridges of the Salient as he believed Haig had instructed him to do. He professed this to his dying day, as opposed to Haig, who insisted that Gough was recommended to aim for a series of limited goals. This misunderstanding eventually led to Gough and his Fifth Army being replaced by General Herbert Plumer and the Second Army, who then conducted a series of 'bite and hold' attacks through the autumn of 1917. (Author's Collection)

Loading shells for a 15-inch heavy howitzer. Howitzers, due to their higher arc and heavier weight, gained great favour as the Great War progressed. Capable of hurling a bunker-penetrating load of high explosive, they were extremely effective at the shorter ranges of the stalemated trench positions. (Author's Collection)

Gas masks on German soldier and horses. Gas masks could protect against the inhalation of poisonous gas such as chlorine and phosgene, however, the introduction of mustard gas presented a new set of problems. As well as being dangerous to inhale, mustard gas also burned and blistered any exposed area of the skin. It devilishly saturated clothing, equipment, and traces even remained active in the soil. By 1917, most gas was launched within artillery projectiles. (National Archives)

Shell bursting outside a flooded and mud-filled British bunker. The epitome of the Passchendaele campaign in 1917, as troops attempt to take cover in a swamp of mud, high water, and devastation while exposed to constant shellfire. By official British Army photographer Lieutenant Ernest Brooks. (National Archives)

German soldiers in a cloud of poison gas. This is probably a training exercise. As the Great War progressed, the use of poison gas became more specifically employed. Usually fired in artillery projectiles to suppress backline soldiers, supply routes, and artillery batteries, it was a grim and fiendish weapon. (Author's Collection)

British Prime Minister David Lloyd George. Replacing Herbert Asquith in December of 1915, Lloyd George was extremely suspicious of General Douglas Haig and the war of attrition. Lloyd George longed to either replace Haig, or change the focus of Britain's war effort, but was unable to find an adequate substitute for either. It was reluctantly accepted that the war would be won or lost on the Western Front and under Haig's command. (Library of Congress)

British soldiers in a sodden, muddy, sandbag-lined trench. Clearly visible are their bayonets mounted on Lee Enfield .303 rifles, the standard issue weapon in the British Army. (Library of Congress, Bain Collection)

Dragging a heavy piece of artillery through the mud by hand. Due to the heavy rains the moving of equipment, men, and supplies became a nightmare of endurance. By British Army photographer Lieutenant John Brooke. (National Archives)

Duckboards leading to the front, used to avoid falling into a hopeless morass of deep, swampy shell holes. Many soldiers drowned upon falling in, especially at night. The photo below is of Chateau Wood by Australian Army photographer Captain Frank Hurley. (National Archives)

Above: Mangled British Mark IV tank. There could be no harder test for the new tracked vehicles than the mud of the Flanders battlefield. (Author's Collection)

Right: General Herbert Plumer conferring with George V. Plumer was a firm believer in the 'bite and hold' method of assaulting the strong German defensive positions. He was methodical and thorough in his preparation for an attack. Plumer successfully conducted the capture of Messines Ridge in June of 1917, and the early autumn successes at Passchendaele before the heavy rains bogged down the attack. (Author's Collection)

Aerial view of the town of Ypres before and after being the centre of constant shelling from artillery. The Pointillist pattern of water-filled shell holes is clearly visible. (Author's Collection)

German prisoners being escorted through the shattered town of Ypres. The walking wounded were the lucky ones. (Reproduced courtesy of the Canadian National Archives; Canada. Dept. of National Defence/Library and Archives.)

long, sobbing moans of agony and despairing shrieks. It was too horribly obvious that dozens of men with serious wounds must have crawled for safety into new shell holes, and now the water was about them and, powerless to move, they were slowly drowning. Horrible visions came to me with those cries, [of men] lying maimed out there trusting that their pals would find them, and now dying terribly, alone amongst the dead in the inky darkness. And we could do nothing to help them.[12]

Of Vaughan's group of 90, only 15 remained.

These attacks continued through the end of August and into September with little or no gain and seemingly no central focus. Meanwhile, Haig was contemplating a change in the operational command of the offensive. Gough and his Fifth Army were clearly not making headway on either the capture of the high ground around the Ypres Salient or the breakout to join the Channel offensive along the Belgian coast. The rain had, of course, made assaulting the determined German defences difficult, but in Haig's mind, more territory should have been captured and more attention paid to the 'bite and hold' method of attack. Therefore, by the end of August, Haig's frustration had reached a terminal point. He was disappointed both in the lack of progress on the capture of Gheluvelt Ridge and in Gough's reluctance to strive for limited advances with reinforced positions. Gough's style of attack had not been rewarded with even the conquest of the first day's objectives, and over 70,000 casualties had been incurred to no substantial geographical or tactical gain. Haig decided to replace him with Second Army commander General Sir Herbert Plumer, who had orchestrated the successful capture of the Messines Ridge in June of 1917. As we have seen, Plumer, another advocate of the 'bite and hold' formula, was the master of methodical and deliberate tactics, relying on thorough preparation before a major assault. Plumer declared he would need several weeks to prepare for the next phase of the battle. He was also hoping for a break in the weather.

In the meantime, the fighting, and the rain, would go on. Attacks on 22 and 24 August achieved nothing except extensive casualties and strengthened Haig's determination to replace Gough, which took place on the 26th. The incessant rain and mud was now completely overwhelming man, machine and beast alike. Typical of the difficulty in attempting to fight a war under these conditions was the comment from Corporal Robert Chambers of the Bedfords regiment, who wrote: 'It was raining like fury. Everywhere a quagmire. Fancy fighting Germans for a land like this. If it were mine I'd give them the whole damn rotten country.'[13]

The taking of Polygon Wood, the heavily fortified area to the north of Gheluvelt Ridge, was essential due to its lethal flanking fire and so equally vital for the Germans to hold. The British, therefore, concentrated repeated energy and resources on the position to gain control of it. It was nigh on impossible. Rifleman G.E. Winterbourne of the Queen's Westminster Rifles describes how the ground could destroy either a man or an assaulting group:

We crept up the night before just after dark...we lay out in shell-holes … When the dawn came, the first wave went over and we could see what had been doing the damage. There was a pillbox in front, and don't know what guns they had in it but they were covering a vast front, and as soon as you appeared they had you. We watched these London Rifle Brigade chaps going for it and dropping all over the place, but they bombed and bombed (used grenades) and eventually the machine-guns stopped. We got up and moved on, over this broken trench and on up the slope. Beyond the trench it was soft going, but seemed to be perfectly good ground – as good as any ground was around there at that time. All of a sudden I put one foot down and next moment I was through the earth and in a bog up to my armpits. Well, our blokes were moving on so fast they didn't see what had happened. I was there absolutely on my own and sinking deeper and deeper, because the more I struggled, trying to get one leg up to get myself out, the deeper I went in. Fortunately the next wave came up and two runners of the 2nd London Fusiliers saw me and stopped. They got on either side and held out their rifles and that gave me some purchase to get out. There was no good shouting for help because there was so much racket going on and shells bursting all around that no one would have heard you. But I was lucky.

Later he related the continuation of the attack and the almost demonic nature of the suckng mud:

We were going through all this awful ground that was just lakes of shell holes filled up with water, with Jerry trenchboards here and there. In a lull in the shelling we heard cries, and there was a poor chap about fifty or sixty yards away. He was absolutely up to his arms in it, and he'd been there for four days and nights – ever since the last attack – and he was still alive, clinging to the root of a tree in the side of this shell hole full of liquid mud. Lieutenant Whitby took three men over to see if they could get him out. But they couldn't get any purchase on the ground because it was all soggy round about. The more they pulled, the more they sank in themselves. Eventually, from somewhere or other, they got a rope, got it under his armpits and were just fixing up a derrick to see if they could hoist him out of it when we had to move on, because there was trouble up in front. All we could do was leave a man behind to look after him. It was another twenty-four hours before he was rescued.[14]

There were now more problems weighing in on Haig and his offensive: political interference, and from the highest quarters. The enormous casualty rates were causing widespread debate in Parliament and in the court of public opinion. The British Prime Minister, David Lloyd George, was questioning the prudence of a continued Flanders offensive, and suggesting that British troops and equipment would be better used on another front – shoring up the Italians against the Austrians, or perhaps a renewal of the failed Gallipoli front. With the stagnation and heavy casualties of the Flanders offensive, the question of allowing Haig to continue, let alone reinforcing the effort, was now under serious consideration. 'I am afraid we have put our money on the wrong horse. It would have been better to have reinforced the Italians,' declared Lloyd George.[15] But Haig had answers for his strategy, tactics and stalled offensive. The British director of intelligence, Brigadier General John Charteris, assured Haig that his information indicated German military morale to be deteriorating and that German manpower could not stand the strain, 'for more than a limited number of months (a maximum of twelve months) provided that the fighting is maintained at its present intensity in France and Belgium'.[16] Attrition to weaken the Germans, even if unable to obtain a breakthrough, would continue to positively push the course of the war to the Allies' overall benefit, provided they were willing to tolerate the cost.

This information only solidified Haig's determination to continue with the Flanders offensive. His new operational commander, Herbert Plumer, requested several weeks to reorganise the offensive using his Second Army as the spearhead, but in the meantime limited attacks to keep the pressure on the German defenders all along the Ypres Salient would continue. Haig was now willing to redirect his Belgian operation along a different tactical path having conceded the mistake of choosing Gough for the original command. Haig would keep the Flanders offensive alive with a firm commitment to the methodical 'bite and hold' formula as practised and perfected by Plumer. It would also help thwart the political threats from Prime Minister Lloyd George, which were interfering with his programme, by purchasing time to deliver success on the battlefield.

THE BATTLE FOR MENIN ROAD RIDGE, SEPTEMBER 1917

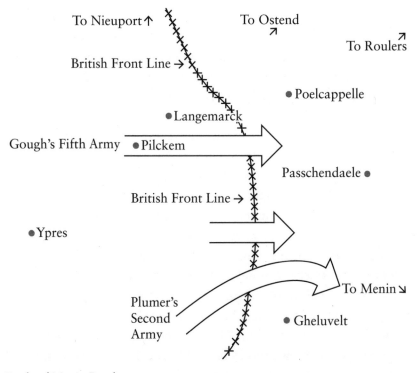

To Nieuport ↑

To Ostend ↗

To Roulers ↗

British Front Line →

● Poelcappelle

● Langemarck

Gough's Fifth Army ● Pilckem

Passchendaele ●

British Front Line →

● Ypres

To Menin ↘

Plumer's
Second
Army

● Gheluvelt

Battle of Menin Road

Haig commented about the situation in his later dispatches by describing it as a regrouping to align with alternative targets, although he was also plainly changing commanders and methods:

> The strength of the resistance developed by the enemy at this stage in the neighbourhood of the Menin Road decided me to extend the flank of the next attack southwards. It was undesirable, however, either to increase the already wide front of attack for which the Fifth Army [Gough's command] was responsible, or to divide between two Armies the control of the attack against the main ridge itself. I therefore determined [to] extend the left of the Second Army [Plumer's command] northwards, entrusting the attack upon the whole of the high ground crossed by the Menin Road to General Sir Herbert Plumer as a single self-contained operation, to be carried out in conjunction with the attacks of the Fifth Army farther north.[1]

The Menin Road was of the utmost importance, both as a possession and as a means of transportation to the front line. Everyone acknowledged this crucial fact. So too was the knowledge of the danger in passing over it, or what was left of it, as it was flanked by endless craters of water-filled shell-holes. The German gunners of course knew of its importance. Driver J. McPherson observed,

> You couldn't do anything about the dead, and there were so many bodies about that you got callous about it. All that time, before the push in September, I was up and down the Menin Road, up and down, up and down, taking ammunition on the backs of horses and mules up to the dump. They had to keep the Menin Road open, because it was the only way you could get up to that sector with horses and limbers, and it was shelled day and night. The Germans had their guns registered on it to a 'tee', and the engineers had to keep filling up the shell-holes. They filled them up with anything. If a limber got

a shell and blown to pieces they just shovelled everything into the crater and covered it over: dead horses, dead bodies, bits of limber – anything to fill it up and cover it over and keep the traffic going.

He describes the loss of shells to the mud:

I was a driver in the artillery and it was our job to get the ammunition up. We could only take limbers so far because of the shell-holes, so we had to go up the rest of the way with a walking squad, leading the horses. Each horse carried four shells, two on either side – and they were the big heavy ones with brass cases. We use to go twenty of us together, leaving the wagon lines at about three o'clock, up to the dump to get our shells, and we reached the guns about seven o'clock at night – if we were lucky enough to reach the guns. We sometimes thought it was a complete waste of time. The gunners never saw half the shells. With the weight of them they were just sinking into the mud, and it was complete waste of ammunition because they couldn't find them.[2]

Such was life, and death, on the Menin Road.

Although lacking definitive objectives, the intermittent British attacks continued unabated through the first three weeks of September, while the Plumer-directed offensive began to take shape. There were several questions and concerns dogging the proposed operation that Haig's high command had to ponder and develop – and the deepest concerns did not involve battlefield tactics. Haig was confronted by the growing political pressure from Prime Minister David Lloyd George and the threat of having the entire Flanders offensive terminated. Lloyd George was no fan of Haig, the Ypres Offensive, or the mounting casualties that were approaching the catastrophic figures of the previous summer's Somme campaign. Lloyd George had threatened not only an alternative front to engage Britain's forces in but also to withhold badly required reinforcements of troops and equipment for the entire Western Front.

Britain as a whole was confronted with a daunting proposition: she had now assumed the unenviable position of being Germany's main enemy, and it would be up to her to stand up to the brunt of German military activity on both land and sea. This was a psychological and physical commitment that had never been anticipated in 1914 when Great Britain marched off to war to help bulwark her French and Russian allies. The United States had entered the war, but would require at least another six months of enlistment and training before fielding an army of any size to begin filling the gaps in the Allies' depleted ranks. Britain was now responsible for both confronting any German offensive and for maintaining sufficient offensive pressure on the Germans to prevent this possibility. This was indeed a formidable task. The prospect of a penetration and breakthrough by the Germans on the Western Front was always lurking. And, in fact, this was to transpire in the spring of 1918 during the German's last-ditch offensive that was only narrowly halted at the Second Battle of the Marne by the combined forces of the British, French and newly arriving American Expeditionary Force.

On the Eastern Front, Russia's initially successful Kerensky Offensive was not only collapsing into military defeat, but into a nightmare of anarchy and revolution. The fate of 'all the Russias' would soon be engulfed by the Bolshevik take-over and the ensuing surrender of the Russians to the Germans at Brest-Litovsk. This would allow for the release of several million German soldiers from the Eastern to the Western Front, providing the impetus for the nearly successful German offensive of early 1918.

Post mutinies and reeling from the almost year-long Battle of Verdun, yet driven by the intense desire to somehow regain the occupied German-held French territory – a desire that under the circumstances the they seemed entirely incapable of accomplishing – the French appeared temporarily impotent and adrift in both strategy and action. At that moment, the French were fortunate to be able to catch their breath while regrouping at Verdun, and then to piece together a summer counter-attack on the beleaguered Verdun front. The presence of the growing British Army and its intended Flanders offensive, along with the anticipated arrival of the freshly minted contingent of Americans and their mountains of equipment and supplies, provided the French with this desperate breathing space to regroup and reorganise.

Within the context of these larger geopolitical strategic considerations, Haig and Plumer had to unpick the tactical conundrum of attacking the German defences at the Ypres Salient. Some sort of innovative strategy to overcome the dynamically difficult scheme of the German defence had to be developed. This was further complicated by the Germans' fierce willingness to aggressively counter-attack and contest every foot of ground. Some sort of original response had to be imagined and applied. To solve this puzzle, Haig turned to Plumer, the general who had done such a remarkable job at Messines Ridge the previous June in the capture of a previously impregnable German position of high ground. Plumer sought reliance in several tried and true tactics that he and his staff believed could dependably produce *limited* gains on the battlefield. He held no misapprehensions – and no misgivings – about the cost that would be incurred in casualties, nor did he harbour grandiose dreams of a breakthrough. Plumer would point to achieving at least some sort of positive gain following the expenditure in lives: lives that Lloyd George believed Haig was entirely too willing to squander for no visible gain.

While fending off political criticism from Lloyd George's administration, Haig continued to speak in relatively vague terms of tactics and objectives. It was now up to Plumer and his staff to provide details for a battlefield success – a success that Haig required if he was to make good on his promise for progress. Having had enough of Gough's direct, unimaginative and, apparently unsuccessful tactics, Haig selected the meticulous Plumer, a stark contrast in both vision and in operation. In fact, Haig and Gough had disagreed right from the start of the Ypres offensive, although neither acknowledged it. This had led to a lack of coordination from the very onset of the campaign. Haig now claimed he knew what he wanted, knew how to do it, and had the man to make it happen in Plumer. Haig later described a hiatus in operations:

> At the beginning of September the weather gradually improved, and artillery and other preparations for my next attack proceeded steadily. Both the extent of the preparations required, however, and the need to give the ground time to recover from the heavy rains of August rendered a considerable interval unavoidable before a new advance could be undertaken. The 20th September was therefore chosen for the date of our attack, and before that day, our preparations had [not] been completed.[3]

General Sir Herbert Plumer was a career infantry soldier who had worked his way up through the ranks. A bushy moustache, round potbelly, and rather droopy posture belied his intelligence, determination, and competence as a warrior. Plumer had distinguished himself at earlier battles in the Ypres Salient, and had proven resourceful and imaginative during the highly successful capture of Messines Ridge. His meticulous and methodical preparation before the Messines attack testified to his stolid yet innovative approach to the First World War dilemma of trench stalemate. Plumer's approach seemed too pedestrian for Haig, hence his initial selection of Gough to lead the entire Passchendaele Offensive. But after a month of enormous casualties, only minor gains, and Gough's reluctance to pursue the offensive, Haig sought fresh thinking. Plumer's methods and leadership, prior to and during the capture of the difficult Messines Ridge operation (*see* Chapter 2), was contrary to the dashing breakthrough hopes envisioned by Gough and Haig. Plumer's plan, if effectively applied and again productive, could now deliver Haig some measure of success in the face of a potential Flanders disaster that was being so seriously questioned in London. Gough's command of the Fifth Army was retained, but the offensive spearhead was now shifted to Plumer's Second Army. In this way Haig horizontally shifted operational direction from Gough to Plumer and, in so doing, gave Plumer the responsibility to salvage success out of the mud and inertia of the first month's desultory results.

Plumer and his staff had several bedrock beliefs. The overall approach should be contingent around the 'bite and hold' purchase of a relatively shallow depth and defined line of desired ground. This line would be well-prepared by an intensive artillery barrage; that barrage would then lift and continue slightly forward and beyond the captured line, shifting deeper to lay down a curtain of protection and disrupting the inevitable German counter-attacks. This initial purchase would then be solidly reinforced before *any* further attacks were considered or ordered. The artillery would be moved forward, and the entire process repeated over the course of the next few days. In this way, artillery would not only service the assaulting infantry with a barrage of moving cover as it attacked, but then protect it by laying down a curtain of shell-fire to prevent penetration by counter-attacking groups (Eingreif). At the same time, improved ranging techniques for enhanced indirect fire (Chapter 6) would allow artillery to silence those rear echelon German cannon that were threatening the newly captured positions. Rather than Gough's desire for a wide, big push and possible breakthrough, Plumer would attack on a narrower front, and only attempt to cross and seize 1000–1500 yards of territory. He would then allow a week to consolidate the position before pressing on with the next short 'bite'.

The method of attack by infantry groups was also being reconsidered; no longer would mass waves of soldiers repeatedly expose themselves in the open while committing to endless charges that frequently bordered on the suicidal. Skirmishers would go forward and probe for weaknesses in the defences, followed by reinforced groups in strength to seize and hold those positions that were captured, to be followed by mopping up units. The attack would pause and regroup while fresh units would come forward. Those isolated defensive strongholds that remained would then be enveloped and destroyed by specially trained groups with hand

and rifle grenades, and the more portable Lewis machine guns. The final phase would involve the immediate construction of support roads and light rail lines to provide for rapid supply to the advancing units. Indirect fire, able to target positions that were out of sight, would be of the highest priority. Air power would play an increasingly important role in observation, reconnaissance, and disruption of German backline reinforcing elements.

At the same time, Haig sought vigorously to solidify his political position, always a consideration, but even more so with Lloyd George chaffing at the stalled Flanders strategy. By outlining the difficulties involved, and the accommodations for improvement applied, Haig defensively proclaimed:

> These arrangements included a modification of our tactics, to meet the situation created by the change in the methods of defence. Our recent successes had conclusively proved that the [German] infantry were unable to hold the strongest defences against a properly mounted attack, and that the Germans increasing the number of his troops in his forward defence systems merely added to his losses. Accordingly, the enemy had adopted a system of elastic defence, in which his forward trench lines were held only in sufficient strength to disorganise the attack, while the bulk of his forces were kept in close reserve, ready to deliver a powerful and immediate blow which might recover the positions over-run by our troops before we had had time to consolidate them. In the heavy fighting of Ypres, these tactics had undoubtedly met with a certain measure of success. While unable to drive us back from the ridge, they had succeeded, in combination with the state of the ground and weather, in checking our progress.[4]

To this challenge, Plumer and his staff drew up their plans to assault and, bit by bit, seize the heretofore-unassailable Gheluvelt Plateau. The reformed flexibility in infantry movement favoured by Plumer would be backed up by a devastating pre-attack barrage of unparalleled ferocity. More guns, specifically more *big* guns, would be employed, and on a much narrower front in order to further increase the concentration of firepower before, during and after the assaults. A more detailed description, from Brigadier General Charles Harrington of the Headquarters of the Second Army, illustrates the plan:

> The waves of attack which were hitherto used, do not give sufficient flexibility, nor are platoons and sections sufficiently under the control of their leaders to deal with sudden opposition likely to be encountered under the new conditions. The leading wave, in one or two lines should be extended to force the enemy to disclose his positions, the remainder in small groups or file ready to deal with unexpected machine-guns or parties of the enemy. It must be impressed on all subordinate leaders that rapidity of action is of paramount importance, and that any delay in assaulting these points adds to the seriousness of the situation and increases the difficulties of dealing with it. Known machine-gun emplacements and defended points are dealt with by parties previously told off for the duty. Careful study of the ground and aeroplane photographs will go a long way towards increasing the 'known' and giving all leaders a clear idea of the points from which opposition may be expected. The rear waves must keep closed-up until No Man's Land [is reached], and gradually gain the distance; after this, officers must be trained to ensure [it] is done.[5]

General Harrington also tells in his memoirs how General Gough was reluctant to attack due to more rain on the night of 19/20 September, but was dissuaded by General Plumer, now in charge of the offensive and confident concerning the morrow's prediction for a dry day in which to attack on the 20th:

> About midnight on the night of 19/20 September, General Gough proposed that operations should be postponed on

account of rain, but General Plumer between 1 and 2 am after consulting his corps and divisional commanders decided to adhere to plan ... 'The attack must go on. I am responsible, not you. Good night and good luck.'[6]

And so, Plumer's offensive commenced. The land designated for the attack was itself nothing but a washed-out, cratered, wreck, as described by a British combatant, Hugh Quigley, at ground level:

> The country resembles a sewage-heap more than anything else, and filled to the brim with green, slimy water, above which a blackened arm or leg might project. It becomes a matter of great skill picking a way across such a network of death traps, for drowning is almost certain in one of them.[7]

This was to be the ground that had to be traversed as the next phase of the campaign ensued.

What was to be called the Battle for the Menin Road Ridge, or the Menin Road, commenced on 20 September in dry and dusty weather, a welcome change from the mainly rain-soaked summer. The weather was going to be a huge joker in the pack as the renewed offensive took shape.

Dry weather meant Plumer's methods for reinforcing the front lines, extending transport routes, and moving the guns forward, could be carried out. It remained physically demanding work, but possible. Rain and the resulting sea of mud, however, could doom the entire operation.

Plumer had called for four tiers of advancement, each to be preceded by the heaviest artillery barrages yet used by the British. There would be breaks of six days between each tier of advance to consolidate the 'bite' and bring the big guns forward. Next would be preparation of roads and light rail to fully access the re-supply chain for the next 'bite'. In this manner, Plumer foresaw the capture of the Gheluvelt Plateau.

As to the importance of the weather, even Haig conceded the need for good weather in his statement of 21 August to the War Office in London:

> If we are favoured with a fine autumn ... I regard the prospect of clearing the coast before winter sets in as still very hopeful, notwithstanding the loss of time caused by the bad weather during the first half of August. At the least, I see no reason to doubt that we shall be able to gain positions from which subsequent operations to clear the coast will present a far easier problem than we had to cope with at the outset of the offensive ... Success in clearing the coast may confidently be expected to have such strategical and political effects that they are likely to prove decisive.[8]

This was optimism in the extreme, as Haig still sought not only gains in Flanders, but the potential strategic link-up with the 'Operation Hush' coast invasion. Some dreams are sometimes hard to let go, and this dream remained. Haig was still hoping to achieve a strategic success, but for now he was counting on Plumer to pull his politically connected chestnuts out of the fire with some tangible gains in Flanders. Following the change in tactical command to Plumer, a steady drumbeat of artillery preparation and infantry attacks continued throughout early September. So erratic and imprecise were these attacks, however, that the German commander on the scene, Chief of Staff General von Kuhl of the Crown Prince Rupprecht Army Group, predicted that the major offensive at Ypres must have concluded and that the British were now content just to settle in to their position for the upcoming winter. But as September gave way to October, and as the weather seemed to indicate a drier pattern, the plans of Plumer and the Second Army began to take shape. Training, rehearsing, and building up ammunition and supplies were followed by a growing intensity of artillery shelling on the German positions. There was to be no relief for either side on the Ypres front. By late September, the narrow attack front of the Gheluvelt Plateau began to rock with the ever-increasing pounding of the preliminary bombardment, reaching a crescendo on the early morning of 20 September.

Plumer not only had more big and medium guns available, but also considerably more shells to lob at the Germans. Narrowing his width of target further increased Plumer's artillery concentration. British improvement in the manufacture of fuses had greatly enhanced ordinance reliability, the better to enable shell detonation at the moment of impact on a designated pillbox or bunker. The deposition of attacking battalions had also been altered in order to better cope with the German system of defence in depth. Instead of two battalions making the initial attack, to be followed up by one battalion to reinforce and push on, the order would be reversed, so that one battalion would seize the position and be reinforced by two battalions to hold and defend the newly gained ground against the inevitable German counter-attacks.

Gas shells would be heavily used to restrain enemy artillery and deny, or at least make more difficult, return fire from the German rear echelon batteries. Surviving bunkers and pillboxes would be dealt with by specially trained combat groups, equipped with the necessary mobile firepower to suppress and destroy the reinforced islands of resistance. Greater emphasis would be placed on preliminary aerial observation to earmark artillery batteries, reserve billets, and defensive strong points. During the attack, air squadrons would be assigned the duty of pinning down both reinforcing infantry units and German air patrols. In the event, the Plumer offensive 'bite' of 20 September would achieve a gain of roughly 1,500 yards in depth, while securing the 'hold' against the German counter-attacks. As planned, the major thrust and goal of the attack was along a slender 4,000-yard front moving up the Gheluvelt Plateau. The overall attacking front would be along an eight-mile-wide area that included Gough's Fifth Army attacking the northern extension of the Ypres Salient. This would place nearly the entire German defensive perimeter under threat, leaving the German commanders unsure as to where the counter-attacking units should be dispatched. The X Corps, consisting of the 41st and 23rd Divisions and the 1st and 2nd Divisions of the I ANZAC Corps, would be responsible for the taking of the primary objective of the Gheluvelt Plateau. A total of nine divisions, engaging over 65,000 troops, were scheduled to attack an overall front of 10,000 yards to hopefully further confuse the Germans as to where to concentrate their reinforcements.

The opening barrage of over 1,275 heavy and medium guns, which included at least 575 heavy and over 720 field guns and howitzers, would be followed by the creeping barrage to escort and lead the attacking units. Plumer laid out one big gun for every 5.1 ft of the 4,000-yard creeping barrage that led up the slope of the Gheluvelt Plateau. Plumer's offensive would utilise over three-and-a-half *million* shells. This was twice the number of shells that the Fifth Army had previously used, and three times the number used by Gough's army for the August attack on Pilckem Ridge. The artillery barrage laid down a solid curtain of explosive metal that virtually prevented any retaliatory fire from the Germans, but also, due to the cloud of dust and earth that was thrown into the air, gave little or no visibility as to what was happening in front of them. Lieutenant Cyril Lawrence observed:

Just look at our artillery. Just look at it, at those countless flashes. See how they stab at the darkness from their hiding places, not in dozens but in hundreds, and yet these are only the heavies, the lighter guns are well up and we cannot see them. See the red glares that light up the country for miles where a Hun shell has landed amongst some cordite. The whole place seems ablaze as far as the eye can see: flash after flash, some singly, some in groups, when a battery fires together, but isn't it all beyond description, beyond belief, even beyond imagination? Feel the vibration and the jolting and hear the ear-splitting, nerve-racking noise of it all. It is not a bit of use trying to talk, or even shout because bellow as you like no one can hear you.[9]

The attack moved forward at 05:40 and within six hours, most objectives were seized and being reinforced against the expected German counter-attacks that were soon to follow. These counter-attacks, however strenuous, were resisted and beaten back. Gough commented in his Fifth Army memoirs:

> As usual in this battle the Germans counter-attacked fiercely. On the V Corps front they launch no less than six counter-attacks. These were either beaten off, or our supporting troops immediately counter-attacked in their turn and once more drove the Germans out. Their losses were very heavy and we captured more than 1,300 prisoners. By the end of the day, we had captured all our objectives with the exception of two farms—an average penetration of 1,000 yards along the front of attack.[10]

German General von Kuhl commented, '...our counter-attack divisions arrived too late. Their blow came up against a defensive position already organised in depth and protected by an artillery barrage.'[11]

The German technique of pouring soldiers into the counter-attack was being engaged with vigour and numbers, and the result was a withering British defence emanating from well organised units that had dug in to their new positions and that were fully backed up by accurately lethal artillery. For once the German tactic was not only failing, but failing in a devastating toll of human sacrifice that exceeded the German ability to provide replacements. The concern expressed by the German staff was obvious, and with the concern came thoughts on how to redeploy their defences in the wake of this defeat.

General Eric Ludendorff commented:

After each attack I discussed the tactical experiences with General von Kuhl and Colonel von Lossberg, sometimes at the front, and sometimes on the telephone ... Our defensive tactics had to be developed further, somehow or other ... in order to gain power, the whole battlefield was to be given more depth than ever ... an unheard of expenditure of force.[12]

The British were beginning to see a breakdown in the German defences, and a possible way through the dilemma of the trench stalemate. Correspondent John Buchan commented:

This day's battle cracked the kernel of the German defence of the Salient. It showed a limited advance, and the total of 3,000 prisoners had been often exceeded in a day's fighting; but every inch of the ground was vital. We had carried the southern pillar on which the security of the Passchendaele ridge depended. Few struggles in the campaign were more desperate, or carried out on a more gruesome battlefield. The maze of quagmires, splintered woods, ruined husks of 'pill-boxes', water-filled shell-holes and foul creeks which made up the land on both sides of the Menin Road was a sight which to the recollection of most men seemed like a fevered nightmare. It was the classic soil on which during the First Battle of Ypres the 1st and 2nd Divisions had stayed the German rush for the Channel. Then it had been a broken but still recognisable and featured countryside; no the elements seemed to have blended with each other to make of it a limbo outside mortal experience and almost beyond human imagining. Only on some of the tortured hills of Verdun could a parallel be found. The battle of the 20th September was a proof of what heights of endurance the British soldier may attain to. It was an example, too, of how thought and patience may achieve success in spite of every disadvantage of weather, terrain, and enemy strength.[13]

The one-day victory, earned and trumpeted as it was, was not without considerable cost. As Plumer had predicted, the Gheluvelt Plateau could be taken, and would be, but it was still at an enormous sacrifice in human life and effort. Lieutenant Firstbrooke Clarke of the North Staffordshires wrote: 'I suppose to people at home it is a fine victory. Well, so it is but they don't see the dead and wounded lying out and they don't have 9.2s bursting every 10 yards away, machine gun bullets scraping a parapet. I lost 17 of my platoon (4 killed) besides the casualties in the rest of the Coy (Company). I was so sick of it and upset that I cried when I got back.'[14]

For the Germans, the British success was obvious and troublesome. Ludendorff commented:

> The enemy managed to adapt himself to our method of employing counter-attack divisions. There were no more attacks with unlimited objectives, such as General Nivelle had made in Aisne-Champagne Battle. He was ready for our counter-attacks and prepared for them by exercising restraint in the exploitation of success.

Ludendorff was conceding the points that Plumer had deemed most essential for a successful attack on any given point: limited objective, immediately reinforced positions, and overwhelming artillery superiority. Ludendorff goes on to further conclude, concerning the Menin Road Ridge battle: 'The enemy's onslaught on the 20th was successful, which proved the superiority of the attack over the defence ... The power of the attack lay in the artillery, and the fact that ours did not do enough damage to the hostile infantry.'[15]

Even with a victory, the casualties to both sides in one day's fighting were enormous, roughly equivalent to the 31 July attacks – although the difference in both ground gained and the spirit of accomplishment was palpable. The British officially suffered more than 20,000 casualties with over 3,000 being listed as killed. The Germans listed more than 25,000 casualties, with over 6,000 listing as missing. Therefore, allowing for the British listing of 3,000 Germans accounted as captured, it may be concluded that the Germans suffered at least 3,000 killed.

According to Plumer's doctrine, the gains would duly be reinforced, fresh road and rail lines would be immediately laid, and the big guns moved forward to engage the Germans for another 'bite'.

12

BATTLE OF POLYGON WOOD, 26 SEPTEMBER–3 OCTOBER

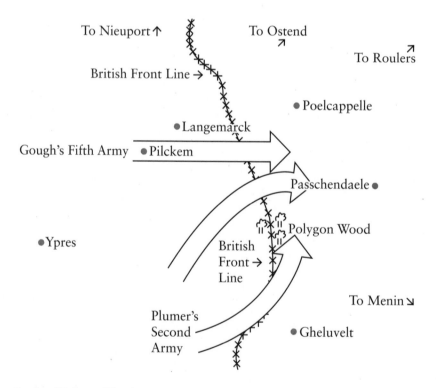

Battle of Polygon Wood

With the Menin Road Ridge secured, General Plumer prepared to continue the advance and sought to take advantage of the dry weather. Four to five days of preparation would be required, followed by another 'bite' of roughly 1,000 to 1,500 yards in depth. This time the goal was the capture of Polygon Wood. Again the overall front would be narrow, 5,000 yards, and the concentration of attack would be limited to an even narrower 1,500 yards of intended capture. If successful, the attack would set the stage for a follow-up swing to the north and the advance on Broodsiende, Poelcappelle, and finally Passchendaele proper. This would then put Haig's army in alignment with the projected drive to the Channel, to merge with Rawlinson's Fourth Army and the arrival of the amphibious forces landing on the coast. The pursuit of 'Operation Hush' as planned would then proceed up the Channel coast. The strategic element of this combined operation was still very much on Haig's greater agenda. His hope was to clear the Channel and the North Sea coast of German submarine bases while simultaneously establishing a position to outflank the German army. Such an outcome would provide generous benefits, both politically and strategically. In terms of operational tactics, however, it would ask another raft of questions. The answers seemed to lie in the continuation of General Plumer's incremental approach. But, in fact, Haig's plans and ideas were already growing beyond Plumer's tactical style.

Excited about the success at the Menin Road, Haig issued the following directions to Plumer and Gough for 26 September, '... the attack is to be carried out on as wide a front as possible ... in order to obtain the tactical advantages of attacking on a wide front.'[1] This somewhat tautological statement – do it this way because it's good – is hardly Clausewitzian in its insight.

This broader approach is not what Plumer had in mind, however, and in the event, the attacking front would be narrower than at Menin Road Ridge. Plumer viewed the attacking fronts as sharpening in focus; Haig now envisioned broadening the front. Plumer proposed assaulting a front of only 8,500 yards as opposed to the previous Menin Road front of 10,500 yards. This would have the added effect of a more concentrated volume of artillery fire – accurate and concentrated artillery being an integral part of Plumer's method. Also reduced would be the anticipated depth of advance, being 500 yards less.[2] As far as getting to the coast and completing 'Operation Hush', the Plumer approach, as successful as it had been, was gaining ground at a slower than pedestrian rate. Success at Polygon Wood would again follow this pattern, both in result and rate.

Accordingly, Plumer's forces began immediately to reinforce the Menin Road Ridge position, lay new rail track to the recently won front lines, and commence a steady barrage on the German lines, using range-finding shelling to prepare for the next push. To confuse the Germans as to where Plumer would strike next, an additional artillery barrage in strength was conducted by the British VIII and IX Corps further to the south of the intended front.

Once again, Plumer would thoroughly rehearse his attacking divisions before the assault and this time the attack would be preceded by five waves of sheltering barrage curtains. The first group of assault troops would be more thinly spaced and more lightly equipped. This group would be sheltered by a wall of iron and explosive fire, providing a curtain of metal, before advancing to seize the German positions. The creeping barrage would then lift to form a protective shield, stranding and isolating the remaining German strongholds and pillboxes while preventing German counter-attacks from entering the protected zone. British reinforcing units would follow in strength, eliminating the German strong points, while the artillery barrage would again be moved forward, this time to strike the German artillery positions and further blunt or destroy immediate German counter-attacks. The goal, as at Menin Road Ridge, was to seize the position, immediately reinforce it, and then quickly seal it with a defending canopy of artillery fire. The planned artillery ration was one big gun for every ten yards of front. Extra ammunition was brought forward before the attacks to assist the assault, but also to better protect the newly gained ground. The thunderous barrages would not only introduce the attack, but preserve the gains that were made.

General Haig accepted Plumer's programme, and ordered an increased number of heavy guns to be assigned for the attack. Along with the heavy artillery, a battlefield unending fusillade of heavy machine gun fire would be used to pin down surviving Germans holding out in pillboxes and other resisting front positions. The Vickers heavy calibre machine gun would be used for this purpose, as machine gun companies would be positioned to lay down a protective blanket cover of devastating firepower. The more mobile advancing units would carry the lighter and more portable Lewis machine guns. The distances for the assaulting soldiers would be shorter, the area of attack narrower, and the focus of both weapons and attacking soldiers greater and more intensely concentrated.

Unbeknownst to Haig and Plumer, the Germans had planned a massive counter-attack of their own for 25 September, the day before Plumer's. The Germans sought to regain ground that they had lost from the Menin Road Ridge engagement the previous week. In keeping with their tactic of holding ground through counter-attacks, German Crown Prince Rupprecht, commander of the Ypres front, was keen to seize lost sections of the Gheluvelt Plateau and its high ground advantage. The Germans also, of course, intended to disrupt the momentum of the British offensive.

The two armies then both proceeded to launch their attacks almost simultaneously. Although the German attacks were repulsed, the results were devastating to the British attacking units massing at the front and poised to go 'over the top' the next morning. The German barrage caught the British by surprise, inflicting heavy casualties just as they were launching their own pre-attack barrage. Clearly the Germans were not collapsing and in fact were still more than able to mount an offensive attack of their own. On the ground, soldier G. S. Hutchinson recorded:

With such energy was the attack pressed that the whole of our line was thrown back. It was impossible to know the position of our troops and how far the German attack had penetrated. Commanders of all formations from those of brigades, even down to Platoons, were out of touch with their commands and with their flanks. The enemy, possessed of the advantage of ground, seems to have been in no such dilemma, for the bombardment lifted, and, as it seemed, with an even greater ferocity smote our communications and every approach to the beleaguered line. British batteries, which in the rear kept up a hurricane fire, from their deep formation, possessed of no new information, although themselves under the heaviest shell-fire, brought down the barrage line with the object of stemming any further infiltration ... the German attack had overrun the Divisional (33rd) right, and made a deep impression on its left ... the 1st Middlesex [and] 93rd Highlanders, held their ground.[3]

Obviously, the Germans remained capable of not only defending, but also of launching devastating attacks of their own. With Plumer's preparation already in place, and the German assault repulsed, Haig decided to go ahead with the British attack on 26 September and the assault proceeded accordingly. As one of the other ranks of the 55th Division observed:

The advance up the slowly rising ridge to Passchendaele once started had to go on, but troops were not going over every day, as on the Somme. Periodical thrusts of greater compass had come to pass, and the creeping barrage. No longer could Jerry lie low in his dug-outs, or in this case his pill-boxes, and know that the lifting of the barrage was an almost infallible signal of our attack. You followed the creeping shells now, and pounced on him still dazed and bewildered. The Somme had not been without its lessons.[4]

At dawn on 26 September, the attack commenced. Plumer's plan was again well prepared and coordinated. The attacks were made across the narrow front and entirely successful with the exception of the heavily and desperately defended position known as Tower Hamlets. Once again, the attacking Tommies were shielded by a creeping barrage of accurately escorting firepower. The successful acquisition was quickly and heavily reinforced, and again the expected German counter-attacks were repeatedly repelled by an overwhelming display of artillery support laying down a curtain of flaming iron. Nine times the Germans counter-attacked and each time they were cut down by smothering artillery fire and the firing from heavily reinforced British positions. However, the British gains did not come without cost as the operation absorbed another 15,000 casualties. Success can be measured in many ways, and these goals won, as welcome to the British as they were, were a mere three-quarters of a mile in depth.

The Germans were continuing to recognise both the success of Plumer's tactics and the failure of their own previously successful 'defence in depth' followed by ruthless counter-attacks. General Ludendorff later commented that the defensive system they had employed would have to be altered, and that, 'the Flanders fighting imposed a heavy strain on the Western (German) troops. In spite of all the concrete protection they seemed more or less powerless under the enormous weight of the enemy's artillery ... There were no more attacks with unlimited objective, such as General Nivelle had made in the Aisne-Champagne battle. He [Plumer] was ready for our counter-attacks, and prepared for them by exercising restraint in the exploitation of success.'[5]

Clearly Plumer's methods were succeeding, even if at a slow incremental rate of advance and with high casualties. Fortunately for Plumer, Haig and the British, the fine, dry weather was holding and allowing favourable conditions for further attacks. This was something that had been lacking in the earlier summer, but there were no guarantees it would continue. Another consequence of the shallow depth of gain was the inability either to capture or completely silence the backline batteries of German artillery. This would plague all future short depth attacks – the inability to knock out the rear garrisons of German heavy artillery. British artillery was obviously improving in aim and capacity and, most importantly, in the tactical acumen to escort the infantry with effective creeping barrage curtains. Nonetheless, the high rates of casualties could only be justified under the heading of winning the war through attrition. The dreadful individual tragedies endured by the ordinary soldier continued unabated. Typical was the report of Lieutenant Alfred J. Angel, 24th London Btn. Royal Fusiliers, 58th Division. Angel describes the condition of the battlefield as his group arrived on the eve of the battle:

> Most of my boys were young Londoners, just eighteen or nineteen, and a lot of them were going into a fight for the first time. Regularly during the night I crawled round to check on my scattered sections, having a word here and there and trying to keep their spirits up. The stench was horrible, for the bodies were not corpses in the normal sense. With all the shell-fire and bombardments they'd been continuously disturbed, and the whole place was a mess of filth and slime and bones and decomposing bits of flesh. Everyone was on edge.

Such was life in the trenches and shell-holes on the Flanders battlefield, but there was also camaraderie and salvation of a kind, as Angel goes on to describe:

> I could hear a boy sobbing and crying. He was crying for his mother. It was pathetic really, he just kept saying over and over again, 'Oh Mum! Oh Mum!' Nothing would make him shut up, and while it wasn't likely that the Germans could hear, it was quite obvious that when there were lulls in the shell-fire the men in the shell-holes on either side would hear this lad and possibly be affected. Depression, even panic, can spread quite easily in a situation like that. So I crawled into the shell-hole and asked Corporal Merton what was going on. He said, 'It's his first time in the line sir. I can't keep him

quiet, and he's making the other lads jittery.' Well, the other boys in the shell-hole obviously *were* jittery and, as one of them put it more succinctly, 'fed up with his bleedin noise'. Then they all joined in, 'Send him down the line and home to Mum' – 'Give him a clout and knock him out' – 'Tell him to put a sock in it, sir.' I tried to reason with the boy, but the more I talked to him the more distraught he became, until he was almost screaming. 'I can't stay here! Let me go! I want my Mum!' So I switched my tactics, called him a coward, threatened him with court-martial, and when *that* didn't work I simply pulled him towards me and slapped his face as hard as I could, several times. It had an extraordinary effect. There was absolute silence in the shell-hole and then the corporal, who was a much older man, said, 'I think I can manage him now, sir.' Well, he took that boy in his arms, just as if he was a small child, and when I crawled back a little later to see if all was well, they were both lying there asleep and the corporal still had his arms round the boy – mud, accoutrements and all. At zero hour they went over together.[6]

On 26 September Lieutenant Angel's battalion went over the top and successfully took their objective. Unfortunately Lt Angel was wounded and lost an eye, the corporal was killed, and the lad crying for his Mum was shot several times – and got to go home.[7]

Even with superior tactics and commensurate gains, nothing was easy, or assumed, in the muck and mire. Lieutenant Colonel Spens of the 5/6th Scottish Rifles led his group forward during the night for the dawn attack. He and his outfit were new to the ground they were assigned and lacked observable markings to calculate their position. He therefore thought it prudent to use a veteran guide to lead the march to their forward stations:

The ground in front was new to us, and guides from the front battalions were asked for. The night was dark and the shelling worse than ever. Battalion headquarters had been established near some friendly-looking tanks, which appeared to be on fairly firm ground at L Farm ... The surrounding ground was a mass of shell holes filled with stinking water and mud and if you fell in you were lost ... it seemed safest to keep to the road ... stretched out in file, in the dark, with the guide and the Colonel in front. For an hour the party followed the lead ... it found itself back at the place from which it had started. The tanks were now a blazing mass of twisted iron. What had gone wrong with the guide? He was obviously lost and had been walking in a circle.[8]

In spite of the high casualties, Haig was excited and optimistic. Progress was being achieved, the weather was now favourable, and more gains could be anticipated. The Germans were fighting fiercely, but they were gradually falling back toward Passchendaele village and sustaining heavy losses along the way. Haig repeatedly predicted a German collapse under the weight of such offensive pressure, as Plumer's Second Army began shoring up its newly gained ground. Haig now sought to immediately prepare and launch the attack on Broodseinde Ridge for the next bite of the attack, as the British inched their way toward the Ridge of Passchendaele. The next attack would be scheduled for 6 October and the target was to be the remains of the village of Broodseinde.

The Germans were also contemplating a change in their defensive alignment, shifting back to the idea of stationing more men along the forward front to better cope with the strength of the British offensives, rather than holding back and attempting to rebound with pounding counter-attacks. The British command, under Plumer's direction, had seemingly discovered a solution to the dilemma of the German defensive system. This forced the Germans to rethink their defensive tactics and caused Ludendorff to begin to question the wisdom of the weak and thinly manned front lines reinforced by in-depth units massed for heavy counter-attacks.

Ludendorff commented that, 'the enemy (has) managed to adapt himself to our method of employing counter-attack divisions.'[9]

This sentiment would be repeated by Ludendorff and different efforts to thwart the British successes would be employed. The restoration of more heavily manned front line trenches would, of course, expose more defending soldiers to initial risk at the point of attack, but the trade-off would be greater ability to fend off the first wave of attackers. It was a difficult equation that shifted back and forth between the opposing armies. This time Ludendorff's solution would meet disaster at the upcoming action on 4 October at Broodeseinde Ridge. Ludendorff also recommended: 'Another tactical detail which was emphasised everywhere was the value of ground observation for artillery. Only by that means could the attacking hostile infantry be annihilated, particularly after penetrating our front, or fire be concentrated on decisive points of the battlefield.'[10] On this point the Germans would continue to excel, since they remained in control of the high ground, such as it was at only 150 ft in elevation.

For Plumer, Gough, and especially Haig, there loomed some other troubling aspects to these seeming 'successes', aspects that would be either overlooked, ignored, or denied by the high command. Most importantly, the successes were dependent on the fair weather that had dried out the battlefield and enabled Plumer's methods to have even a reasonable chance for success. Secondly, although Plumer's tactics were proving to be successful, the overall gains were marginal at best, and considering the cost in application of equipment and men, they were actually extravagantly expensive. Various critics have pointed out that success at this rate would have the British Army in Berlin by no sooner than 1930! Worst was the cost in casualties; a cost of 6,000–10,000 casualties for every 1,000 yards was exceedingly difficult to absorb in manpower and to accept by political or humanitarian definition. Even conceding that the Germans were losing equal or greater numbers (the war of attrition argument), just how much of a 'victory' march such as this could be tolerated by the public, or by the manpower resources required for its completion? It was a daunting thought. Hence, Haig's constant desire to salvage the plan to reach the coast, link up with amphibious forces, and flush the Germans off the coast. They could then proceed to roll up the northern edge of the German flank in Belgium and, theoretically, win the war. Haig was almost giddy with enthusiasm for the resurrection of his original strategy. It was a high hope, but extremely tenuous.

The same issues were being contemplated and wrestled with by Ludendorff and the Germans, who again framed the overall picture in strategic, rather than tactical, terms:

> ... the 26th [September and the Battle for Polygon Wood] proved a day of heavy fighting, accompanied by every circumstance that could cause us loss. We might be able to stand the loss of ground, but the reduction of our fighting strength was again all the heavier. Once more we were involved in a terrific struggle in the West, and had to prepare for a continuation of the attacks on many parts of the front ... The depth of penetration was limited so as to secure immunity from our counter-attacks, and the latter were then broken by the massed artillery.[11]

In Haig's view, the British were winning the 'war of attrition' and inflicting backbreaking losses on the Germans, while at the same time regaining the opportunity to achieve a breakthrough and turn the German flank through northern Belgium. Haig was so confident that he summoned Admiral Reginald Bacon, commander of the British Navy's Dover Patrol, from Britain to peg a date for uniting his infantry in Flanders with the amphibious landings. Haig was still holding on to the possibility of clearing the coast of the German U-Boat threat and was pleased when told that tides would be favourable until early November – giving Haig another month to accomplish the mission, assuming the fair weather held up. This optimism was keyed on the fair weather window continuing to prevail, and on London's acquiescence over the high casualty rate. However, 'Operation Hush' was officially cancelled on 14 October. The onset of more rain and the full realisation of the fact that the Passchendaele campaign was struggling caused the grand scheme to be taken off the table. Since 31 July, Haig's two-month offensive had already consumed 86,000 British casualties for the gain of only 3.5 miles. Haig now somehow envisioned a corresponding advance to complete the capture of the Passchendaele heights within just *two weeks*, followed incredibly by a further gain of nearly *five more miles* and the capture of the Roulers railhead, to be then further extended another 25 miles to the Belgian coast and the necessary amphibious link-up! It sounded like a pipe dream, a wilful delusion. And it all assumed dry weather for the next month.

The optimism is revealed by the comments in a letter home from Major General John Monash, commander of the 3rd Division ANZAC forces at Ypres, on 24 September as the assault to capture Polygon Wood was reaching its successful conclusion:

> You have heard by now that the campaign for the Passchendaele Ridge ... started on the 20th. First ANZAC is having the first go, and we shall come later. First and 2nd Divisions did the first 'push' brilliantly; day after tomorrow 4th and 5th Divisions will come through them and do a second push; and in early October ... later get on the Passchendaele Ridge proper. The fighting done in this 'push' by the Australians has been most brilliant in every way ... We have been four weeks' re-organisation and training in most beautiful rolling country, mostly in beautiful autumn sunshine ... I dined with him (Haig] and Lieutenant General Kiggell, chief of general staff, and Major General Butler, deputy-chief of general staff. There were only four of us present. So you may imagine some very important and confidential matters were discussed, about which I need say no more than that there is no question that we are very rapidly wearing down the German military power, and now it is a question of time and weather.[12]

The last sentence is the most telling: the belief that the Germans were worn down and on the verge of a collapse, and that it was a question of 'time and weather'. Both of these conclusions were frightfully over-optimistic. The Germans were anything but worn down, and the weather was going to grant Haig and the British only one more day of fair weather for the attack on Broodseinde Ridge. It would then take another month of slogging through endless mud and rain and cold to 'get on' to Passchendaele Ridge proper, as hoped by Monash.

The next bite and hold would be for Broodseinde Ridge. The mild weather would temporarily hold and success would be repeated, but the rain would begin again and the timetable for the Flanders offensive would then swing back the other way. The hell of Passchendaele would not only continue but become worse.

13

THE BATTLE OF BROODSEINDE, OCTOBER 1917

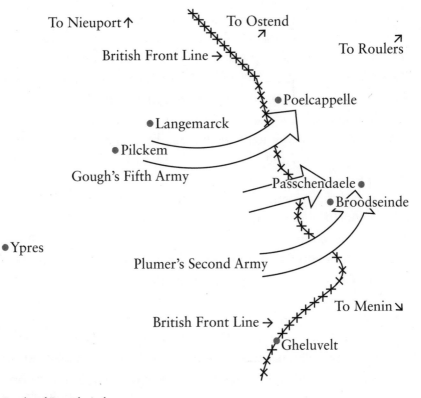

To Nieuport ↑   To Ostend ↗

British Front Line →

To Roulers ↗

● Poelcappelle

● Langemarck

● Pilckem

Gough's Fifth Army

Passchendaele ●

● Broodseinde

● Ypres

Plumer's Second Army

To Menin ↘

British Front Line →

● Gheluvelt

Battle of Broodseinde

The Battle of Broodseinde Ridge epitomised the success and failure of General Sir Hubert Plumer's tactics and General Sir Douglas Haig's strategy. The attack, the third in Plumer's methodical and incremental method of attacking and gaining limited but achievable objectives, was the most successful of his Second Phase attacks. It once again featured careful planning, limited objectives (roughly 1000–1500 yards forward), and an enormously heavy opening bombardment of massed artillery upon a narrow assault front. The attack had originally been scheduled for 6 October but Haig was growing increasingly concerned about the weather. To capitalise on the dry period that the British and Plumer had been enjoying, the attack was moved up to the 4th. Eight British divisions were committed to the 06:00 assault. Among the British troops were units of the I and II ANZAC Corps, three Australian divisions and one from New Zealand. As dry as the last month had been, the night before this attack saw heavy rainfall that had to be endured while positioning for the assault. This would not prevent success at Broodseinde, but it was to plague the British for the next six weeks. They were repeatedly challenged to get the assault troops to the front line in good order before an attack, due to the heavy rain and resulting lakes of mud.

Once again the Germans were soundly driven back from their front line positions and effectively prevented from recovering their positions during the inevitable counter-attacks. The Germans were now at a loss as to how to prevent the seemingly inevitable British encroachment. Broodseinde Ridge and what was left of Zonnebeke village were captured by mid-morning. More of the Gheluvelt Plateau was secured and some attacking units began pushing on to the village of Poelcappelle. The frustrated Germans were fully aware of their limitations and bewildered as to how to halt the British and their methodical advances. Nothing seemed to work for the Germans; neither the familiar German counter-attacks, nor a variety of defensive re-alignments and adjustments. Nothing seemed able to prevent the British from gradually swallowing up bites of territory. The bites were small, but steady nonetheless, and also lethal. Heavy casualties were severely draining German reserve units and the British seemed to have an unlimited supply of soldiers to pour into repeated attacks.

Ludendorff again commented on this situation, and his responses were beginning to sound very familiar:

> The depth of penetration was limited so as to secure immunity from our counter-attacks, and the latter were then broken up by the massed fire of artillery. After each attack I discussed the tactical experiences with General von Kuhl and Colonel von Lossberg, sometimes at the front, sometimes on the telephone. This time I again went to the fronts in order to talk over the same questions with officers who had taken part in the fighting. Our defensive tactics had to be developed further, somehow or other. We were all agreed on that. The only thing was, it was so infinitely difficult to hit on the right remedy.[1]

The trade-off to these repeated short thrusts and successes was twofold. Yes, the British were still inflicting enormous casualties on the Germans and taking objectives. Granted, the taking of the Broodseinde position had taken only one 'easy' day of fighting, but it had still accounted for another 20,000 British casualties. This was a huge number for the minimal gain of only 1,000 yards of penetration. As pointed out earlier, for this rate of gain and corresponding cost in human life, the Allies were not getting much closer to Germany but were racking up an enormous 'butcher's bill'. Nor was it, again, even remotely threatening a breakthrough. And it was not, much to the British high command's chagrin and denial, forcing an imminent German collapse in morale. British high command continued to predict a German collapse, but the Germans were fighting as hard as ever. And they retained the capability to pack a violent counter-offensive punch even if they were not successful in recovering lost ground. Added to this was the weather factor that would continue to hover over the entire theatre of operation and made every phase of the offensive so obscenely difficult. The frightful cost in casualties, and the corresponding expenditure of equipment and munitions, should have cast a black shadow over any optimism being generated by the short advances. And this was in good weather. Yet optimism reigned supreme. Such was the flip side of the victory achieved by Plumer at Broodseinde.

For the British and their ANZAC companions, the Battle of Broodseinde would go well. The one-day effort would be preceded not by a lengthy bombardment but instead by a hurricane barrage at 06:00 during the jump-off hour. The tactic would work splendidly and Plumer's objectives would be secured almost immediately; by noon, Broodseinde would be in British control. However, during the night before the assault, clouds would roll in and by morning the wind would whip up a rain squall to end what had been several days of dry weather. W. J. Harvey, 24th Battalion, 2nd Australian Division, describes what it was like to await 'going over the top' in the early morning:

> They pounded our position with high explosives, including minenwerfers and eight-inch shells, and we had tremendous casualties. It was the heaviest shell-fire the battalion had ever encountered on the jumping-off line. It was hardest on our battalion and on the 21st next to us. We had forty killed, including two of our platoon officers, and taking into account the wounded a third of our men were put out of action. Everyone kept their nerve, although it was a terrible strain to lie there under that sort of fire without being able to do a thing about it, knowing that there was a terrible struggle ahead and that we'd be going into it well under strength. It seemed an eternity before our own guns opened up and we got the order to advance.[2]

At Broodseinde the Germans attempted two tactical shifts: a morning offensive on the British lines that coincided with the British attack, and a return to massing their defenders in greater strength at the frontline trenches to blunt the British attack. Both manoeuvres failed. The British successfully thwarted the

German attack while again destroying, in large numbers, the German defenders manning the reinforced forward line. To a devastating extent, and with comparative ease, the British overran the German frontline defences and rapidly captured and reinforced the Broodseinde objectives by noon of 4 October. Ominously, it also began to rain, at first a drizzle during the night before and into the early morning of the attack (3 to 4 October), and more steadily during the day. It was a harbinger of what was to come.

On the German side, Ludendorff was deeply concerned and disappointed but did not consider the situation hopeless. Seeking adjustments to his defensive configuration to combat the British tactics he commented:

> The infantry battle commenced on the morning of the 4th. It was extraordinarily severe, and again we only came through it with enormous loss. It was evident the idea of holding the front line more densely ... adopted after my last visit to the front in September, was not the remedy. I now followed my own judgement without asking for further outside opinions, and recommended the Fourth Army to form an advanced zone, that is to say a narrow strip between the enemy's front line and the line which our troops were to hold by mobile defence. The enemy would have to cross this strip in making his advance, and our artillery would have time to get onto him before he could reach our main line of resistance. The great difficulty lay in withdrawing the garrison of the advanced zone in case of attack, and in bringing the artillery back to our own line.[3]

The result of the Germans' simultaneous early morning attacks that ran headlong into the British attack, coupled with the Germans experimenting with the renewal of massing their defenders at the forward-most front, led to terrible carnage, as described by Captain Edwin Trundle of the 26th Australian Battalion:

The joke about this last attack is that Fritz had planned a large attack to take place precisely at the same minute as ours ... However, we blew first and gave him the shock of his life. His having massed troops for an attack like this only made our victory all the greater as they were caught in our artillery barrage and cut to pieces to say nothing of the huge number of prisoners we got. Well, when I went up after the attack had succeeded, and went over the ground where Fritz had been formed up ready to attack, I saw one of the 'best' sights I have seen in the war. Where the Huns had been massed and formed up for the attack they lay there dead in thousands – it was grand to see them – good dead Huns absolutely in piles. I have never seen so many 'stiffuns' before, and it is only when you see sights like this that one realises what a hiding Fritz is getting. Every other shell hole in their area had a dead Hun or part of one in it and some had as many as five in them.[4]

Clearly the Germans were at a loss as to how to cope with the British methods but they remained determined, desperate, and resourceful in their desire to force the British to pay a high price in lives for any gain. Soon the elements in the form of rain and cold would come to the Germans' rescue; not that fighting in the mud would be any easier for them than the British, but at least they would not be attacking and attempting to move through the rain-sodden fields to gain positions. The weather and abominable conditions would again clearly aid the defenders.

However, Haig was still completely optimistic as to the developments and success of the enterprise and immediately called for follow-up attacks by 10th October. So confident was Haig, he again ordered Plumer and Gough to plan on launching a breakout attack, and again to activate the four divisions of cavalry and be prepared to sweep through the upcoming opening of the German lines on 10 October. 'Operation Hush' was yet again back on the agenda, as more assaults were hurriedly prepared in spite of some misgivings on the part of both Plumer and Gough. They both sought to postpone the next set of attacks for at least another week's preparation, and to stand in readiness to exploit the expected German collapse that intelligence repeatedly predicted.

With the German collapse so widely anticipated, Haig now had his sights set on an advance of at least eight miles to the railhead of Roulers and wanted his forces to be prepared immediately to seize the heights of Passchendaele. So optimistic was Haig, he informed Fourth Army commander General Sir Henry Rawlinson, stationed in the northern tier of Belgium along the coast, and Admiral Sir Henry Jellicoe, to prepare to connect with his advancing armies. The combined forces would then unite and sweep up the Channel and North Sea coast and begin the envelopment of the entire German northern flank. Such was the extravagant thinking on the part of the British high command after the success of Plumer's third bite and hold attack.

Optimism abounded as the British leadership felt the time had arrived to capitalise on the perceived German collapse.

Writing home again on 7th October, General Monash reviewed the situation with confidence:

Great happenings are possible in the very near future, as the enemy is terribly disorganised, and it is doubtful if his railway facilities are good enough to enable him to re-establish himself before our next two blows, which will follow shortly and will be very severe. My next objective will be Passchendaele, unless the 66th [Division] succeed in getting so far in the next battle … Our success [on 4 October] was complete and unqualified. Over 1,050 prisoners and much material and guns. Well over 1, 000 dead enemy counted, and many hundreds buried and out of reach. We got absolutely astride of the main ridge. Both corps and army declare there has been no finer feat in the war.[5]

Such was the rosy optimism of the British high command.

Haig's diary underscores all of these points:

In order to not to miss any chance of following up our success if the enemy were really demoralised, I met with Plumer and Gough and with their staff officers in my house in Cassel at 3pm. Plumer stated that in his opinion we had only up-to-date fought the leading troops of the enemy's divisions on his front. Charteris, who was present, thought that from the number of German regiments represented among the prisoners, all divisions had been seriously engaged and that there were few available reserves.[6]

All of this would prove to be wishful thinking. When combined with the incessant rain now falling, a disaster for the attacking British over the next month's action was waiting to unfold. Nonetheless, Haig continued in his euphoric thoughts and added: 'After full discussion I decided that the next attack should be made two days earlier than already arranged, provided Anthoine [the French General] could also accelerate his preparation.'[7]

There were other positive factors. The tank was beginning to make its presence felt in tactical ways. The dry weather had allowed the tank to operate on the previously unnavigable swamp and many Germans were deathly afraid of the iron monsters. A captured German officer on being asked why he surrendered, responded: 'There were tanks – so my company surrendered – I also.'[8]

Tanks, although not yet of strategic value or capable of a full breakthrough, were making a difference. When used in large enough numbers and in correct and prudent tactical situations, and with the weather and terrain permitting, their presence was beginning to have a positive effect beyond just the enemy's fear of the iron beasts. Optimal weather and terrain conditions were a prerequisite, particularly on a battlefield as torn apart and flooded as was Flanders at this time.

Earlier in the summer, and beset by impassable swampy conditions, tanks had come under much criticism due to their ineffectiveness in battle and tendency to break down. They had therefore been repeatedly held back due to the foul conditions of the poor roads and flooded shell holes that prevented them from navigating the morass of no man's land. But the persistence of General Maxse's XVIII Corps finally found a measure of vindication on 4 October at Broodseinde when twelve tanks succeeded in assuming their role as the juggernaut to lead infantry in a widely successful capture of heavily entrenched German positions. The big Mark IV tanks, with their hefty six-pound cannon, were able to combine with supporting infantry using lighter weight Lewis machine guns, to devastate previously stoutly defended objectives. Haig and his high command duly noted that the combined units, operating in mutual assistance, were most impressive. Haig's positive impression probably led to his willingness to accept the Cambrai plan later that year. In late November 1917 at the Battle of Cambrai, aided by dry weather and an unscarred battleground, the tank and infantry combination would be featured in another highly successful attack. Commanders were gradually, and often grudgingly, realising that when used en masse, and assisted by trained infantry over appropriate terrain, the tank could have a huge impact.

Major W. Watson recorded the success of the tanks:

> ... we were greatly handicapped in attacking either the south-east edge of the Houthulst Forest or the Passchendaele Ridge itself from the northwest. Further, the only two main roads in the neighbourhood passed through the village ... The attack was scheduled for 4 October. Marris (commanding No. 10 Company) brought his tanks into St. Julien and camouflaged them among the ruins. St. Julien, though now still easily within close field-gun range, was now respectably behind the line.

As the tanks moved forward it was clear what a difference the armoured vehicles could make on the battlefield. Watson reported:

The attack was incredibly successful. Of Marris's twelve
tanks, eleven left St Julien and crawled perilously close all
night along the destroyed road. At dawn they entered the
village with infantry and cleared it after difficult fighting. One
section even found their way along the remains of a track
so obliterated by shellfire that it scarcely could be traced on
the aeroplane photographs, and 'bolted' the enemy from a
number of strong points.[9]

The tanks were proving their worth, but it is significant to note
that, in the above observation, the tanks' success involved a mix
of infantry and armour together in what was going to become
'combined arms' operations. Neither arm was as successful
independently as they were when used in combination. This
was an important and critical lesson that was being learned and
tactically developed.

At Broodseinde, at least for one day, everything had gone well
for the British. The Battle of Broodseinde had moved the British
another 1,000 yards closer to Passchendaele Ridge and left them
only a mile-and-a-half away from Passchendaele village. It had
been the third consecutive 'victory' by Plumer using the limited
'bite and hold' technique.

W. J. Harvey of the 24th Battalion, 2nd Australian Division
described the view from the heights of the Broodseinde Ridge that
had now been secured from German control: '...the whole field
was under observation, and as we gazed back over the country we
could see quite plainly the movements of our own units on various
duties – guns, transport, men, the lot. The ridge was a prize worth
having.'[10]

As low as the 'high' ground was in Flanders, it was still high
enough to dominate the adjacent area. Captain W. Bunnig of the
24th Australian Battalion was amazed at what he was able to see
as he surveyed the surrounding area from this freshly captured
'high' ground:

When I got to top of Broodseinde Ridge it was really surprising to see before you the green fields of Belgium. Actual trees! Grass and fields of course churned up a good deal by barrage shells – but as far as we were concerned it was open country! Then to look back, from where we came, back to Ypres ... There was devastation. Then I could see why our own gunners had had such a gruesome time. You could see the flashes of all the guns, from Broodseinde right back to the very Menin Gate.[11]

The Australian Official History described Broodseinde:

An overwhelming blow had been struck, and both sides knew it. The objective was the most important yet attacked by the Second and Fifth Armies, and they had again done exactly what they planned to ... This was the third blow struck at Ypres in fifteen days with complete success. It drove the Germans from one of the most important positions on the Western Front; notwithstanding their full knowledge that it was coming, they were completely powerless to withstand it ... coming on top of the achievements of September 20th and 28th, its success was of an entirely different order.

Continuing in this vein, the review excitedly went on:

For the first time in years, at noon on 4 October on the heights east of Ypres, British troops on the Western Front stood face to face with the possibility of decisive success ... Let the student ... ask himself, 'In view of the results of the three step-by-step blows, all successful, what will be the result of three more in the next fortnight?'[12]

To further encourage and seduce Haig into believing that his recent successes had him poised on the brink of a strategic breakthrough came the report of captured German documents. They revealed Ludendorff's policy of staging massed defenders at the immediate front line of defensive positions, a situation that had enabled British artillery to pulverise large numbers of German defenders as the attacks began and allowed not only the decimation of many defenders, but fairly easy capture of the targeted positions. It was a made-to-order advantage for the attacking British. Unfortunately for them, however, these German field orders, having been tried and proven to be failed tactics, had been countermanded and abandoned.

Under the assumption that they remained in effect, Haig remarked:

The enemy has suffered severely, as was evidenced by the number of prisoners in our hands, and by the number of his dead on the battlefield, by the costly failure of his repeated counter-attacks, and by the symptoms of confusion and discouragement in his ranks. In this connection, documents captured in the course of the battle of the 4th October throw an interesting light upon the success of the measures taken by us to meet the enemy's new system of defence by counter attack. These documents show that the German Higher Command had already recognised failure of their methods, and were endeavouring to revert to something approximating to their old practice of holding their forward positions in strength.[13]

Haig went on to comment in his diary how optimistic he was as to the need to be prepared for a rapid break out if the opportunity arose. Speaking about a conversation with Plumer and Gough, Haig reiterated: 'I pointed out how favourable the situation was and how necessary it was to have all the necessary means for exploiting any success gained ... if the enemy counter-attacks and is defeated, then reserve brigades must follow after the enemy and take Passchendaele Ridge at once.'[14]

Such was Haig's delight at the prospects heading into mid-October. Plumer's three consecutive successes, the inability of the Germans to halt the limited British advances under thunderously heavy artillery barrages, and the belief that the Germans were about to collapse, were all to coalesce into the confident belief that a rapid continuation of the offensive would soon bring victory to the Allies on the Flanders front. The question now became, how soon would the attack be renewed and how quickly could Passchendaele Ridge be taken before the rains returned? That answer was soon to come, and Haig was anxious to get on with it.

14

THE BATTLE OF POELCAPPELLE, OCTOBER 1917

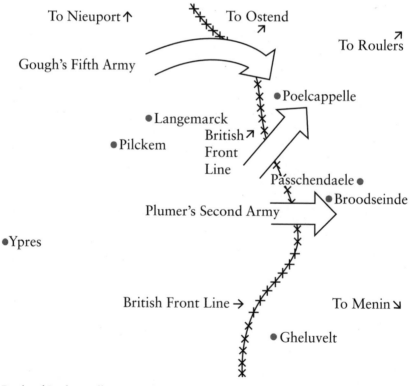

Battle of Poelcappelle

The overwhelming confidence following the success at Broodseinde seemed not only to confirm Plumer's methods and Haig's strategy of the offensive, but also to encourage a surge of optimism for the future. Breakthrough and victory now seemed almost inevitable. Haig was swayed by many factors: German losses in terms of both casualties and surrender rate; the seeming inability of the Germans to defend against Plumer's tactics; the reports of the collapse of German morale; and the increasingly successful momentum of the British attacks. For Haig, all of this evidence seemed to point to a an imminent British victory, or at least a war-winning turning point on the Western Front. Those hopes would be brutally dispelled at the Battle of Poelcappelle as the British resumed their relentless Flanders offensive and the push to occupy the Passchendaele Ridge objectives, now only a mile-and-a-half away.

Initially, there was debate over when the next attack should take place. Haig was so excitedly optimistic that he pressed for only a two-day wait before the next large-scale attack. This went contrary to Plumer's firm desire for methodical preparation in bringing forward the big guns, organising a proper supply train of material and fresh equipment to the staging area, and thoroughly briefing the attacking units as to objectives, tactics, and recognition of German positions and strengths. Unfortunately, the usually adamant Plumer was willing to concede to Haig on the urgency to follow up immediately on the gains from the previous attacks, as well as the assumption that the Germans were on the verge of collapse. Haig felt that it was important to maintain momentum and not allow the recoiling Germans the chance to recover and regroup. At a meeting between Haig, Gough and Plumer, held 5 October, the decision on the date for the next attack was moved forward. Haig believed the current German weakness to be so acute that only two days' preparation would be required to smash through the weakened German line. Plumer successfully pleaded for at least one more day of preparation, pressing for 9 October. Haig was adamant, however, in maintaining the active profile of the offensive. In response to Plumer and Gough's reluctance, Haig conceded that due to the weather, the readying of cavalry and tanks to exploit a breakthrough would be postponed.[1]

Meanwhile, the weather continued to deteriorate. Rainfall had begun on 4 October and had persisted, further swamping the battlefield. There is no *official* documentation of either Gough or Plumer objecting to Haig's urging for a prompt renewal of the offensive, however, Gough later recounted that he was decidedly opposed to going forward at this time due to the weather, German resistance, and the condition of the battlefield. Other than Gough's later memoirs, there exists no documented evidence of this prudent, if perhaps retrospective, recommendation. This lack of caution on the part of Plumer also seems strange, since he had previously been so insistent on the absolute necessity of essential preparation. Perhaps he too was caught up in the heady gains of the previous month's operation. Plumer's Chief of Staff, Tim Harrington, spoke to the newspaper correspondents on the eve of the battle and emphasised 'how strongly he was in favour of continuing the battle, and that one or two more bangs [and[the cavalry would be ready to go through'.[2]

This too appears both tactically and strategically short-sighted, given the enormous cost in men and material that had already been consumed in what was actually a very insignificant conquest of territory. Add to that the continued inability to even begin to connect with the Channel offensive, 'Operation Hush', which had been the original strategic goal of the Flanders offensive. Plumer's hitherto insistent strategy and tactics of detailed preparation seem to have been discarded in the delirium of the Broodseinde success. The Broodseinde progress, coming on the heels of the previous two successes, became the rationale for the case of instantly embarking on the next phase of attacks.

General Monash of the ANZAC Corps reported in a letter home to his wife dated 15 October:

I am inclined to believe that the plan (to attack on 9 and again on 12 October) was fully justified, and would have succeeded in normal weather conditions. It could have succeeded, however, in the hands of first-class fighting divisions whose staff work was accurate, scientific and speedy ... But Higher Command decided to allow us only twenty-four hours, and even under these circumstances with normal weather conditions, we might have succeeded. However, a number of vital factors intervened, and I personally used every endeavour to secure from the corps and army commanders a twenty-four hours' postponement. The Chief [Haig], however, decided that every hour's postponement gave the enemy breathing time, and that it was worth taking the chance of achieving the final objective for this stage of the Flanders battle.[3]

In the event, Plumer did obtain one more day's preparation, which, due to the return of the incessant rains, became hopelessly inadequate for the task. The rain had flooded the approach roads and prevented any meaningful follow-up for advanced gun placement, forwarding supplies, and troop deposition. Far different from the Broodseinde success, the attack on Poelcappelle was going to be under-gunned, under-prepared, and dreadfully difficult in the face of a determined German defensive posture. Poorly supplied artillery, due to time and weather constraints, would prevent adequate softening up of German positions and provide insufficient barrage protection for the advancing infantry.

General E. C. Amsty of the Royal Artillery wrote:

Seldom has the supply of ammunition, food and water to guns in action presented greater difficulties. It could not be done to batteries more than 150 yards from the main roadways. The journey by pack animals, the only possible form of transport from the wagon lines to the guns, instead of taking the normal hour, might require anything from six to sixteen hours. If animals slipped off the planks into the quagmire alongside, they often sank out of sight. On arrival, shells had to be cleaned of the slime coating before they could be used. The heavy wastage from sickness was not surprising, for the flooding both in the wagon lines and gun positions forced men to sleep on wet blankets or sodden straw ... The effective strength fell rapidly, and lack of numbers made reliefs impossible, just when they were most needed. The heavy artillery suffered almost as much from the conditions as the field [artillery].[4]

The continuous rainfall did not abate. Tanks were obviously useless in the conditions and the movement of men and material to the front was all but hopeless. Any objectives taken were soon to be quickly and decisively reclaimed by furious German counter-attacks. The offensive became a tangle of foul weather, merciless rain and mud, and withering German resistance. The Germans were anything but ready to surrender en masse.

Private Norman Cliff of the 1st Grenadier Guards captured the difficulty with his vivid description of the attack:

The approach to the ridge was a desolate swamp, over which brooded an evil menacing atmosphere that seemed to defy encroachment. Far more treacherous than the visible surface defences with which we were familiar, such as barbed wire; deep devouring mud spread deadly traps in all directions. We slashed and slithered, and dragged our feet from the pull of an invisible enemy determined to suck us into its depth. Every few steps someone would slide and stumble and, weighed down by rifle and equipment, rapidly sink into the squelching mess. Those nearest grabbed his arms, struggled against being themselves engulfed and, if humanly possible, dragged him out. When helpers floundered in as well and doubled the task, it became hopeless. All the straining efforts failed and the swamp swallowed its screaming victims, and we had to be ordered to plod on dejectedly and fight this relentless enemy as stubbornly as we did those we could see. It happened that one of those leading us was Lieutenant Chamberlain, and so distraught did he become at the spectacle of men drowning in mud, and the desperate attempts to rescue them that suddenly he began hysterically belabouring the shoulders of a sinking man with his swagger stick. We were horror struck to see this most compassionate officer so unstrung as to resort to brutality and our loud protests forced him to desist. The man was rescued, but some could not be and they sank shrieking with fear and agony. To be ordered to go ahead and leave a comrade to such a fate was the hardest experience one could be asked to endure, but the objective had to be reached, as we plunged on, bitter anger against the evil forces prevailing piled on to our exasperation. This was as near to Hell as I ever want to be.[5]

Such were the abominable conditions facing the British soldiers as they endeavoured to attack the Poelcappelle objective. It was certainly not for want of trying by the British soldiers, who were willing to repeatedly attack in the face of the most appalling conditions. These conditions, along with fatigue, and the sheer difficulty in just surviving, were beginning to take a toll on the British as much as the defending Germans – a fact that cannot be overlooked.

General Sir William Birdwood, commander of the I ANZAC Corps, revealed the two sides of the psychologal coin: the intense desire to succeed pitted against overwhelming adversity:

My men were weak and tired, and when Plumer consulted me I had to advise against any further advance. However, since only one division of my Corps was to be involved in the next stage, and since the other Corps Commanders were in favour of pushing on, Haig decided to go. In a sense, I was reminded of our final effort to capture Sari Bair at Gallipoli, for here again it was a case of 'so near and yet so far'. Haig's view was that if we held the main Passchendaele Ridge overlooking and commanding all the country to the east, this would involve so decisive a break in the German line that our cavalry could be used to good effect; and there is little doubt that if the weather had held, and if we had been able to prepare and rehearse our advance as carefully as in the first three stages, we should have been able to take Passchendaele. But the weather defeated us.[6]

Major W Watson of D Battalion, Tank Corps, clearly explained the difficulty for tanks in the Flanders morass. Personally inspecting the route his tanks would need to take heading into the next attack he reported:

On the 6th [three days in advance of the attack] Cooper and I made a little expedition up the Poelcappelle Road. It was in desperate condition ... The enemy gunners had shelled it with accuracy. There were great holes that compelled us to take to the mud at the side. In places the surface had been blown away, so the road could not be distinguished from the treacherous riddled waste through which it ran. To leave the road was obviously certain disaster for a tank. Other companies had used it, and at intervals derelict tanks which had slipped off the road or received direct hits were sinking rapidly in mud. I could not help remembering that the enemy must be well aware of the route which so many tanks had followed into battle.[7]

Tank squadrons were only able to advance along the already nearly impassable roads – really nothing more than slightly reinforced mud tracks – as they attempted to reach the front. Any derelict tank prevented the entire column from advancing. Blocked and stalled tanks then became easy targets for German gunners. Broken tanks had to be moved and cleared so that other tanks and soldiers could continue to proceed forward. At Poelcappelle, the entire affair became a confused tangle of deserted debris, shattered and broken equipment, and dead and wounded men and animals.

A Tank Corps Brigade Engineer Officer summed up the day's frustration in his crew's attempting to retrieve stalled or damaged vehicles:

I waded up the road, which was swimming in a foot or two of slush; frequently I would stumble into a shell-hole hidden by the mud. The road was a complete shambles and strewn with debris, broken vehicles, dead and dying horses and men ... As I neared the derelict tanks, the scene became truly appalling. Wounded men lay drowned in the mud, others were stumbling and falling through exhaustion, others crawled and rested themselves up against the dead to raise themselves a little above the mud. On reaching the tanks, I found them surrounded by the dead and dying; men had crawled to them for what shelter they could afford. The nearest tank was a female [smaller version of the Mark IV]. Her sponson doors were open. Out of these protruded four pairs of legs; exhausted and wounded men had sought refuge in this machine and dead and dying lay in a jumbled heap inside.[8]

Tanks, therefore, were going to be virtually useless during the Poelcappelle attacks. After numerous breakdowns and inability to traverse the mud, it was decided to use the tanks as forward retrieval vehicles for abandoned or sunken big guns and to haul them into forward positions. Captain Hickey's tank squad was pressed into this emergency role and accomplished some meaningful tasks while being otherwise unable to cross the battlefield and participate in the fight.

There seemed to be no immediate prospect of storming the Passchendaele Ridge with our tanks. Any plan for using them as fighting weapons appeared to have been abandoned. In an endeavour to find a job for tanks, my two were being sent forward to be used experimentally as tractors for hauling guns and supply sledges. Very soon after our arrival at Birr X -Rd, we had a chance to show what we could do. A lorry had gone off the road ... one of [my tanks] succeeded in pulling the lorry on to the road again. Similarly, a 6 inch howitzer was unditched at Birr X-Rd.[9]

Leading up to the attack, 7 October saw a full-blown gale of cold and drenching rain. Thousands and thousands of rain-filled shell holes covered square miles of landscape. Every section of the Flanders battlefield was flooded and oozing Creeks and streams overflowed It was within this mud bath and through driving torrents of rain that gun crews attempted to negotiate impassable tracts to relocate their cannon and supply them with the necessary shells – all the time under constant German artillery fire.

The rain did ease somewhat on 8 October with some sun and wind, and Haig hoped it would dry out the battlefield. He wrote to his wife about the conditions: '... bright and clear with a high wind which is drying the ground nicely. But yesterday's rain made the mud bad beyond Ypres in the low ground, and stopped all the guns we wanted getting forward, but we have enough for tomorrow's attack.'[10]

It was a deeply mistaken conclusion concerning the provision of big gun firepower. It was not only an incorrect evaluation of the circumstances, it was woefully wishful thinking for the poor attacking infantry. October, with shorter days and considerably cooler temperatures, was not so easily going to dry out the sodden 'earth'. In fact, October and November were destined to be some of the rainiest autumn months on record. The night before the attack saw rain again falling, so that on 9 October men were unable to reach their jump-off points. The dawn attack was through ponds of water hampering any movement to cross no man's land, and all the while under heavy shellfire. The miserable attempts to slog through deep, thick, swampy conditions took place both before and during their assaults.

Lieutenant P. King of the 2/5 Battalion, East Lancashire Regiment decribed the perilous journey:

It was an absolute nightmare from the start. Often we would have to stop and wait for up to half-an-hour, because all the time the duckboards were being blown up and men being blown off the track or simply slipping off – because we were all in full marching order with gas masks and rifles, and some were carrying machine-guns and extra ammunition. We were all carrying equipment of some kind, and all had empty sandbags tucked down our backs. We were loaded like Christmas trees, so of course an explosion nearby or just the slightest thing would knock a man off balance and he would go off the track and right down into the muck ... It had taken us more than twelve hours to get there [the jump-off point]. The Colonel had led the battalion up the track – Colonel Whitehead, a very terse man, a very brave man. And he said to me, 'Get them into the attack.' I passed it on to the NCOs, who gave the orders: 'Fix bayonets. Deploy. Extended order. Advance!' We went over into this morass straight into a curtain of rain and mist and shells, for we were caught between two barrages ... the machine gun fire from the Germans was frightful. They were simply spraying bullets all over the place. We could hardly move because the mud was so heavy there that you were dragging your legs behind you, and with people being hit and falling and splashing down all around you, all you can do is keep moving and look for some form of cover. The casualties were very heavy and after we'd realised that the position was absolutely hopeless ... we were there for more than twenty-four hours and the rain and the shelling never stopped the whole time.[11]

The struggle was understood by British military leadership as well. Brigadier General Sir James Edmonds explained:

The difficulty was to get the assaulting troops to the jumping-off tapes at all, and in some sort of a condition to make an attack ... It must be emphasised again, too. that in all that vast wilderness hardly tree, hedge or wall or building could be seen ... nor any scrap of natural cover other than the mud-filled shell holes.[12]

At Poelcappelle, unlike the previous three Plumer-planned assaults there was a lack of overwhelming artillery support. This lack could be filed under multiple categories: lack of necessary observation of targets due to the weather, lack of properly placed and resupplied artillery positions due again to the weather, deterioration of equipment due to extended use without maintenance and replacement, and insufficient time to accomplish all of the above due to the overly optimistic energetic enthusiasm of high command following the recent successes experienced during the early autumn attacks by Plumer.

Minus the necessary artillery coverage and coupled with the mud slowing advance to the German lines, attacking infantry were confronted with a vanishingly small opportunity for success. This time there would be no swift achievement of objectives followed by rapid consolidation. With the exception of the northern flank, none of the initial objectives was seized. The creeping barrage was soon lost due to the slow pace of the advance that was unavoidable due to the conditions and heavy German gunfire. The weather, and its effect on so many other aspects of operation, could not be altered – but before assaulting the Poelcappelle position, it certainly should have been taken into account in a more pragmatic and realistic way, considering the history and terrain of the area.

Not to be deterred by the lack of progress on the first day's assaults, Plumer and Haig, despite the now pouring rain, decided to pursue the offensive the following day. A similar negative result ensued. So meagre were the results that even the ever-optimistic

General Charteris, head of intelligence and one of Haig's staunchest supporters, commented:

> I was out all yesterday at the attack. It was the saddest day of the year. We did fairly well, but only fairly well. It was not the enemy but mud which prevented us doing better. There is now no chance for complete success here this year. We must still fight on for a few weeks more, but there is no purpose in it now as far as Flanders is concerned.[13]

Such was the bleak outlook of one Haig's greatest advocates and upbeat members of the British high command.

Allied air superiority was reduced in value due to the prevailing weather. It was all but cancelling aerial observations, so vital to the accuracy of locating targets and allowing for the pinpointing of artillery firepower. Airplanes were grounded, observation was limited, and targeting became difficult. Artillery had previously been the essential ingredient for the barrage protection of Plumer's attacking infantry. In sum, there was less artillery backing the attack, and less accuracy from the guns that were available. The infantry was suffering on all counts. Incredibly, they were ordered to continue their assaults throughout the week.

Going forward under these appalling conditions of slashing rain, cold and mud, and at all times the enemy gunfire, had a harrowing effect on the morale of those exposed to the brutal environment. Major C. L. Fox of 502nd Field Company, Royal Engineers, mentioned the slender strand of discipline that prevented the utter breakdown of morale during the nightmare:

> There was no ground to walk on; the earth had been ploughed up by shells not once, but over and over again, and so thoroughly that nothing solid remained to step on, there was just loose, disintegrated, far-flung earth, merging into slimy, treacherous mud and water round shell holes so interlaced that the circular form of only the largest and most recently

made could be distinguished. The infantry in the outposts moved hourly from shell hole to shell hole, occupying those that had just been made and which had not, in consequence, yet filled with water. All honour to them ... covered with mud, wet to skin, bitter cold, stiff, and benumbed with exposure, cowed and deadened by the monotony of 48 hours in extreme danger and by the constant casualties among their mates, they hung on to existence by a thin thread of discipline rather that by any spark of life. Some of the feebler and more highly strung deliberately ended their own lives.[14]

Lacking reliable communication, and again largely due to the weather, Plumer assumed his units were achieving success similar to the previous three battles. When troops were ordered forward to reinforce and further penetrate imagined gains, they instead discovered confusion, disarray, or Germans occupying the supposedly captured objectives. The 42nd Australian Battalion, moving forward to relieve the British 66th Division, found only mayhem, scattered remnants of the 66th, and plenty of Germans holding the position.[15]

Lieutenant W. G. Fisher of the 42nd Division was sent forward to scout and report what was going on in Ravebook Valley:

The slope was littered with dead, both theirs and ours. I got to one pillbox to find it was just a mass of dead, and so I passed on carefully to the one ahead. Here I found about 50 men alive, of the Manchesters. Never have I seen men so broken or demoralised. They were huddled up close behind the box in the last stages of exhaustion and fear. Fritz had been sniping them off all day and accounted for 57 that day – the dead and dying lay in piles. The wounded were numerous – unattended and weak, they groaned and moaned all over the place ... Finally the company came up – the men done after a fearful struggle through the mud and shell holes, not to speak of the barrage which the Hun put down and which caught numbers. The position was obscure – a dark night – no line – demoralised Tommies.[16]

In view of these events and lack of success, on the evening of 11 October General Gough telephoned Plumer and recommended the attacks be postponed due to the weather and lack of success to that point. Plumer, however, responded that upon speaking with his corps commanders, he was convinced that the offensive should continue and: 'phoned back at 8 pm to say they considered it best for the attack to be carried out'.[17]

And so it was for another day, and to absolutely no gain.

The Battle for Poelcappelle had turned into a disaster. In terms of weather, casualties, and success, it was an unremitting failure. Poor planning and preparation, atrocious conditions, and a renewed defensive posture by the Germans, combined to remind Haig and the British that the Germans were perhaps not yet ready to break. The attacks would sputter on for several days until what followed would be termed the First Battle of Passchendaele. The rain was now continuous and the transport system hopelessly bogged down. But even now, Haig believed that the Germans were ready to crack. He firmly believed that just one more push would gain the long-sought breakthrough.

BATTLE OF PASSCHENDAELE (FIRST ATTEMPT) AND DIVERSION BATTLE OF LA MALMAISON

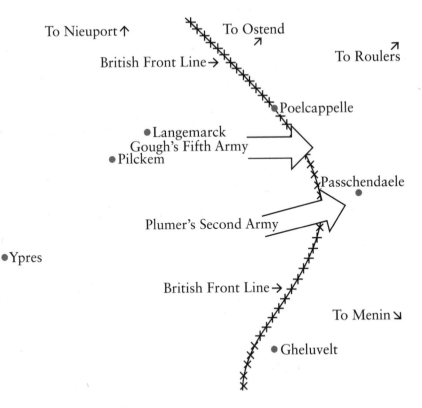

To Nieuport ↑   To Ostend ↗

British Front Line →

To Roulers ↗

● Poelcappelle

● Langemarck
Gough's Fifth Army
● Pilckem

Passchendaele
●

Plumer's Second Army

● Ypres

British Front Line →

To Menin ↘

● Gheluvelt

First Battle of Passchendaele

The goal of General Haig to capture the Passchendaele Ridge and the village of Passchendaele had now become an end unto itself. Haig desired nothing less than control of the high ground before the onset of winter. Passchendaele Ridge would now be taken in spite of the weather, casualties, or strategic significance. The conquest would require another month of vicious fighting, in the harshest of elements, and over the same flooded field of mud and swamp that had been the hellish terrain for the last two months of bitter engagements.

In an ironic twist of outcomes begetting objectives, Haig was now trying to prevent the British Army from having to endure the winter in the low valley of swamp, mud, and lakes of water-filled shell holes, whilst under the eyes and guns of the Germans perched upon the elevated Ridge of Passchendaele. But, of course, the British Army was in that predicament because of Haig's insistence on engaging a Flanders offensive and pursuing it to to the uttermost. They were now within range of the Ridge but unable to proceed further due to the tenacious German defence. Entirely lost was the original strategic goal of clearing the Channel coast and turning the German flank. Instead, three months of campaigning had placed the British Army in a position where only more attacking would alleviate the agony of remaining in their vulnerable situation. The alternative would be to withdraw to a more defensible, and drier, position by abandoning the Ypres Salient, and forfeit the summer and autumn's modest gains that had placed them where they now were, at the base of Passchendaele Ridge. Therefore, to justify the incredible sacrifices that had been invested, Haig became obsessively determined to capture the ridge at all costs, thus validating the offensive and its expenditure in men and material.

Coming off the bitter disaster at Poelcappelle, Haig was determined to achieve a positive outcome and was not to be denied. The attacks on Passchendaele Ridge would continue until the ridge was taken. It would not be easy and there would be no cooperation from the weather.

Steady rain through the day and night made movement to the front a nightmare of effort. The struggle was to get close enough to the front the night before in order to reach a forward position to either attack or relieve those in the forward positions. Between the constant rain and German shelling, the task was a hard, semi-blind one; as described by Signaller Sydney Fuller, 8th Battalion, Suffolk Regiment:

> We left the pillbox about 11:45 pm and moved forward towards our position for the attack, following a duckboard track all the way, the only possible way of getting over the ground, which was a waste of shell holes many of which were nearly full of water. Even on the duckboards progress was slow and difficult. Many boards had been broken by the enemy's shells and in some cases had been destroyed or broken away. Now and again somebody would step on a duckboard which was balanced like a see-saw with the result that he fell in the mud and water. It was impossible to see in front of one's feet and a light would only have brought a worse evil – shelling.[1]

Lieutenant Harold Knee, 1/1st Battalion Hertfordshire Regiment, reported the conditions and corresponding effect on the morale of his unit as they moved up through their own lines to the front:

> A rain of shells on both sides caused some panic, and the men began to trot after having settled their steel helmets a little to that side on which the iron rain was falling most. The stretcher bearers were cursed for their slow pace by those in the rear who could not rudely pass by – the track being so narrow with shell holes full of water waiting to receive their carcasses should they happen to slip. 'Mind the hole' or 'Wire overhead' or 'Duckboard gone' – these

mutterings, groans, and something akin to gasping sobs, as we shuffled our way along in the inky blackness punctuated by the flashing of gunfire and aerial flares. The whole area had been turned into a huge sea of mud and water which was continually being churned up by shells large and small; shell holes almost lipped one another and some were deep enough for a man, or indeed a mule, to drown. It was a particularly sticky squelching kind of mud which could not have been negotiated without the aid of duckboards which had to be frequently replaced. The nerves of even the strongest of men were known to give way under the strain of helping, or being helped, out of this slough of despond and some had to be brutally kicked, tugged and lugged to their feet as they lay nerve-shattered in the mud asking only to be left there to die.[2]

On 12 October the ANZAC Corps was once more called upon to attack in the pouring rain. Artillery coverage was again weaker than during the drier assaults conducted in September and early October. Preparation to gain Passchendaele Ridge and progressive attempts to take the village of Passchendaele commenced throughout the week leading up to the main attack on 12 October. An Australian officer described the conditions as the preparation began and culminated in the morning attack:

On the night of the 11th we marched off at 6:30 pm and walked till 5 am on the morning of the 12th ... Before 5 am we had lost men like rotten sheep, those who survived had most marvellous escapes. I nearly got blown to pieces scores of times. We went through a sheet of iron all night and in the morning it got worse. We attacked at 5:25 and fought all day, at times we were bogged up to our arm pits (in mud and water) and it took anything from an hour upwards to get out. Lots were drowned in the mud and water.[3]

As at Poelcappelle, the lack of a concentrated barrage wreaked havoc on the attacking assault troops. Well-aimed artillery fire was impossible. Air reconnaissance was limited at best and nonexistent when the weather was foul. Enough ammunition to maintain a steady and constant barrage was difficult to supply to the gun batteries due to the inability to bring forward ammunition through the morass of mud. The result was a valiant effort by gunners and their batteries under horrific conditions, yet they were incapable of properly supporting the attack.

Bombardier Bertram Stokes, 3rd Brigade, New Zealand Field Artillery, describes the frustration:

At 5:00 very dark, raining and blowing, we went up to the gun, about 400 yards away. And what a job it was getting there through the mud and sometimes falling into the water-logged shell holes. The gun was just on muddy open ground, no shelter at all. The previous evening we had scoured the vicinity for some timber to put the gun wheels on and also a log for the gun trail [rear part of the gun carriage that rests on the ground]. The ammunition was dirty and had to be cleaned. All this in the rain and cold. So the eventful hour came, 05:25, 12th October 1917. We commenced firing and after every shot the gun dug into the mud as also did the trail. It was a case of making adjustments after every shot and this was very hard work. Numbers of our boys [assault infantry] who had been wounded were coming back – walking wounded – and we being the first they encountered stopped at our gun for assistance. At one stage our gun resembled a small Dressing Station. They all had the same story to tell, of trenches filled with water, of men bogged down in mud, of the wire not being cut because our full artillery fire was not available, and also of shells simply ploughing into the mud without exploding. There was little we could do other than say a word of cheer and comfort and send them on.[4]

Those Tommies returning to the front line discovered not only lack of progress forward, but in many instances that the assault had been blunted, pinned down, and been driven back while waiting for relief or reinforcement. Lieutenant Walde Fisher, 42nd Battalion AIF describes the effect on morale as the failures during the attempts at Poelcappelle and First Passchendaele unfolded:

Our units sank to the lowest pitch of which I have ever been cognizant. It looked hopeless – the men were so utterly done. However, the attempt had to be made, and accordingly we moved up that night – a battalion ninety strong. I had 'A' Company with twenty-three men. We got into position somehow or other – and the fellows were dropping out unconscious along the road ... We found the line instead of being advanced, [was now] some 30 yards behind where we had left it – and the shell stricken and trodden ground thick with dead and wounded ... some of the Manchesters were there yet, seven days wounded and not looked to. But men walked over them – no heed was paid to anything but the job. Our men gave all their food and water away, but that was all they could do. That night my two runners were killed as they sat beside me, and casualties were numerous again ... [blown out of my shell hole twice, so I shifted to an abandoned pillbox. There were twenty-four wounded men inside, two dead Huns inside ... in various stages of decomposition. The stench was dreadful.[5]

The 3rd Australian and New Zealand divisions were called upon to seize the village of Passchendaele situated on the high ground of Passchendaele Ridge, which had now become a trophy that Haig was determined to capture. The New Zealand Division suffered heavily, losing 2,700 men in four hours on what has been termed 'New Zealand's blackest day'.[6]

Private Leonard Hart of New Zealand's Otago battalion described how depressing it was to come upon the crest of a ridge only to discover: 'a long line of practically undamaged German concrete machine-gun emplacements with barbed wire entanglements in front of them fully fifty yards deep ... Dozens got hung up on the wire and shot down before their surviving comrades' eyes.'[7]

Gunner B. O. Stokes, 13th Battery, New Zealand Field Artillery explained:

C and D went forward first, and didn't they have a time getting them through the sea of mud and slush! They had to have eight horse teams to do the job ... a sound of a shell coming over told us it was going to land very near. We crouched to the earth, and the shell landed only 3 yards away ... there lay four of our boys dead ... You can't imagine how we felt. The shelling didn't cease for another half-hour. Shelling. Shelling. Shelling ... The wind and rain lashing down. The horses screaming and rearing and plunging down into the mud as the shells exploded all around us.[8]

Private W. Smith, Machine Gun Company, 2nd Otago Regiment, 2nd New Zealand Brigade:

We made a bad 'blue' [decision] in sticking to the main ... road. It certainly looked the best part to get a footing on – covered with inches of mud, of course, but with a fairly firm footing underneath. I suppose Fritz had anticipated this. As we started up the road we were caught in enfilade fire from the big pillboxes in the low ground to our right. People were dropping all the way. Then, as we turned the corner on top of the rise, we saw this great bank of wire ahead, maybe 100 yards away. A rat couldn't have got through that. The bombardment should have cut the wire but it hadn't even dented it. Not that we could get near it anyway, for it was positively spitting fire ... more than half of us fell.[9]

Once again Major General John Monash of the ANZAC Corps would describe the frustration and disappointment in his letters home to his wife. Perhaps his feelings were even stronger than indicated in his words concerning the course of the First Passchendaele attack that had deteriorated into another abysmal disaster. Dated October 15, it reads:

Just in degree that the battle of 4 October was brilliantly successful, so were the operations of 12 October deeply disappointing, although the 3rd Australian Division did magnificently under the most adverse circumstances. It is bad to cultivate the habit of criticism of higher authority and, therefore, I do so now with some hesitation, but chiefly to enable you to get a correct picture of what the situation was … Considerable rain began to set in 6 October. The ground was in a deplorable condition by the night of 8 October, and, in consequence, the 66th and 45th Divisions who had taken up the role of the 3rd Australian and the New Zealand divisions, failed to accomplish more than about quarter of a mile of the projected advance. Even in the face of this the Higher Command insisted on going on, and insisted, further, that the uncompleted objectives of the fourth phase should be added to the objectives of our fifth phase; so that it amounted to this, that Russell [NZ Commander] and I were asked to make and advance of 1¾ miles. The weather grew steadily worse on 10 and 11 October. There was no flying and no photographing, no definite information of the German re-dispositions, no effective bombardment, no opportunity of replenishing our ammunition dumps; and the whole country from Zonnebeke forward to the limits of our previous captures was literally a sea of mud, in most places waist deep … My casualties have been rather heavy.[10]

In a letter of 18 October, Monash was even more pronounced in his feelings: 'Our men are being put into the hottest fighting and are being sacrificed in hair-brained ventures, like Bullecourt and Passchendaele, and there is no one in the War Cabinet to lift a voice in protest. It all arises from the fact that Australia is not represented in the War Cabinet...'[11]

These sentiments were reinforced by those who were selected to spearhead the attack on the field and provide the barrage for those doing the assaulting. The Official History reflects those observations:

> The artillery barrage intended to support the advance of the New Zealand Division, weak and erratic at the start, became even thinner and more ragged as the troops advanced up the slope, howitzer shells burying themselves in the sodden ground and merely splashing the pillboxes with fountains of mud. In consequence, the New Zealanders found themselves confronted with broad belts of unbroken barbed wire entanglements ... This splendid division lost a hundred officers and 2,635 other ranks within a few hours in brave but vain attempts – its only failure – to carry out a task beyond the power of any infantry with so little support, and had gained no ground except on the left.[12]

Another example of the result of this lack of artillery preparation comes from the division report commenting on the futility of the 18th Division in attacking the machine gun nests that remained lethally intact:

> The fact of there being no preparatory bombardment undoubtedly enabled the enemy to employ more machine guns in the front line than would have been the case had they been subjected to a bombardment. Some of these machine guns pushed close to our front line and [were] missed by our barrage ... All reports agree that the volume and intensity of machine gunfire encountered by our troops yesterday were far heavier than on any recent battle day.[13]

Trapped in the mud, pinned down by heavy machine gun fire, and lacking a substantial artillery barrage either to screen them in front or protect them later, the infantry could make no progress in the offensive. Objectives, if approached, were not taken and most units were unable to advance at all. Casualties were heavy, German resistance was stout, and any positive results were negligible. The rain refused to slacken and the Passchendaele Ridge remained firmly in German control.

The conditions were just as difficult for the German defenders, except of course they weren't obliged to move. German Lieutenant Ernst Junger vividly described the scene from the German lines at this time:

> ... to the right and left of us shells splashed down in the swamp and sent vast mud mushrooms ... Everywhere we saw traces of death; it was almost as though there wasn't a living soul anywhere in this wasteland ... From time to time one of us would disappear up to the hips in mire, and would certainly have drowned but for the presence of his comrades.

Men on both sides were in the hands of the capricious fates when the big shells began to fall from the sky, as Junger continues: 'I fled to a nearby farmhouse, and went inside ... That evening, precisely the same chain of events, only this time I stayed in the open, as the rain had stopped. The next shell flew into the middle of the collapsing farmhouse. That's the role of chance in war. More than elsewhere, small cause can have a vast effect.'[14]

Similar to the frustrating endeavour at Poelcappelle, British progress was hopelessly bogged down. The weather refused to cooperate. The attempt to secure Passchendaele Ridge had failed. Once again, British tanks were of no use, and as long as the rain-soaked weather and swampy conditions remained they would continue to struggle. D. E. Hickey of H Battalion, Tank Corps, described how day after day, during and after the Battle of First Passchendaele, his crew checked the routes that might be used for the tanks to go forward:

The road here was deserted. There was not a living soul to be seen ... I passed a hand sticking up. Its owner had evidently been buried by a shell ... At the point I reached there was a water filled crater stretching almost across the road. Five or six tanks could have sunk in it easily. Floating on the surface of the water were several dead bodies. As I gazed forward across a black expanse of mud where no life was visible, the desolation of the scene reminded me of a cold grey sea and deserted shore.[15]

Clearly tanks would not be traversing this road until the rains ceased, the ground dried out, and the track was somehow reinforced.

In desperation, the British tried everything to make a go of the assault. Hickey went on to describe how he and his crew watched the troops heading up the line:

From forward in the salient on our way back to our dugout each evening at dusk, we used to pass the men going up to the firing line. They marched in single file along the side of the Menin Road. Their sallow faces haunted me. For many it would be their last journey. We were looking forward to the end of our fruitless labours, floundering in the mud around Ypres ... then there was a sudden reversal of plan. Two tanks were to take part in an attack.[16]

British casualties at First Passchendaele totalled another 13,000 men – virtually an entire division – and as at Poelcappelle, for no consequential gain. Rainfall had nearly doubled every day for three consecutive days: 2.5 mm on the 10th, 4.9 on the 11th, and 7.9 mm on the 12th of October, the day of the assault. Soldiers were literally drowning in rain and mud. Frustration was mounting while morale was crumbling. For the second time in a week, the vaunted tactics of Plumer had not just been thwarted, but defeated at great cost. High casualties were this time not reflected in any meaningful advantage. The autumn was growing later, days were growing shorter, temperatures were falling, and the rains were not abating. Haig's position could be compared with that of a single soldier, as recorded by the Commander of the 7 Seaford Highlanders:

> One man left the front line wounded slightly at dusk on the 12th and on the morning of the 13th was discovered stuck fast in a shell hole a few yards from where he started. Repeated efforts were made to get him out with spades, ropes, etc. At one time 16 men were working at once under enemy view. But he had to be left there when the Battalion was relieved on the night 13th/14th. What became of him is unrecorded.[17]

Haig and his offensive were deeply mired in the mud. Haig recorded in his diary the obvious truth:

> Our attack, launched at 5:25 am on the 12th October between the Ypres Roulers Railway and Houthulst forest, made progress along the spurs and higher ground; but the valleys of the streams which run westward from the main ridge were found to be impassable. It was therefore determined not to persist in the attack, and the advance towards our more distant objectives was cancelled.[18]

Haig was also bitterly disappointed and discouraged that the French had still not yet begun their renewed offensive action at the Chemin des Dames Ridge in north-western France. French General Philippe Petain had promised a diversionary offensive to relieve pressure from the Flanders front, where Haig and the British had been hopelessly engaged for the past three months, in part to support the French as they recovered from their mutiny. The French had managed gradually to recover from the mutinies of early and mid 1917, had regrouped, reorganised, and re-energised their forces, and had been conducting limited offensives to assist the British in Belgium. The northern flank in Flanders, between Rawlinson's Fourth Army and Gough's Fifth Army, had seen several successful attacks by the French under General Francoise Anthoine to support the overall British Flanders operation. The French had been ably supported by their reliable heavy artillery and had achieved some minor gains through western Belgium while protecting Gough's left flank.

As the French regained strength and confidence, Haig had hoped for Petain to launch a major aggressive action in north-western France along the Aisne River. This was an area south of the junction where the French and British forces merged and just south of 1916's four-month Battle of the Somme. This French offensive had been planned to draw off German reserves from Flanders and help the British achieve their Flanders drive to the Channel coast. After all, reasoned Haig, the British had assaulted the Germans for four months on the Somme in 1916 to relieve the enormous pressure on the French at Verdun, and were engaged in another three-month bloodbath in Flanders to help relieve pressure on the French after their disastrous Nivelle offensive in the spring of 1917. It was the hopelessly futile Nivelle offensive that had spawned the French army's mutiny and the ensuing refusal by the French infantry to attack in response to the suicidal offensive that they had been required to endure.

Petain had carefully restored the French army into fighting shape and sat poised once again to launch an offensive operation along the Aisne River, scene of Nivelle's spring disaster. With the French back on their feet more or less, Haig had met with Petain and thought there had been agreement for a French return of the favour and an attack, even if limited in scope and scale, to assist the British who were desperately attempting to achieve some sort of positive outcome in Flanders before winter set in. The anticipated attack was to be at La Malmaison and led by French General Maistre. It would draw German attention away from Flanders and away from Haig's next offensive target set for Cambrai, France, in late November.

The British debacle at Poelcappelle had underscored the need for such a diversion, and the postponement of the French effort during the First Battle of Passchendaele only further heightened Haig's disappointment as the British continued to struggle against both the rain and the determination of the Germans. When the attack at La Malmaison did come on 20 October, it proved to be highly successful both tactically and as a drain on German reserves. The well-coordinated and executed attack captured 1,200 German prisoners and 300 field guns, and in addition pushed the Germans off the Chemin des Dames Ridge while also capturing the fortress of La Malmaison. The offensive, which lasted a week, was seen as an important result with regards to the return of French fighting strength and spirit. It bolstered confidence that the French were willing to renew their assistance to future Allied offensives. Even so, Haig was beside himself at the delay and postponement, which he saw as contributing to his own frustrating situation in Flanders. The La Malmaison diversion overlapped the First Battle of Passchendaele and what became known as the Second Battle of Passchendaele, as Haig and the British also regrouped: changing commanders, rotating troops, and revising their tactics.

After four months of vicious fighting under the most extreme conditions, where they suffered at least 250,000 British and Commonwealth casualties, Haig was finally willing to concede that his goal of gaining the mere 25 miles to the Channel coast and linking up with Rawlinson's Fourth Army was impossible. Also discarded was the goal to clear the Germans off the Channel coast, turn the German northern flank, and set the stage to win the war. Clearly, these early summer objectives were now completely out of reach. Haig's immediate goal now was simply to seize the Passchendaele Ridge and shut down the offensive.

He was finally prepared to end the Flanders operation and was already planning his surprise attack at Cambrai, France, for later in the year using massed tanks. Haig was determined to maintain the offensive momentum and keep the pressure on the Germans. But first, the Flanders situation had to be concluded. Haig commented in his diary: 'Owing to the rain and bad state of the ground, General Plumer decided that it was best not to continue the attack on the front of his Army'.[19]

Haig and his staff were now in agreement and, at a conference held 13th October, the decision to consolidate their position and temporarily shut down the offensive was determined:

I held a conference at Cassel at noon with Generals Plumer, Gough, their staff officers, (and) Kiggell, Nash, Birch, Charteris, Davidson ... The Army Commanders explained the situation; all agreed that the mud and the bad weather prevented our troops getting on yesterday. I said that our immediate objective was the mass of high ground around Passchendaele. Once this was taken the rest of the ridge would fall more easily. The Canadians would join the Second Army at once for the next attack ... The enemy seems to have increased the number of his machine guns in front. We all agreed that our attack should only be launched when there is a fair prospect of fine weather. When the ground is dry no opposition which the enemy has put up has been able to stop our men. The ground is so soft in places the D.G.T. (Director of Ground Transport Nash) told us, that he has light engines (train locomotives) on the 60cm (light) railways sunk up to the boilers in the mud. The track has completely disappeared.[20]

It had taken almost four months of the most intense fighting to recognise what should have been obvious. It is difficult to imagine that some of these conclusions concerning weather and dry ground should just now have been reached and accepted, since so many of the attacks over the last several months had been conducted in the same atrocious conditions of rain and mud.

Just as the aforementioned unknown soldier was pathetically pinned in the mud, so too was Haig trapped in the quagmire of his Passchendaele offensive. He needed to extricate himself and his army from a highly untenable position. Having used up the ANZAC troops to no avail at Poelcappelle and First Passchendaele, Haig would now draw upon another contingent of Commonwealth soldiers, the rested and available Canadian Corps, to wrest himself and his largely exhausted army out of a sticky situation.

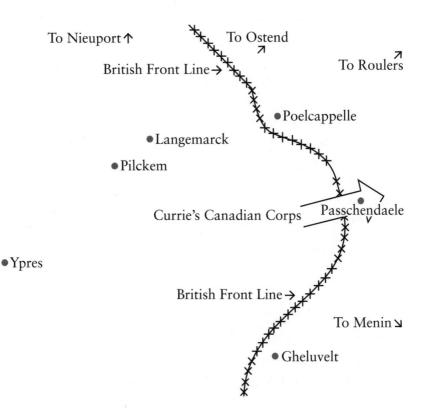

Second Battle of Passchendaele

16

BATTLE OF PASSCHENDAELE (SECOND ATTEMPT) OCTOBER–NOVEMBER

General Haig was, as we have seen, determined to seize the high ground of Passchendaele Ridge before the end of the campaign.

By this time the persistent continuation of wet weather had left no further room for hope that the condition of the ground would improve sufficiently to enable us to capture the remainder of the ridge this year. By limited attacks made during intervals of better weather, however, it would still be possible to progress as far as Passchendaele, and in view of other projects which I had in view, it was desirable to maintain the pressure on the Flanders front for a few weeks longer.

He added,

To maintain his defence on this front the enemy had been obliged to reduce the garrison of certain other parts of this line to a degree which justified the expectation that a sudden attack at a point where he did not expect it might attain a considerable local success. The front for such an attempt had been selected, and plans had already been made. But certain preparation and movements of troops required time to complete, and the 20th has been fixed as the earliest date for the attack.[1]

Lieutenant General Sir Arthur Currie and the Canadian Corps, consisting of four infantry divisions comprising 70,000 soldiers, would be the ones asked to pull the BEF's chestnuts out of the fire. Supremely successful at Vimy Ridge and Hill 70, the Canadian Corps was acknowledged as perhaps the strongest of the British fighting units. Currie had previously demonstrated his rugged insistence on thorough preparation and planning. Now he was asked by Haig to plan the attack that would *finally* seize the Passchendaele Ridge and village and end the interminably difficult campaign of Third Ypres/Passchendaele. Currie was reluctant to take on the operation, using his Canadian independence to express his reticence. However, Haig was able to convince Currie of the need to have some kind of positive end to the engagement and Currie accepted the task.[2] Evoking the same philosophy and demands as General Plumer in August, Currie insisted he would do so *only* after what he deemed to be sufficient artillery support was fully provided, along with the necessary means to supply and invest his assault. Even so, Currie bluntly responded to Haig that to be successful would probably cost another 16,000 casualties, but that the Canadians could and would do it. And so they did – both achieving the goal and suffering the casualties.

General Currie would not be rushed. In accepting the command to take Passchendaele Ridge, he demanded improved networks of transport; reinforced and re-equipped artillery; and three methodical stages of attack. He made a personal inspection of the artillery situation and found it to be wanting. Cannon were worn out and in need of repair or replacement due to the strenuous demands of the past three months. The constant exposure to the wretched weather conditions had also taken its toll. The number of available guns, in all calibres, was now woefully insufficient for Currie's requirements. The resupply system for men, machines and weapons would have to be ovrhauled and upgraded before any attacks could take place. The attacks would be carried out in three separate assaults, and each would be divided from the next by *at least* three days in order to properly prepare for the next phase of advance. There would be no imprudent decision to seize the moment and go for a quick breakthrough. All were now in agreement that this was not going to happen. There would be absolutely no thought of an attempt to short-circuit the procedure of securing and holding each objective before pushing on with the next. Haig had little choice but to agree.

Currie concluded that the attacks from his Canadian Corps should attempt to seize the Passchendaele Ridge in a series of short and heavily reinforced segments. Gough's Fifth Army would provide flanking support directly to Currie's north and Plumer's Second Army would provide assistance directly to the south of Currie's main thrust. As mentioned, before any attacks commenced, Currie, with his background in artillery, did an analysis of his available artillery and discovered that not only was he lacking sufficient big gun firepower for his offensive, but that many guns were improperly placed. Less than two-thirds of the available artillery was deemed serviceable after a summer and autumn of continuous use.[3]

Brigadier General E. W. B. Morrison personally inspected the artillery assets and reported his findings. Of the 250 listed heavy cannon, only 227 could be located and of those, 89 were damaged and out of action. Of the 306 18-pounders, more than half were out of action.[4] The artillery situation would have to be rectified with more guns and more balanced positioning. A narrow attack zone for the final push on Passchendaele Ridge would require, but also make easier, an accurate pre-attack ranging and aiming programme to securely escort the assaulting waves of attackers with an effective creeping barrage. Along with the demand for more guns came the requirement of reinforcing roads to better manoeuvre the guns into place and to better keep them fed with ammunition. Currie's chief engineer, General W. B. Lindsay, was assigned the task of reorganising the logistical support to provide upgraded transport and communication. If the Canadians were to accomplish the seizure of the Passchendaele Ridge, it would require a restoration of a dependable supply system and transport connection; Currie would do everything to see that it was provided.

Attacking troops would be moved forward at least three days in advance to prevent delays in the launch of the attacks and to better acclimate the attacking soldiers to the still brutal conditions of the sodden front. Three dates were selected for the advance: 26 October, 30 October, and 6 November. Not surprisingly, Haig had hoped for earlier dates, Currie for later, and this compromise was reached. In preparation for the offensive, several battalions were put to work repairing and reinforcing roads and supply depots to the front. Attacking soldiers were then thoroughly briefed on locations, objectives, and tactics to the maximum extent possible.

The opening attacks began on 26 October. Even with improved artillery firepower, fresh troops, and improved supply and material preparation, the going was still bitter, wet, and costly. General Gough, commanding the supporting Fifth Army, reported:

> On the 26th all three Armies [Second, Fifth, and French] attacked again, but it rained heavily during the night and the ground in front of the Fifth Army was becoming almost impossible, and very little progress was made either by us or by the Second Army. The state of the ground had been frightful since the 1st of August, but now it was getting absolutely impossible. Men of the strongest physique could hardly move forward at all and became easy victims to the enemy's snipers. Stumbling forward as best they could, their rifles also soon became so caked and clogged with mud as to be useless.[5]

The flanking attacks under Gough, Plumer and Anthoine were of limited success. Six Allied divisions on the flanks absorbed over

8,700 casualties.[6] To them the first step resembled the previous difficulties of the last month when Plumer abandoned his strict 'bite and hold' and had pressed on against his own better judgement. General Haig, as usual, was more optimistic about the progress:

> In the evening General Gough communicated with General Kiggell GCS that he found the ground on his front so very bad that he recommended delaying operations until frost set in! ... In my opinion today's operations at the decisive point (Passchendaele) had been so successful that I was entirely opposed to any idea of abandoning the operations till frost set in. If wet continues, a day or two's delay may be advisable before we launch the next attack ... the Canadians had established themselves securely on the small hill south of Passchendaele ... the operations of our Allies on this day were limited to establishing bridgeheads across the floods of the St Jansbeek (stream). These were to be the jumping off places for the second stage of the Canadian offensive.[7]

As usual there was confusion in the reports about just how much ground had been gained and how many casualties had been sustained. The 44th regimental history attests to the first day's grim accounting:

> Stretcher bearers work doggedly in the almost hopeless task of caring for the countless wounded who mingle with the dead in advanced positions. Parties of men lose direction in the darkness and wander to and fro in the mud, trying to find their units. The toll of killed and wounded mounts steadily under the everlasting bombardment of enemy guns.[8]

Gains on the 26th amounted to only a modest 500 yards at a cost of over 3,400 Canadian casualties. This had been Currie's and the Canadian's goal for the initial step up the Passchendaele Ridge and it had been achieved. However, Currie was returning to a strict 'bite and hold' format as used by Plumer during his September and October successes, before being lulled, or cajoled, by Haig into abandoning the tactic and returning to recklessly impetuous attacks seeking to seize an imagined initiative and potential breakthrough. Currie would not be so seduced, instead sticking to his programme that called for consolidation of the line, accurate determination of the progress that was accomplished, and complete preparation before the next series of assaults to open his second stage of the advance.

On Currie's left flank the Fifth Army, under Gough, struggled as it attacked through a shallow valley of flooded swamp while under withering gunfire, suffering 2,000 casualties in mercilessly difficult conditions without any tangible gain. Both Generals Maxse and Cavan (Fifth Army) gauged the difficulty and fearing a return to earlier disasters, concluded progress was impossible. They recommended to Fifth Army Commander Gough, who in turn personally broached the idea with Haig, to defer until a frost hardened the ground. On 30 October, through pouring rain, the Fifth Army was again assigned flanking attacks to protect the main Canadian thrust in the centre, and again suffered repeated losses and setbacks. Meanwhile, in the centre and at the foot of Passchendaele Ridge, the Canadian soldiers on the fighting line experienced similar frustration and heartache.

Private R. Lebrun, 16th Machine-Gun Company, 4th Canadian Division:

> We went on a main plank road, which was a mistake because the Jerry planes were buzzing about, and we were bombed incessantly. It raised havoc with the horses and mules, the trucks and limbers – we lost a lot them and most of the day we spent trying to get reorganised. As we neared the front the officers mapped out their headquarters in an old German pillbox, and then they picked out another spot nearer the front for a delivery point for ammunition, water and rations. This was as far as the mules were allowed

to venture. There had been a lot of casualties among the mules and they were trying to conserve them, but it seemed to us that their attitude was that one mule was worth twenty good men. We had to take a careful note of this dump, because they were putting us into the line, and every morning two or three of us had to get down there and carry our supplies to our shell-hole and dug outs at the front ... I had that duty the very first morning we were there. It was only a quarter of a mile or so from the front, and the whole way was nothing but shell-holes with bodies floating in them. It always seemed worse when you didn't see the whole body, maybe just legs and boots sticking out from the sides. The shelling never let up. The very first trip back on the morning of the 25th, the day before the first attack, I heard someone nearby calling for help. I dodged round a shell hole and over a few hummocks before I saw him. It was one of our infantrymen and he was sitting on the ground, propped up on his elbow with his tunic open. I nearly vomited. His insides were spilling out his stomach and he was holding himself and trying to push all this awful stuff back in. When he saw me he said, 'Finish it for me, mate. Put a bullet in me. Go on. I want you to. Finish it!' He had no gun himself. When I did nothing, he started to swear. He cursed and swore at me and kept on shouting even after I turned and ran. I didn't have my revolver. All my life I've never stopped wondering what I would have done if I had.[9]

LeBrun continued:

The infantry attacked early in the morning of 26 October. We had been ordered to fire 500 rounds every twenty minutes throughout the previous night at targets in front. We were right out in front of the line, and the mud was so deep in our shell holes that we had to put at least six boxes of ammunition underneath us – .303 ammo with 1,000 rounds to a box – just to stand on to get out of the mud. We had to keep filling our belts with ammo. Whenever we did that, we put our groundsheets across to cover the shell holes while we loaded up. At dawn the infantry went on past us, and we elevated our sights to cover them.[10]

The Germans, believing that the British offensive was to be shut down for the season, quickly realised that another major attack was underway. German officer Ernst Junger recorded on the morning of the 26th the early signs of the renewed attack:

The morning of 26 October were filled by drumfire of unusual severity. Our artillery too redoubled its fury on seeing the signals for a barrage that were sent up from the front. Every little piece of wood and every hedge was home to a gun, whose half-deaf gunners did their business ... As wounded men going back were making exaggerated and unclear statements about a British advance, I was sent off to the front at eleven o'clock with four men, for more accurate information. Our way led through heated fire ... We passed numerous wounded men, among them Lieutenant Spitz, the commander of the 12th, with a shot in the chin. Even before we got to the command dugout we came under well aimed machine-gun fire, a sure sign that the enemy must have forced our line back.[11]

British Private A.V. Conn:

I just raised the bottle [of rum] to my lips when I felt a terrific blow on my right arm. I never heard the shell burst, but it was a 5.9 which had dropped very near our shell hole. My mate who had taken my place [as lookout] fell back into the shell hole; his head was shattered and cracked right open; he fell past us into the water in the bottom of the shell hole ... I stared stupidly at my arm; the jagged pieces of white bone were poking through a great gash in my forearm, my wrist was open and the blood was welling through and down my side; also there [was] a large wound on my right shoulder ... They always said that you never heard the shell that was going to hit you.

Fortunately, Conn was able to make his way to a dressing station.[12] He continued:

Mud: we slept in it, ate in it. It stretched for miles, a sea of stinking mud ... we lost a quarter of a million men in this sector; many thousands of them were unidentified. The dead buried themselves. The wounded died in it. Men slithered around the lips of huge shell crater filled with mud and water. My first trip to this awful place was [at night]. For it was at night that men crept out of their holes at Passchendaele like rats ... Each side of the [duckboard] track lay the debris of war. Passchendaele, the mud sucked them down deeper and deeper ... Finally dawn broke, a hopeless dawn. Shell holes and mud. Round about rifles with bayonets fixed in the mud marking where men had died and been sucked down. It was daylight when we started back and the things that were now revealed to us in the light of day. All had their stories to tell [of] men who had struggled back only to give up and die when their strength failed them. Many had been pushed off the track to the sides to sink partly in the mud. There were mules and horses whose very intestines were spewing out of their swollen bloated bellies like long coils of piping. Here an arm and leg. It was a nightmare journey. The dead, their yellow teeth bared in ghastly grins, friend and foe alike were all clothed in the same filthy mud.[13]

On the left flank the Fifth Army was ordered to partake in yet one more attack to seize the Houthulst Forest, a particularly well-defended German position – it was to be their final assault at Third Ypres. Gough was not pleased with the result:

> The Fifth Army had, however, to take part in one more attack. On the 30th October ... we attacked with part of two divisions, but being in the low ground and operating in the valleys of the small streams that run westwards off the ridge, we could not get far forward – an advance of 300 yards or so being the limit of the day's objectives.[14]

From time to time the rain would stop, or lessen – 14 and 15 October had been rain free, and other days saw diminished amounts, but the accumulation could not be overcome. The shorter and now colder days, combined with the shattered canal and drainage system of the Flanders farm fields, merged to create a completely hopeless bog of flooded desolation. Fresh Canadian troops and marginally better weather would not necessarily be enough. The struggle remained as difficult as it had been; the conditions and the determined German resistance had not in any way diminished to make progress any easier, much less inevitable. It was going to be a long and brutal slog up the ridge.

Attacks were renewed on 30 October as reported by the Commanding Officer of 58 Division, listing the countless reasons why more success was not attained:

> ... more difficulty was experienced in maintaining communication on this occasion than I have hitherto experienced during the war ... Many messages sent back by runners who got bogged and were shot down. The majority of the company signalers were hit ... Pigeons were saturated in mud and water and couldn't fly. No contact aeroplane went out ... the ground was impassable and so powerless were the troops to manoeuvre that they were shot down whilst stuck in the mud ... the barrage was ineffective and troops were unable to keep up with it ... oblique

hostile M.G. [machine gun] fire was very effective ... the only Lewis Gun which succeeded in getting into action was useless in three minutes because of the mud ... all uncovered rifles were useless, all covered rifles ditto within ten minutes ... power of manoeuvre was nil ... to sum up the situation, neither *fire nor movement* was possible, and any prospects of success under these conditions was nil.[15]

After the fighting of 30 October, Haig concluded that Gough's Fifth Army had had enough and it was withdrawn. Casualties, frustration and the relentless pressure of the Ypres sector had finally been recognised as having taken its toll. If not broken, they certainly were battered and bruised to a point of total exhaustion. Likewise, it was no picnic in the centre for the Canadians moving against the Passchendaele Ridge. Any hint of better weather didn't lessen the stubborn resistance of the Germans holding the high ground. The Germans were refusing to budge an inch so that the slightly better weather provided little consolation for the attacking Canadians.

The 5th Canadian Rifles summary stated: 'The two preceding days had been fine and the shell-torn ground dried somewhat, enabling the men to pick their way over fairly solid ground around the lips of the shell craters.'[16]

However, Private J. Pickard of the 7th Winnipeg Grenadiers reported: 'The bombardment was murderous – ours and the Germans – and they weren't only flinging over shells, they were simply belting machine-gun fire for all they were worth ... The shells were falling thick and fast and by some sort of capillary action the holes they made filled up with water as you looked at them.'[17]

The 2nd Canadian Battalion history recorded:

Tense and expectant for hours, the men now rose from their cramped position and, in perfect formation, ploughed heavily forward behind the barrage. They overran the trench which, earlier in the morning had caused them so much worry, only to find that ... trench mortars had disposed of this enemy garrison effectively. An officer and about a dozen Germans, machine gun and all had been destroyed ... The lift of the barrage brought the shells smashing amongst them, sending the enemy to cower for protection within their thick concrete walls. Before they could emerge, No. 1 Company was on top of them ... the enemy had already been subjected to some tremendous punishment and they required little persuasion to surrender.[18]

And Corporal H. C. Baker commented:

The buildings had been pounded and mixed with the earth, and the shell exploded bodies were so thickly strewn that a fellow couldn't step without stepping on corruption. Our opponents were fighting a rearguard action which resulted in a massacre for both sides. Our boys were falling like ninepins, but it was even worse for them. If they stood up to surrender they were mown down by their own machine gun fire aimed from their rear at us; if they leapfrogged back they were caught in our barrage.[19]

Lt Colonel C. E. L. Lynn wrote:

It rained torrents all day, we were fighting at 3:30 this morning in a perfect deluge, until I was soaked and coated in mud. The mud which was horrible before became absolutely impassable. I had to get 2 guns into new places, one stuck muzzle deep in mud, and for hours defeated our most frenzied efforts. Finally the Hun strafed blue hell out of us unceasingly throughout the day ... just as it got dark, and I was changing my sodden garments, one of the dugouts got blown in with a direct hit, and out we went in mud and dark to excavate the survivors! The place was absolutely wrecked, the wonder was that a single occupant was left alive. Horrible groans from inside and with great difficulty we at last extracted some battered looking figures and hurried them off on stretchers to the dressing station during which process, we all, including the wounded me, fell repeatedly into shell holes full of water, cost me 5 casualties which makes a great difference as I am only keeping two or three men per gun up in the unsavoury spot. We returned to our shelter and found it, alas, submerged, torrents of rain – awful life.[20]

As October met November, it became a race against time and the onset of winter. Haig was also in a hurry to capture Passchendaele Ridge as quickly as possible because he was about to spring another sudden and swift offensive further south in France, at Cambrai. He calculated that the Germans would remain concentrated and vigilant in Flanders and was confident that he could surprise them with a quick attack in north-western France. The Cambrai attack had been well planned for some time and involved the use of a large force of several hundred tanks (over 400 Mark IVs, the latest and most capable model) over ground that had not been repeatedly pulverised. Therefore, Haig sought to complete the conquest of the Passchendaele objectives, shut down the Flanders offensive as soon as possible, and move on to a new area of operation with a mass attack of tanks supported by coordinated artillery and infantry. The Cambrai offensive would initially be very successful, and prove to be a landmark in tactical and technological warfare. The Cambrai assault was scheduled for 20 November, so it became imperative for Haig that Currie get on with his Passchendaele push, seize the high ground, and keep the Germans occupied in Flanders.

With Gough's Fifth Army withdrawn after its fruitless and costly first two segments of the assault, Haig turned over the final push up the Passchendaele Ridge to the Canadians. The Canadian front had now narrowed to a tapering 2,000-yard zone of savagely intense fighting. The Canadians would take the ridge and the village virtually unsupported by other units. Using a thunderously dominating, well-rehearsed creeping barrage of powerful and well-directed artillery, the Canadian infantry advanced in a series of short and methodical 'bite and hold' steps. On 6 November and through 10 November, the Canadian Corps along with the British 1st Division, determinedly fought its way up the slope of Passchendaele Ridge, finally occupying all of the ridge except for Westrozebeke village and an adjoining section of the ridge edge on the northern spur 1,000 yards north. There was nothing left of the villages and what debris remained was swamped in the deluge.

On 10 November, and in pouring rain, the flattened, rain- and mud-soaked village of Passchendaele was taken by the Canadian Corps and the offensive of Third Ypres/Passchendaele was terminated. Currie had promised that his Canadian Corps could take the ridge in three steps, and they had achieved their goal through nearly three weeks of bitterly contested fighting. Currie had also predicted 16,000 British and Commonwealth casualties in the accomplishment, and that number was almost exactly what the attackers suffered in their achievement.

The result

And so, it was done. The high ground of Passchendaele village and ridge was taken. In that landscape there was now nothing left except the shell holes and the swamp. A cold, pouring rain completed the desolate conditions of the location. Currie himself considered the Passchendaele Ridge a worthless piece of ground.[21] The British Army now held the 200-ft heights that commanded the nearby swampy sea of mud. What had been gained? A breakthrough had not been accomplished, the railhead at Roulers had not been reached, and the Belgian coast was nowhere near. Haig's dream of turning the German northern flank of the Western Front was just that, a dream. Denied these grand accomplishments, Haig was rightfully worried that his army would end up being stranded and exposed in the miserably shattered valley of mud in front of Passchendaele Ridge. Remaining in that position would have left the British under constant German observation and easily raked by her guns. Haig's decision had been to continue assaulting Passchendaele Ridge in spite of the high costs in casualties.

Assuming they could not spend the winter in this terrible position, the choice became to retreat to higher and drier ground and a safer, more defensible position; or to continue to attack and take Passchendaele Ridge. Haig had chosen the latter, rather than give up ground that had been so dearly and desperately taken. Remaining in the low, wrecked and swampy valley was out of the question. Therefore, seeking to 'successfully' conclude the battle before winter fully set in, Haig sought to have his army out of the valley and on to the high ground of Passchendaele Ridge. This had now been achieved but again at heavy costs in casualties, and only barely before winter weather became even worse.[22]

In three-and-a-half months of brutal fighting, the Ypres Salient had only been moved forward five miles beyond the town of Ypres, and the Salient still remained a salient. In fact, the point of attack had continually narrowed as the attacks ground on. By the time Currie and the Canadians made their final charge to seize Passchendaele, the massed artillery and infantry assault upon the German front had sharpened to a mere 2,000 yards, barely more than one mile in width. In depth the guns were reaching 4–5 miles, meaning an incredible amount of iron was expended upon a shallow area of former farm and pasture that rested near a low ridge containing the demolished village of Passchendaele.

Since early summer the British Army had accepted at least another 275,000 casualties in some of the heaviest and most difficult fighting of the war; and the advances had still not reached as far as Gough's optimistically hoped for red line projected for the Day One attacks, a distance of 6,000 yards beyond the original British lines. With November upon Haig and his weary army, the thought of continuing the offensive in the face of increasingly cold and wet weather, let alone the condition of the battlefield itself, forced a halt to the operation.

But there was, of course, more to the 1917 Flanders campaign than just capturing the village of Passchendaele, even if the grand strategies for Haig's offensive had failed to develop. The French had gained desperately needed time to reorganise their army, rebuild their morale, and move beyond the mutinies. The Germans had somehow never learned about the French mutinies, reflecting a woefully inadequate system of intelligence. Germany had also been reminded again of the fierce determination displayed by the British infantry and the increasing lethality of the British artillery. The Germans were confronted with a British Army that was large, willing to fight and absorb extreme casualties.

Haig's faith in the war of attrition had again meted out merciless losses to both British and German soldiers alike, although the Allies were better situated to withstand such blood-soaked punishment. The Russians had also been provided time to recover and reorganise, but instead, had spiralled into virtual anarchy and suffered a revolution before pulling out of a war they never had any business entering.

On the plus side for the Allies, due to Germany's imprudent return to a policy of unrestricted submarine warfare, the vast resources of the United States, including a budding million-man army, were on the way and due to begin arriving in substantial numbers by spring 1918.

Some of Passchendaele's lessons would not go unlearned. As the Germans feared, the Allies would not wait long to go on the offensive again. Before the Battle of Passchendaele had ended, Haig was already making plans for his next attack, a limited advance in northern France, just north of the area that witnessed the 1916 Somme campaign. It would feature the use of the growing tank force, and this time the terrain would be more suitable for the slow-moving armoured vehicles.

Passchendaele had proven that repeated attacks over ground that was hopelessly destroyed and chewed up by artillery, and especially when saturated in mud, was a difficult, if not impossible, road to victory. And the use of the tank in the bog was a waste of the weapon's potential. Therefore, a drier and more tank-friendly field would be required to take full advantage of the tank's power and usefulness.

The attack at Cambrai in late November 1917 would demonstrate the potency of a large-scale tank offensive when properly blended with appropriate infantry and artillery. It would point the way to the future and a return of more mobile warfare. A plan developed by tank advocate Major General J. T. C. Fuller using nearly 450 Mark IV tanks would be an important part of a thrust to make significant gains.[23] The Cambrai engagement would receive much publicity in the British and American press for its bold and innovative use of the tank, allowing the British to capture several miles of territory in only one day of fighting, more than in over three months fighting at Passchendaele. Surprisingly, the Germans remained unimpressed with the tank and its potential as a tactical force, and German tank development remained limited throughout the rest of the war. The Germans would take other lessons from the Passchendaele campaign.

From the other side of the trenches, the German position, although not much rosier, was one of relief. We may criticise the British for repeatedly attacking in Flanders, but doing so obviously forced the Germans to defend. They had no other option. To pull back would automatically risk conceding the Belgian North Sea coastal ports of Ostend and Zeebrugge and the valuable submarine bases that the Germans were placing such great faith in. In fact, their ill-advised decision to return to unrestricted submarine warfare was imposing strategy and tactics upon the *Germans*, rather than the enemy.

By refusing to abandon their Belgian positions, the Germans were trumpeting their willingness to stand and defend as a principle.[24] That defence would be as bitter, difficult and costly to the Germans as it was to the British in attacking. Although the casualty figures for both sides are disputed, it is safe to say that the Germans also suffered at least a quarter of a million casualties and probably more.

The Germans were in a desperate situation and they knew it. Their biggest error was not responding to peace feelers and attempting a compromise settlement with the Allies before the war was lost. There was a movement within the Reichstag for an armistice and an accompanying peace, but it surely would have meant concessions on territory. The German Chancellor, Theobald von Bethmann-Hollweg, had been receptive to this, but the consideration was entirely rejected by the dominant duo of Hindenburg and Ludendorff, the primary exponents of the renewal of unrestricted submarine warfare that was going to raise the stakes for either victory or defeat.[25]

With the collapse of Russia, the Germans would gain roughly an extra one million soldiers from the Eastern Front, plus reaping the spoils of the captured Russian territories – concessions given up by the new Soviet Russian government in the Treaty of Brest-Litovsk in February 1918. Having blocked the British in Flanders, the Germans now held several high cards, however, their overall position remained perilous. The British blockade of German ports was slowly strangling Germany of goods and materials, and there was a shortage of food at home and at the front. The German navy, bottled up in the German ports, was now disgruntled, inactive and bordering on either mutiny or revolution, and the Allied armies were poised again to go on the offensive bolstered by American reinforcements. A turning point had been reached and a decision had to be made. Yet the Germans rejected the opportunity to accept a compromise that would allow them to get out of the war with at least some gains and their empire intact.

Generals Hindenburg and Ludendorff, assuming more and more political as well as military control, had insisted on the removal of German Chancellor Bethmann-Hollweg, due to his supposed willingness to listen to peace suggestions from the Reichstag in July 1917. By supporting his generals Hindenburg and Ludendorff, Kaiser Wilhelm II had virtually abandoned his own leadership role and would soon have to face the ultimate consequences of defeat; surrender and abdication. Without any civilian moderation to temper the rule of the military, the Kaiser was painting himself and Germany into a diplomatic corner that could only be recovered by a complete battlefield victory. For their part, Ludendorff and Hindenburg would choose an all-out offensive to break the stalemate in an attempt to defeat the Allies on the battlefield and win the war. Five months later, in March of 1918, the Germans would launch their spring offensive and the British would evacuate the Passchendaele Ridge and abandon much of their Salient position, conceding the very ground that had cost the British Army over a quarter of a million casualties during the previous year's effort. The German bid for winning the war would come within a whisker of success but would be blocked, in part, by the very strategy they themselves engendered.

The unrestricted submarine warfare that brought the US into the war in the spring of 1917 would now come back to haunt the Germans. The American army was pouring into France at 250,000 soldiers a month, along with their mountain of supplies and resources, and this would tip the balance of the war in the Allies' favour, ensuring the Allied victory.[26]

A strong argument can therefore be presented as to the positives of the Flanders campaign in terms of the entire war picture. What is difficult to excuse, however, is Haig's compulsion to continue the Passchendaele battle beyond the fair weather gains by Plumer's advances in early October. With winter weather increasing, with heavy rain falling, with the Germans stubbornly resisting, and the battlefield an inoperable moonscape of mud, the prudent decision to call a halt to the campaign by at least no later than mid-October and the nasty defeat at Poelcappelle would seem to have been obvious.

Instead, Haig ignored not only the above-mentioned conditions, but the advice of nearly all his trusted advisers and commanders. His stubborn belief in the imminent collapse of the German army could not have been based upon anything other than wishful thinking, as the German defence refused to show any signs of breaking. It would, instead, be six more weeks of ferocious fighting under hellish conditions. The minimal reward would be the remains of the destroyed village of Passchendaele and the occupation of its blood- and mud-soaked ridge. For this, it is difficult to excuse Haig and his insistence on continuing the operation into November.

17

CONCLUSION

What had been the goals of this 1917 Flanders Offensive, the Third Battle of Ypres, and now commonly referred to as the Battle of Passchendaele? Why had it come to this, and what had been accomplished?

We began this book in search of answers as to why, and to how, Passchendaele was fought the way it was; once again we *must* place the question within the context of the entire identity of the Great War. Passchendaele must be examined from a number of qualifying perspectives:

(1) The Great War,
(2) The Western Front in 1917,
(3) The political environment and responsibilities of the Lloyd George government,
(4) The personal ambition and philosophy of General Douglas Haig.

An added factor that is commonly overlooked, but one that has been included here as often as possible, is:

(5) the *German* view of the war and their response to the strategic riddle, and the corresponding obligation of the Allies to react.

Several of these motives go hand-in-hand and intersect in importance and necessity. But, at the same time, some of these same answers positively refute the need and requirement of corresponding demands, and are in acute opposition to each other. This then sets up conditions for the tragic consequences that ensued during this four-month struggle. The argument has continued to this day.

The tragedy of the Great War itself has already been discussed: the needless nature of its inception, the careless disregard of the possibilities that lurked, and the reckless enthusiasm of both those in the highest levels of government and the most common and ordinary of civilian stations. It was a mistake, plain and simple, and the repercussions of which have reverberated for several generations and probably will continue well into the future. From the obvious and immediate physical death toll of over 10 million human beings and the grief of their respective families and society, to the spread of the post-war pandemic of 'Spanish Flu' that killed more than the war itself, to the collapse of the European social and economic structure and the onset of the Great Depression, to the Second World War, to the rise of the communist Soviet Union and the Cold War, to the splintering of the political stability of the former Austro-Hungarian Empire in Europe, and the Ottoman Empire in the Middle East – it was a disaster of the highest magnitude. So in terms of the Great War, the debacle of Passchendaele was one more catastrophic episode in the list of many convulsive events of that war, a prelude to the calamities that would follow. Once locked into the Great War, the tumultuous battles that ensued were merely a parade of orchestrated slaughters following each other in a progression of greater and greater crimes of industrialised murder and societal destruction.

Once engaged by the world's *enlightened* powers there would be, and could be, no backing off. The weight and impact of the insanely fought encounters at Verdun, Somme, and Passchendaele cannot be explained in rational terms. They took on a momentum all of their own: tragic, diabolical, and inexplicable. Who could conceive of such madness, and for what possible gain would the madness and tragedy be justified? Obviously no one; and, just as obviously, for no justifiable reason.

Many fine authors and historians have studiously and brilliantly written to explain why this war needed to be fought, and their arguments are quite cogent and well taken, but none of these explanations have succeeded in justifying the *extent* of violence and waste that the Great War expended to achieve whatever necessary ends the war may have actually hoped to accomplish. So in terms of the Great War, Passchendaele extended what had been spawned by the origins of the war itself. It personified the enormous strength of the opponents, the determination of the combatants, and the excesses of the entire endeavour. It was a microcosm of all that the First World War represented and inspired – its violence, its frustration, and its futility.

Approaching the second point, and isolating Passchendaele within the context of the war itself, this conflict fully amplified the difficulty in capturing any position, of developing any avenue of breakthrough, or achieving any specific tactical and strategic goal – in this case the clearing of the German-held channel ports in Belgium. Certainly the idea of clearing the channel ports was a definable, worthwhile consideration; and the bending of the northern flank of the Western Front was a significant stategic ambition. The conception of a combined operation with the Royal Navy's amphibious landing was imaginative and held great potential but, as in so many prior attempts to open the war to manoeuvre, the effort was hampered by the circumstances of overwhelming obstacles, the biggest being the strength of the opponent. Once past the entire question of the Great War itself, the idea for the assault on the Flanders ridges and the sweeping of the Belgian coast, had merit.

And also on the second point, in terms of the Western Front, this is where the reality of the First World War battlefield comes into play. Attack, and achieving goals through the attack process, was not practical, or successful – period. This had been demonstrated time and again, and at great cost in lives and resources. The potential manifold benefits of the Flanders campaign were apparent, but the positive benefits to be gained were not automatically attained by the mere initiation of the programme. This goes far to explain the repeated arguments by Haig, and others, resorting to the value and necessity of a 'war of attrition': the relentless grinding down of an opponent into submission and defeat. Unfortunately, such a strategy, besides lacking imagination, implies the equally relentless and grinding down of one's own forces.

The charnel houses of Verdun, Somme, and Passchendaele are testaments to this fact. When confronted with the lack of tactical gain, Haig and his lot were always ready to renew the assertion of victory through attrition. The Germans had attacked at Verdun, had recognised this failure in strategy, and after a year of horrific losses and no gain, had given up that attempt. The Germans, therefore, chose to defend the positions they held – the captured territory of France and Belgium. Granted, they incurred heavy losses in those defences but, had they been more sensible in their diplomatic imagination, they could have conceivably negotiated an earlier settlement and retained some of their early war gains. The Allies, on the other hand, France in particular, were attempting to win back their lost territory – even from the 1870–71 Franco-Prussian War – and were forced to attack in order to evict the Germans from their soil. But attacking, whether for legitimate reasons or not, was nonetheless a losing proposition.

The British attacked at the Somme and Flanders for tactical reasons, but also in the important strategic attempt to cover the predicament in which the French army had placed themselves. The British operation can, therefore, be partially explained in terms of strategic need, even if questioned in terms of tactical method. As to the motive for the incredible expenditure in lives and resources to expel the Germans from France and Belgium, one must pose the question as to what length a nation is willing to spill its treasure and blood for a specific piece of soil.

For Great Britain the sacrifices at the Somme, and again at Passchendaele, become considerably more justifiable when considering their alliance with the French. The necessity of providing relief for the French army struggling to recover from the potential war-losing disasters of Verdun in 1916, and the 1917 mutinies, was paramount. The equation was clear – for Germany to be defeated, France must avoid defeat. Therefore, British support was mandatory. In fact, German strategy was hinged on knocking either France or Britain out of the war. Being wedded to its commitment, Britain was now compelled to support the French in their time of need. As to the decision of taking on the responsibility of being an ally of Belgium and France in 1914, Britain's early entrance begs the question as to the ultimate wisdom of their original reasoning. Great Britain discovered it was now increasingly beholden and assuming the responsibility of a major land power with all the incumbent cost in manpower, resources and downright prudence.

If the object was to win the war, then the importance of fighting the Germans on the Western Front would have to be accepted and, with it, the associated costs. It was the primary location where the Allies could physically engage the Germans, the powerhouse of the Central Powers and, for that matter, of all Europe. To defang and defeat Germany would mean more than just starving her into surrender. It would require reducing her military capacity and defeating her on the battlefield; hence, the enormously long and brutal battles of the Western Front. This was where the war would be lost or won.

This would be conclusively proven in 1918, when the spring offensives launched by the Germans pierced the Allied lines to within fifty miles of Paris, before being halted and defeated at the Second Battle of the Marne. The Germans had shot their bolt and the Allies immediately seized the initiative. The shattered and exhausted German offensive would be reversed by the combined Allied counter-attacks that now featured one million fresh American soldiers. The American army, arriving every month in large numbers, joined the Anglo-French armies that would drive the Germans all the way back to the German border and force them to seek a war-ending armistice. The war had boiled down to which side would survive the atrocious battles of attrition and then have enough stamina to produce a victory on the Western Front. Even then, after four years of devastating attrition, it would require the arrival of the Americans with their enormous capacity for resources and fresh manpower to turn the tide.[1]

It should be pointed out that the American General John Pershing, upon fielding his large and inexperienced army, stubbornly repeated the very same tactical mistakes that his predecessors had committed earlier in the war.

Pershing and his staff sent thousands of willing and anxious American soldiers to a needless death in countless fruitless charges against heavily defended German positions equipped with modern weapons. As Winston Churchill later commented on the American soldiers: 'Half-trained, half-organised, with only their courage, their numbers and their magnificent youth behind their weapons, they were to buy their experience at a bitter price.' But they arrived in greater and greater numbers and the fountain of fresh American manpower seemed limitless. The drain on German troops and resources proved overwhelming; they could not be stretched any further.[2]

This then leads us to the third point, the political question. As previously implied, for all of Lloyd George's blustering over Haig's attritional tactics, the fact was Lloyd George was a fighter. Yes, he sought to rein in Haig's wasteful use of soldiers, and yes, he held back half a million soldiers from Haig during 1917 to avoid more careless waste of manpower, and yes, he talked up attacking Turkey, or Mesopotamia, or Italy. But in his heart, he understood that the Western Front was the battleground to engage and defeat the Germans. Lloyd George realised that Germany's near victory in the spring of 1918 was a clarion call for change and that necessary change included an insistence on a unified command structure with a French general – therefore *not* Haig – to command it. That man proved to be the capable Ferdinand Foch.[3]

Lloyd George was sick of the huge losses but, more importantly, he was sick of the huge losses without any gain to show for the investment. This was the nub of the issue. Lloyd George was politically safe on the home front, the weary and reluctant Asquith having been removed, but the results of failing to demonstrate any return for the horrific costs being absorbed was Lloyd George's real fear and worry. He sought to win the war, and that would mean a radical shift in the Allied command structure. Lloyd George had shown his political instincts by becoming Prime Minister, and now he employed that asset with his faith in unified command under Foch. It was to prove a correct judgement.

Lloyd George, never a fan of Haig, understood that in a complementary capacity to Foch, Haig's stubborn willingness to sustain heavy casualties could be tolerated and, if properly channelled, could succeed. Following the repulse of the German offensive, Haig was free to wage a war of manoeuvre against an opponent who was depleted and on the ropes. With the French and Americans applying effective pressure in eastern and northern France, the British under Haig drove the Germans back to the Rhine and forced the armistice. Lloyd George would ride Haig's 100-day victory to Germany's surrender, but it was made possible by the unified command under Foch, and supported by the fresh compliment of America's numerous reinforcements.

Lloyd George helped forge the peace settlement at the Versailles Peace Conference in 1919 that did much to promote and precipitate the Second World War. Politics in international affairs does matter, and has drastic repercussions. Not that Lloyd George's efforts can necessarily be blamed for that future – to that honour goes the naïve idealism of American President Woodrow Wilson, and to the vindictive treaty of retribution imposed upon Germany by the victorious French.

Now to the fourth point and the actions of General Douglas Haig: debate about this issue has raged for a century, and will go on long after and beyond this book's scope. In simple terms, Haig has his supporters and his detractors. His supporters believe Haig fought the war that was handed to him, and fought it the only way it could be fought in the circumstances. The war of attrition was brutal, but a 'success' nonetheless, coinciding with Britain's blockade to starve Germany of food and resources. When Germany exhausted her last reserve of energy on the spring offensive of 1918 and nearly won the war, it was Haig who kept his cool, developed a capable defence, and then reversed the advantage into a brilliant 100-day campaign of nine consecutive victories to the Rhine River that brought Germany to her knees and surrender.[4] All of this is true, but is that the whole story?

For other historians, the wasteful tactics of Haig are not only inexcusable but empty of any imagination or success. Haig's tactics basically consisted of endlessly pounding an opponent, with the resultant cost to his own attacking army. Evident by the irrefutably appalling numbers of casualties, there were absolutely no definable tactical or strategic victories for this investment in lives until war's end. Nor is there any hard evidence to prove that attrition worked better than either the Royal Navy blockade of German ports, or the arrival of the American army near the end of the war, both being extremely significant in the Allied victory. During the Somme campaign, Haig began to repeatedly support his tactics by the only argument that could justify his seemingly reckless use of manpower – the plea that he was following the tragic demands of a war of attrition. Both the Somme and Passchendaele offer substantial evidence that after some initial gains, the indefatigable Haig squandered tens of thousands of British and Commonwealth soldiers. The continued ordering of futile charges continued, even after his commanders' recommendations to halt the slaughter, which fell on the deaf and stubborn ears of Haig. For this, many believe Haig should be held responsible, and judged as negligent.

Finally, one should not overlook the foolishness of the German high command. The German chancellor, Bethmann-Hollweg, was passionately against the use of unrestricted submarine warfare, fearing, and rightfully so, the entrance of the United States into the war. Also, as a true diplomat looking out for the best interests of his nation, Bethmann-Hollweg was in compliance with the Reichstag's willingness to at least consider and debate a compromise peace solution and end the war.[5] This was anathema to the stubbornly narrow Hindenburg-Ludendorff philosophy of no other goal than a victory over the Allies on the battlefield. Both Hindenburg and Ludendorff had threatened to resign if Bethmann-Hollweg was not removed. The Kaiser could have accepted the resignations and sought a peaceful settlement, as humbling as that might have been. But, to retain his leading generals, the Kaiser complied and Bethmann-Hollweg was removed.

This virtually assured US entry into the war and defeat for the German Empire. Having failed in his foreign policy at the beginning of the war, the Kaiser chose to allow those whom he retained, Hindenburg and Ludendorff, the option to completely destroy his empire at the end of it. The Kaiser's decisions, reflected in the policies of Hindenburg and Ludendorff, would lead to the inevitable end of his reign. The Kaiser, by acceding to Hindenburg and Ludendorff's demands and granting them control of policy, was virtually setting up his own downfall and signing his abdication.

In retrospect, the major powers, France, Britain and Germany, faced an insoluble problem with regard to attack and defence. The British had developed a method to gain ground, although at such a high price in casualties for so small a gain in territory as to be not only negligible, but simply fruitless. This fact was either never realised, or at least not admitted to, by Haig and his co-commanders. For the Germans, the problem was the reverse – they could defend nearly any position and blunt any offensive but, again, at a price that was outrageous in terms of casualties and resources. This was the dilemma of the Western Front. One side could attack and advance, but with no appreciable gain of territory, while the other side could endlessly defend, but with a huge cost in manpower and material.

Ironically, it was the defending Germans who would point the way and demonstrate the method and possibility of tactically breaking the stalemate with their spring 1918 offensive as they penetrated the Allied lines in several places and nearly won the war. However, their tactical success did not convert into a strategic victory. Using their temporary manpower advantage to grease their tactical advancement in combined arms only hastened Germany's expenditure of energy, resources, and manpower in the failed offensive to win the war. It also allowed the Allies to capitalise on the now limited German strength and depth to adequately defend. Germany had spent her reserves in an all-out bid for victory and had come up short. The Allies now held the whip hand of superior resources and manpower, especially with the massive American entrance into the war. With German power depleted and spent, the Allies were able to mount their own counter-offensive and defeat the worn out German army. The German advantage in tactics had led to the Allied success in strategy, as their overall advantage in men, resources and depth finally blossomed into victory.

The Kaiser allowed his generals, as brilliant as they were in tactics, to overlap their military authority in matters that they had little experience of or insight into, politics and foreign affairs. It would lead to their defeat. The British, on the other hand, desperately tried to manage their generals and keep them under control. When politicians edged into military matters, it frequently ended in failure, such as at Gallipoli in 1915. But Prime Minister Lloyd George was able to retain a tight enough leash on Haig to encourage a more pragmatic, unified command under Foch. Great Britain and the French, through adroit use of diplomacy (and the brilliant work of Admiral Reginald 'Blinker' Hall, the Director of Naval Intelligence, in exploiting the infamous Zimmermann Telegram) were able to help nudge the United States into their corner, and then show enough patience to prolong the war until the arrival of the American army to tip the balance toward the Allied cause.

The Battle of Third Ypres/Passchendaele was of a magnitude that defies description. In a war of volcanic energy and cataclysmic repercussions, its horrific character of mindless slaughter, fought in the pit of an abysmal rain-soaked swamp, staggers the imagination. Quotes from those who lived through it give only a hint of the madness and agony that was endured. It was an appalling tragedy of immense scope, concentrated within a tiny area of Flanders. The courage and determination shown by those who fought and died there cannot be denied – only marvelled at from the distance of over a century. The tragedy for those who dedicated and sacrificed themselves to such an endeavour is that they could not be rewarded with an appropriately meaningful result to justify such a heroic action.

CHRONOLOGY

1914
August 1914 – the Great War begins

September – German invasion of France and bid for early victory
 is halted and defeated at First Battle of the Marne

Autumn – First Battle of Ypres

1915
Spring – British offensive at Nueve Chapelle

Spring – Second Battle of Ypres, first use of poison gas

Autumn – British offensive at Loos

Winter – Douglas Haig assumes command of BEF

1916
February to December – Battle of Verdun

July to November – British offensive at the Somme

1917
April – United States enters war

Spring – French offensive at Chemin des Dames

Spring – French Army begins a mutiny on Western Front

Spring – British offensives at Arras, Vimy Ridge, and Messines Ridge

July-November – Third Battle of Ypres/Passchendaele

31 July – 2 August Battle of Pilkem Ridge

15–25 August Battle of Hill 70 and renewed Battle for Gheluvelt Plateau

16–18 August Battle of Langemarck

20–25 September Battle of Menin Road Ridge

26 September–3 October Battle of Polygon Wood

4 October Battle of Broodseinde

9 October Battle of Poelcappelle

12 October Battle of First Passchendaele

26 October–10 November Battle of Second Passchendaele

20 November The Flanders/Third Ypres/Passchendaele campaign is declared closed by Haig

November – Battle of Cambrai in northern France

1918

Spring–summer – German offensive almost captures Paris

July – Second Battle of the Marne halts German advance

Summer–autumn – Allies counter attack and drive the Germans back, the '100 days' and Allied victory

11 November – Armistice and the defeat of Germany

1919

June – Treaty of Versailles signed in Paris

SELECT BIBLIOGRAPHY

Addington, Scott, *First World War Weapons,* (History Press, 2014)

Bridger, Geoff, *The Great War Handbook*, (Pen and Sword, 2009)

Cave, Nigel, *Passchendaele, Ypres*, (Pen and Sword, 1997)

Carver, Michael (ed.), *The War Lords*, (Weidenfeld and Nicholson, 1976)

Clarke, Dale, *World War I Battlefield Artillery Tactics*, (Osprey, 2014)

David, Saul, *Military Blunders*, (Carroll and Graf, 1997)

DeGroot, Gerard, *Christian Science Monitor* (article), (2014)

Dooley, William G. Jr, *Great Weapons of World War I*, (Army Times Publishing, 1969)

Dupuy, T. N, *A Genius for War*, (Hero Books, 1984)

Evans, Martin, *Passchendaele, the Hollow Victory*, (Pen and Sword, 2005)

Finnegan, Terrence J., *Shooting the Front: Allied Air Reconnassance in the First World War*, (The History Press, 2011)

Ferguson, Niall, *The Pity of War*, (Penguin, 1998)

Fussell, Paul, *The Great War and Modern Memory*, (Oxford University Press, 1975)

Groom, Winston, *A Storm in Flanders*, (2002)

Hart, Peter, *The Great War*, (Oxford University Press, 2013)

Holmes, Richard, *The Western Front*, (BBC Books, 1999)

Holt, Toni and Valmai, *Western Front-North*, (Pen and Sword, 2004)

Johnson, J. H., *Stalemate!*, (Arms and Armour Press, 1995)

Jones, Archer, *The Art of War in the Western World*, (Oxford University Press, 1987)

Jorgensen, Christopher (ed.,), *Great Battles*, (Parragon Publishing, 2007)

Junger, Ernst, *Storm of Steel*, (Penguin, 1920)

Keegan, John, *The Faces of Battle*, (Penguin 1976)

Keegan, John, *The First World War*, (Alfred A. Knopf, 1998)

Livesey, Anthony, *Historical Atlas of World War I*, (Henry Holt, 1994)

Macdonald, Lynn, *Passchendaele*, (Penguin, 1978)

McNab, Chris, *Passchendaele 1917*, (History Press 2014)

Macksey, Kenneth, *Technology in War,* (Prentice Hall, 1986)

Mallinson, Allan, *Too Important for the Generals,* (Bantam Press, 2016)

Marshall, S.L.A., *World War I,* (American Heritage, 1964)

Neiberg, Michael S., *The Western Front 1914–1916,* (Amber Books, 2008)

O'Shea, Stephen, *Back to the Front,* (Avon Books, 1996)

Parker, Robert J., *British Prime Ministers,* (Amberley, 2011)

Paschall, Rod, *The Defeat of Imperial Germany,* (Da Capo Press, 1994)

Price, W. R., *Gunner on the Somme,* (History Press, 2016)

Prior, Robin and Wilson, Trevor, *Passchendaele, the Untold Story,* (Yale University Press, 1996)

Ramsay, David, *Blinker Hall, Spymaster: The Man who Brought America into World War I,* (Spellmount, 2009)

Ross, Stewart, *War in the Trenches,* (Wayland Publishers, 1990)

Russell, Thomas, *America's War for Humanity,* (L. H. Walter, 1919)

Sheffield, Gary, *A Short History of the First World War,* (Oneworld Publications 2014)

Sheffield, Gary, *The Chief, Douglas Haig and the British Army,* (Aurum Press, 2011)

Sheffield, Gary, *The First World War in 100 Objects,* (Andre Deutsch, 2013)

Simkins, Peter, *The First World War, the Western Front,* (Osprey, 2002)

Steele, Nigel and Hart, Peter, *Passchendaele, the Sacrificial Ground,* (Cassell, 2000)

Stevens, Philip, *The Great War Explained,* (Pen and Sword, 2012)

Stewart, Cameron, *A Very Important Officer,* (Hodder and Stoughton, 2009)

Strohn, Matthias, (ed.), *World War I Companion,* (Osprey, 2013)

Strong, Paul and Marble, Sanders, *Artillery in the Great War,* (Pen and Sword, 2011)

Terraine, John, *The Western Front 1914–1918,* (Arrow Books, 1964)

Travers, Tim, *The Killing Ground,* (Pen and Sword, 1987)

Warner, Phillip, *Passchendaele,* (Sidgwick and Jackson, 1987)

Wilson, G. Murray, *Fighting Tanks,* (Seeley Service, 1929)

Wiest, Andrew, *The Western Front 1917–1918,* (Amber Books, 2008)

Winter, Denis, *Haig's Command,* (Penguin, 1991)

Winter, Denis, *Death's Men,* (Penguin 1978)

APPENDICES

Approximate size of British and Commonwealth First World War army units and usual commanding rank
All figures are optimum and all units were frequently under-sized due to illness, injury and death.

Platoon	50 men	lieutenant
Company	250 men	captain
Battalion	1,000 men	lieutenant colonel or major
Regiment	2000 men	colonel
Brigade	4000 men	brigadier general
Division	12,000 men	major general
Corps	50,000 men	lieutenant general
Army	200,000 men	general

British and Commonwealth Order of Battle

Commander-in-Chief, Field Marshal Sir Douglas Haig.
Second Army, General Sir Herbert Plumer.
Fourth Army, General Sir Henry Rawlinson.
Fifth Army, General Sir Hubert Gough.

I Corps, Lieutenant General Sir Arthur Holland.
II Corps, Lieutenant General Sir Claud Jacob.
V Corps, Lieutenant General Sir Edward Fanshawe.
IX Corps, Lieutenant General Sir Alexander Gordon.

X Corps, Lieutenant General Sir Thomas Morland.

XIII Corps, Lieutenant General Sir William McCracken.

XIV Corps, Lieutenant General Earl of Cavan.

XV Corps, Lieutenant General Sir John due Cane.

XVIII Corps, Lieutenant General Sir Ivor Maxse.

XIX Corps, Lieutenant General H E Watts.

Canadian Corps, Lieutenant General Sir Arthur Currie.

I ANZAC Corps, Lieutenant General Sir William Birdwood.

II ANZAC Corps, Lieutenant General Sir Alexander Godley.

Guards Division, Major General G. P. T. Fielding.

1st Division, Major General E. P. Strickland.

3rd Division, Major General C. J. Deverell.

4th Division, Major General T. G. Matheson.

5th Division, Major General R. B. Stephens.

7th Division, Major General T. H. Shoubridge.

8th Division, Major General W. C. G Heneker.

9th (Scottish) Division, Major General H. T. Lukin.

11th Division, Major General H. R. Davies.

14th (Light) Division, Major General V. A. Couper.

15th (Scottish) Division, Major General H. F. Thuillier.

16th (Irish) Division, Major General W. B. Hickie.

17th (Northern) Division, Major General P. R. Robertson.

18th (Eastern) Division, Major General R. P. Lee.

19th (Western) Division, Major General C. D. Shute acting to 19 June, Major General G. T. M. Bridges wounded 20 September, Brigadier General W. P. Monkhouse acting to 22 September, Major General G. D. Jeffreys.

20th (Light) Division, Major General W. Douglas Smith.

21st Division, Major General D. G. M. Campbell.

23rd Division, Major General J. M. Babington.

24th Division, Major General L. J. Bols.

25th Division, Major General E. G. T. Bainbridge.

29th Division, Major General Sir B. de Lisle.

30th Division, Major General W. de L. Williams.

33rd Division, Major General P. R. Wood.

34th Division.

35th Divison.

36th (Ulster) Division, Major General O. S. W. Nugent.

37th Division, Major General H. Bruce Williams.

38th (Welsh) Division, Major General C. G. Blackader.

39th Division, Major General G. J. Cuthbert to 20 August, Major General E. Feetham.

41st Division, Major General S. T. B. Lawford.

42nd Division.

47th (1/2nd London) Division (TF), Major General Sir George Gorringe.

48th (1st South Midland) Division, Major General R. Fanshawe.

49th (1st West Riding) Division (TF), Major General E. M. Percival.

50th (Northumbrian) Division (TF), Major General P. S. Wilkinson.

51st (Highland) Division, Major General G. M. Harper.

55th (1st West Lancashire) Division, Major General H. S. Jeudwine.

56th (1st London) Division, Major General F. A. Dudgeon.

57th (2nd West Lancashire) Division, Major General R. W. R. Barnes.

58th (2/1st London) Division, Major General H. D. Fanshawe to 6 October, Major General A. B. E. Cator.

59th (2nd North Midland) Division, Major General C. F. Romer.

61st (2nd South Midland) Division, Major General C. J. Mackenzie.

63rd (Royal Naval) Division, Major General C. E. Lawrie

66th (2nd East Lancashire) Division, Major General Hon. H. A Lawrence.

1st Canadian Division, Major General A. C. Macdonell.

2nd Canadian Division, Major General H. E. Burstall

3rd Canadian Division, Major General L. J. Lipsett.

4th Canadian Division, Major General D. Watson.

1st Australian Division, Major General H. B. Walker.

2nd Australian Division, Major General N. M. Smith.

3rd Australian Division, Major General Sir John Monash.

4th Australian Division, Major General W. Holmes killed 2 July, Brigadier General C. Rosenthal Acting to 16 July, Major General E. G. Morgan-Sinclair.

5th Australian Division, Major General J. Talbot Hobbs.

New Zealand Division, Major General Sir Arthur Russell.

NOTES

Prologue
1. Wiest, Andrew. *Western Front 1917–1918*, p. 92 and Macdonald, p. 203, Lt. P. King 2/5th Btn., East Lancashire Regiment
2. Hawkes, Jaquetta, *Mortimer Wheeler: Adventure in Archaeology*, pp. 57-58
3. Stewart, J. and Buchan, J. *The Fifteenth (Scottish) Division, 1914–1919*, p. 156
4. Bill, C.A., *The 15th Battalion, The Royal Warwickshire Regiment in the Great War*. p. 159, cited from *Stalemate* Johnson, J. H.
5. Junger, Ernst, *Storm of Steel*, p. 19
6. Livesey, Anthony, *Historical Atlas of World War I*, p. 128
7. Prior and Wilson. *Passchendaele*, p. 27 and pp. 150-151
8. Robertson, William, *Soldiers and Statesmen 1914-1918*, vol. 2
9. O'Shea, Stephen, *Back to the Front*, p. 42 and Groom, Winston, *A Storm in Flanders*, pp. 224–225

Chapter 1
1. Wiest, *The Western Front 1917–1918*, pp. 52-53

Chapter 2
1. Simkins, Peter, *The First World War*, p. 35
2. Ferguson, Niall, *The Pity of War*, p. 293
3. Holmes, Richard. *The Western Front*, p. 180
4. Holmes, p. 180

Chapter 3
1. Holmes, p. 59
2. Johnson, J. H. *Stalemate*, pp. 132-133

3. Simpson cited in Holmes, p.192

4. Holmes, p. 192

5. Holmes, p. 160

6. Holmes, p. 160

7. deGrotte, Gerard. *Christian Science Monitor* article

8. Sheffield, Gary, *The First World War in 100 Objects*, p. 100

9. Holmes, p. 168

10. Holmes, p. 168

11. Parker, 'Somme', p. 158

12. Holmes, pp. 167-168

13. Holmes, p. 168

14. Kapitan Kalepsky of Infanterie Regiment 86, *Artillery in the Great War*, p.137

Chapter 4

1. Parker, *British Prime Ministers*, p. 85

2. Michael Neiberg, *World War I Companion*, p. 27

3. Warner, Phillip. *Passchendaele*, p. 42

4. Travers, *Killing Ground*, p. 207

Chapter 5

1. Addington, Scott, *Weapons of WWI*, p. 30.

2. Addington, p. 127

3. Haig's dispatches, p. 142

4. Dooley, William, *Great Weapons of WWI*, p. 185

5. Dooley, p. 194

6. Dooley, pp. 137-138

7. Dooley, pp. 137-138

8. Sheffield, p. 100

Chapter 6

1. Belgium Military Recovery Program

2. *British Artillery*, Clarke/Dale, Osprey

Chapter 7

1. Hankey, Lord. *The Supreme Command 1914–1918*, p. 137 cited from *Stalemate*

2. Holmes, p. 175

3. Wiest, p. 64

4. pp. 15-16 Evans and p. 68 McNab

5. Holmes, p. 179

6. Holmes, p. 179

7. Evans citing Ludendorff p. 15
8. Evans p. 15
9. Warner p. 51
10. Holmes, p. 168
11. Severn, Mark, (pseud.), for author and Western Front gunner Franklin Lushington *The Gambardier*
12. McNab, Chris, *Passchendaele*, p. 78
13. Edmonds, p. 149, cited from *Stalemate*
14. Warner, pp. 224-225
15. Warner, p. 225

Chapter 8

1. Holmes, p. 181
2. Hart, Peter, *The Great War*, pp. 353-354
3. Hart, p. 354
4. Sheldon, J. *The German Army at Passchendaele*, pp. 52-53 and Hart, p. 356
5. Keegan, John, *First World War*, p. 361
6. MacDonald, p. 103
7. John Buchan in *Nelson's History of the War, Vol. XX*, cited from *Stalemate*, p. 144
8. MacDonald, pp. 115-116
9. Keegan, p. 361 citing Farndale, p. 204
10. Johnson, p. 145
11. Junger, p. 161
12. Junger, p. 175
13. Junger, p. 176
14. Barton, Peter, *Battlefields of the First World War*

Chapter 9

1. Hart, p. 358
2. Hart, p. 359
3. Dannocks, Daniel, G., *Welcome to Flanders Fields*, p. 245
4. Canadian Great War Project, 102nd Battalion daily field diary
5. Ludendorff, Erich, *My Memoirs, 1914–1918* cited by Hart, pp. 360-361
6. Robert, Andrew, *Smithsonian*, July 2016

Chapter 10

1. Holmes, p. 185
2. Wiest, p. 83
3. Haig's dispatches, p. 118
4. Falls, C., *History of the 36th Ulster Division*, cited in *Stalemate*, p. 146

5. Haig's dispatches, p. 118
6. Haig's dispatches, pp. 118–119
7. Gibbs, Philip, cited in *Stalemate*, pp. 146-147
8. MacDonald, Lynn, pp. 148–149
9. Gough, General Sir Hubert, *The Fifth Army*, 1931
10. Keegan, WWI, p. 363
11. Keegan, WWI, p. 363
12. Keegan, WWI, pp. 363–364
13. Holmes, pp. 185–186
14. Macdonald, pp. 143–144
15. Macdonald, p. 147
16. Holmes, p. 186

Chapter 11
1. Haig's dispatches, p. 119
2. Macdonald, p. 177
3. Haig's dispatches, p. 121
4. Haig's dispatches, p. 120
5. Hart, pp. 360–361
6. Evans, Martin, *Passchendaele, the Hollow Victory*, p. 81
7. Evans, Martin, p. 82
8. Haig, War Office Report, 21 August 1917
9. Hart, p. 361
10. Terraine, John, *The Road to Passchendaele*, p.262
11. Holmes, p. 187
12. Terraine, p. 279
13. *Nelson's History of the War*, John Buchan, Vol. XX
14. Holmes, p. 187
15. Ludendorff, Erich, *War Memoirs*, Vol I, 1929

Chapter 12
1. Haig's memo to Gough and Plumer OAD Operational records, 21/9/17, Prior and Wilson p. 125
2. Prior, Robin and Wilson, Trevor, *Passchendaele, the Untold Story*, p. 128
3. Hutchinson, G. S., *The Warrior*
4. Wiest, p. 87
5. Wiest, p. 89
6. Macdonald, pp. 179–180
7. Macdonald, p. 183
8. Evans, pp. 99–100

9. Wiest, p. 89
10. Evans, p. 105
11. Evans, p. 104
12. Evans, pp. 97–98

Chapter 13

1. General Erich Ludendorff, General Headquarters, cited in *The Great War*, Hart, Peter, p. 362
2. MacDonald, pp. 197–198, and Evans, p. 108
3. Evans, p. 113
4. Steele and Hart, pp. 238–239
5. Evans, p. 113
6. Evans, p. 113
7. Evans, p. 114
8. Prior and Wilson, p. 137
9. Evans, p. 112
10. Evans, p. 110
11. Evans, p. 110
12. *Official History of Australia in the War of 1914-1918* (1921)
13. Haig's dispatch, October 1917
14. Evans, p. 105

Chapter 14

1. Prior and Wilson, p. 160
2. Prior and Wilson, pp. 160-161
3. Evans, pp. 115-116
4. Amsty, E. C. *History of the Royal Artillery 1914–1918*, p. 189. Amsty Papers, cited in Prior and Wilson, pp. 159–160
5. Cliff, Norman, *To Hell and Back with the Guards*, p. 83 cited in Hart, pp. 365–366.
6. Birdwood, *Khaki and Gown: an Autobiography*, p. 316 cited in McNab, p. 113.
7. Evans. p. 115
8. Steele and Hart, p. 272 (from William-Ellis, C. *The Tank Corps*)
9. Evans, p. 123
10. Evans, p. 117
11. Mcdonald pp. 203–204 and Wiest p. 92
12. Brigadier General Sir James Edmonds, *History of the War: Military Operations, France and Belgium 1917*, Vol II
13. Evans, p. 122 and notes from GHQ from General Charteris
14. Steele and Hart, p. 259

15. Steele and Hart, p. 273
16. Steele and Hart, pp. 273–274
17. Evans, p. 124

Chapter 15

1. Steele and Hart p. 275
2. Steele and Hart, pp. 275–276
3. Holmes, 'Western Front', p. 191, anon.
4. Steele and Hart, p. 276
5. Hart, pp. 366-367
6. Holmes, p. 191
7. Holmes, p. 191
8. Evans, pp. 124–125
9. Evans, p. 125
10. Evans, pp. 128–129
11. Evans, pp. 129–130
12. Edmonds, Brigadier General Sir James, *Official History*, pp. 341–342
13. Maxse Papers, XVIII Corps, Report on Operations of 12th October 1917
14. Junger, pp. 196–199
15. Evans, p. 137
16. Evans. 135
17. Prior and Wilson, p. 169
18. Haig's Diary, Evans, p. 130
19. Haig's Diary, Evans, p. 130
20. Haig's Diary, cited in Evans, p. 130 and McNab p. 125

Chapter 16

1. Haig's Diary, cited in Evans pp. 130-131
2. Keegan, p. 367.
3. Wiest, P.96
4. Evans, p. 132
5. Evans, pp. 139–140
6. McNab, p. 130
7. Haig's Diary, cited in Evans p. 140
8. Evans, p. 141
9. Macdonald pp. 226–227
10. Macdonald pp. 226–227 and Evans pp. 138–139
11. Junger, p. 197
12. Wiest, p. 96
13. Wiest, p. 96

14. Evans. p. 142

15. 174 Brigade (58 Division), Preliminary Report on Operations of 30th October 1917 58 Division War Diary, August-November 1917. Prior and Wilson p. 176-177

16. 5th Canadian Mounted Rifles, Summary of Operations, Oct. 30-31 1917, 8th Canadian War Diary Jan–Dec 1917. Prior and Wilson p.176

17. Private J. Pickard, Winnipeg Grenadiers, from Macdonald p. 224, and, Prior and Wilson p. 176

18. W. W. Murray, *The History of the 2nd Canadian Battalion (East Ontario Regiment) Canadian Expeditionary Force in the Great War, 1914–1919* from Prior and Wilson p. 178.

19. Corporal H. C. Baker, 28th North West Battalion, (quoted in Macdonald p. 226) from Prior and Wilson, p. 179

20. Letters of Lt Colonel C. E. L. Lyne) Prior and Wilson p. 181

21. Paschall, Rod, *The Defeat of Imperial Germany*, p. 77

22. Paschall, p. 76

23. Pashcall, p. 105

24. Steele and Hart p. 28–29

25. Dupuy, Trevor, *A Genius for War*, p. 167

26. Dupuy pp. 167–168

Chapter 17

1. Carver, Michael, ed., *War Lords*, Stone, Norman pp. 74–75

2. Roberts, Andrew, *Smithsonian* July 2016

3. Dupuy, p. 175

4. *War Lords*, Terraine, John, p. 41

5. Dupuy, p. 166

ACKNOWLEDGEMENTS

First I would like to thank the friendly people in the towns and villages of Flanders. Their gracious cooperation during my visits was most warmly received. In particular, among many, I am delighted to mention Steve Douglas at the 'The 'British Grenadier Bookshop' in Ypres, and my excellent personal guide Roger Steward, for their knowledgeable and generous guidance while touring the Passchendaele battlefield. Special thanks must go to my trusted copy editor Cathy Stagg who worked so diligently to prepare the final manuscript, and as always, the crew at Amberley Publishing for their dedicated effort. Special thanks must be included for my project editor Jonathan Reeve, whose encouragement, inspiration, and advice was most greatly appreciated. I would most of all like to thank my wife Sheila and our son Robbie for their endless patience through the writing of this book.

Although the attempt was made to carefully review and correct every detail, any errors of facts or interpretation in this book are entirely mine.

INDEX